ABOUT BACH

About Bach

Edited by Gregory G. Butler,
George B. Stauffer, and
Mary Dalton Greer

UNIVERSITY OF ILLINOIS PRESS · URBANA AND CHICAGO

Library of Congress
Cataloging-in-Publication Data

About Bach / edited by
Gregory G. Butler,
George B. Stauffer,
and Mary Dalton Greer.
p.   cm.
Includes bibliographical
references and index.
ISBN-13: 978-0-252-03344-5
(cloth : alk. paper)
ISBN-10: 0-252-03344-2
(cloth : alk. paper)
1. Bach, Johann Sebastian, 1685–1750—
Criticism and interpretation.
2. Music—18th century—History and
criticism. I. Butler, Gregory. II. Stauffer,
George B. III. Greer, Mary Dalton.
ML410.B13A36   2008
780.92—dc22   2007046831

Dedicated
with affection
to
Christoph Wolff
Scholar, Mentor, Friend

This volume
was made possible by
the financial support
of
Walter B. Hewlett,
David W. Packard,
and
William H. Scheide.

CONTENTS

AFTER BACH

PREFACE

Philipp Spitta, author of the monumental nineteenth-century biography *Johann Sebastian Bach* (Leipzig, 1873–1880), once explained his passion for his subject by pointing out that Bach was a composer "whose life and works have occupied a considerable portion of my own." Certainly Christoph Wolff could make a similar claim, since his equally monumental *Johann Sebastian Bach: The Learned Musician* (New York: W.W. Norton, 2000) represents a lifetime of scholarly involvement with Bach and his musical art.

But Wolff has devoted himself to other things as well: to examining and editing the music of Mozart, Schubert, Brahms, and Hindemith; to leading the Graduate School of Arts and Sciences at Harvard University; to directing the Bach-Archiv in Leipzig; to playing the organ and harpsichord; and to teaching. Indeed, in this last endeavor Wolff has proven to be almost as industrious as Bach himself, training and guiding the next generation of PhD students, first at the University of Toronto, then at Columbia University, and finally at Harvard University. Just as Bach brought up his pupils on his own pieces for clavier, since they were "the most instructive" (as his son Carl Philipp Emanuel once put it), so Wolff has passed on his craft to his students in the form of his own *exempla classica*, a steady stream of brilliant books and essays that serve as models of the best in musicology. It is with affection and gratitude that students and colleagues of Christoph Wolff celebrate his sixty-fifth birthday with the present collection of essays, *About Bach*.

The volume begins with two studies of Bach's forebears. Kathryn Welter looks at a manuscript liturgical guide written by Johann Pachelbel, one of Bach's most important predecessors, and draws him more strongly into the tradition of master teachers, while Mary Dalton Greer discusses the Old Testament foundation of the family tree that Bach drew up in 1735 on the occasion of his fiftieth birthday.

In the second section, devoted to Bach's vocal music, Alexander J. Fisher looks at Bach's application of a process similar to parody technique in the cantata *Ein ungefärbt Gemüte*. Fisher terms this process "combinatorial modeling" and explores its context and implications. Daniel R. Melamed then examines the place of unison chorale texture as an important marker in Bach's concerted vocal music. The precise formulation of Christ's last words on the cross in the St. Matthew Passion is clarified in an etymological and textual study by Michael Ochs, and William H. Scheide proposes the wedding cantata *Sein Segen fliesst daher wie ein Strom* as a possible source for parodied arias in the B-Minor Mass.

ix

In the middle section, Hans-Joachim Schulze reveals Johann Friedrich Schweinitz as a Bach student who established a collegium musicum in Göttingen on the model of his teacher's university ensemble in Leipzig. Jen-yen Chen focuses on Bach's second-youngest son, Johann Christian, and his role in the development of the so-called "church symphony."

Bach's instrumental music is the focus of the fourth part of the book. Gregory G. Butler returns to the Art of Fugue for another look at the scribes and engravers of the original edition, to shed light on Bach's intentions regarding the contents and final disposition of the collection. Ton Koopman takes issue with commonly held assumptions concerning how Bach realized figured basses and offers advice for modern-day players, and George B. Stauffer explores the music performed by Bach's Collegium Musicum, showing that Handel's opera arias and secular cantatas were frequent fare in Leipzig in the 1730s and 1740s. Finally, Andrew Talle, in a detailed scrutiny of another intriguing print, *Clavierübung* I, discusses the difficulties of pinpointing which, if any, of the numerous extant exemplars of the original edition might have served as Bach's personal copy.

The influence of eighteenth-century musical practices on those of the nineteenth century is the topic of the three concluding essays. Robert Hill presents acoustical research bearing on Carl Reinecke's interpretation of a slow movement by Mozart, while Mark Risinger surveys oratorio practices in London after Haydn through a close reading of a concert program from 1814. Finally, Douglass Seaton brings the volume to a close with a look at the posthumous fate of the B-A-C-H motive in Schumann's Symphony No. 2 in C Major.

The editors would like to thank the contributors for taking time from their busy schedules to write essays for this volume. We would also like to extend gratitude to Walter B. Hewlett, David W. Packard, and William H. Scheide for financial support that made this publication possible, and to Barbara Wolff for her behind-the-scenes guidance and advice. We are indebted, too, to David Wolff for setting the music examples, to David Chapman for compiling the index, and especially to Willis Regier, director of University of Illinois Press, and his staff for guiding the book through production and keeping the project on track. In closing, we want to express once again our appreciation to Christoph Wolff, scholar, educator, administrator, musician, and mentor extraordinaire.

Gregory G. Butler
George B. Stauffer
Mary Dalton Greer

ABBREVIATIONS

BC   *Bach Compendium: Analytisch-bibliographisches Repertorium der Werke Johann Sebastian Bachs.* Edited by Hans-Joachim Schulze and Christoph Wolff. Leipzig and Frankfurt: Edition Peters, 1985– .

BDOK   *Bach-Dokumente.* Edited by Werner Neumann and Hans-Joachim Schulze. Kassel: Bärenreiter/Leipzig: VEB Deutsche Verlag für Musik, 1963–2008. 6 vols.

BG   *Johann Sebastian Bach's Werke* [Bach-Gesamtausgabe]. Edited by the Bachgesellschaft. Leipzig: Breitkopf & Härtel, 1851–1899. 49 vols.

BJ   *Bach-Jahrbuch.*

BWV   *Thematisch-systematisches Verzeichnis der musikalischen Werke von Johann Sebastian Bach* [Bach-Werke-Verzeichnis]. Edited by Wolfgang Schmieder (rev. ed.). Wiesbaden: Breitkopf & Härtel, 1990.

DTB   *Deutsche Tonkunst in Bayern* (rev. ed.) Wiesbaden: Breitkopf & Härtel, 1967– .

DTÖ   *Denkmäler der Tonkunst in Österreich* (rev. ed.). Graz: Akademische Druck- und Verlagsanstalt, 1960– .

KB   *Kritischer Bericht* (critical report) of the *Neue Bach-Ausgabe.*

NBA   *Johann Sebastian Bach: Neue Ausgabe sämtlicher Werke* [*Neue Bach-Ausgabe*]. Edited by the Johann-Sebastian-Bach-Institut, Göttingen, and the Bach-Archiv, Leipzig. Kassel: Bärenreiter/Leipzig: Deutscher Verlag für Musik, 1954– .

NBR   *The New Bach Reader: A Life of Johann Sebastian Bach in Letters and Documents.* Edited by Hans T. David, Arthur Mendel, and Christoph Wolff. New York: W.W. Norton, 1998.

P   *Mus. ms. Bach P*, Staatsbibliothek zu Berlin—Preußischer Kulturbesitz, Musikabteilung. Partitur (score).

RISM   *Répertoire International des Sources Musicales* (Publié par la Société Internationale de Musicologie et l'Association Internationale des Bibliothèques Musicales, 1971–).

St   *Mus. ms. Bach St.*, Staatsbibliothek zu Berlin—Preußischer Kulturbesitz, Musikabteilung. Stimmen (parts).

Before Bach

A Master Teacher Revealed

Johann Pachelbel's Deutliche Anweisung

Kathryn Welter

For musicians of the Baroque Era, the ability to teach and attract students was essential to establishing their reputations, supplementing their incomes, and helping them to fulfill their myriad duties in church, city, or court positions. In Germany, the teaching tradition is well illustrated by Johann Pachelbel, whose treatise *Deutliche Anweisung* verifies his position in the long line of *Lehrmeister*, or master teachers, that began in the seventeenth century with Jan Pieterszoon Sweelinck and continued with Pachelbel's colleagues Dieterich Buxtehude and Johann Adam Reinken and successors Johann Heinrich Buttstett, Johann Christoph Bach, and Georg Böhm. This impressive chain of pedagogues culminated with Johann Sebastian Bach.

Johann Pachelbel has long been known to church musicians and scholars as an organist and composer. In his time he was also a renowned teacher. For instance, Buttstett, his most famous Erfurt student, specifically referred to Pachelbel as his "master teacher."[1] Although historians have focused mainly on Pachelbel's accomplishments as a performer and composer, his achievements as an instructor are equally important, for they shed light on the central role that teaching played in transmitting Baroque musical traditions.

For Pachelbel and many of his fellow pedagogues, we have very little evidence of actual teaching methods, except for a few manuscript collections copied and circulated among students and occasional descriptions by students in letters or publications. The *Deutliche Anweisung*, one of Pachelbel's little-known writings, offers evidence that bears directly on his teaching practices. Written in Nuremberg sometime during the last decade of Pachelbel's life,[2] the *Anweisung* is an organ-instruction manual in the composer's hand that was most likely intended for personal reference and student instruction (Plate 1).[3] Its full title runs as follows:

> *Deutliche Anweißung. Wie man durchs ganze Jahr bey wehrenden Gottesdienst, so wohl in den Vespern als Tagambt, bey S: Sebald mit der Orgel zu intonieren und zu respondiren sich zu verhalten habe.* [Detailed Instruction. How one should use the organ to intone and respond during the Holy Church Service throughout the entire year, in Vespers as well as in Daily Worship at St. Sebald's Church.]

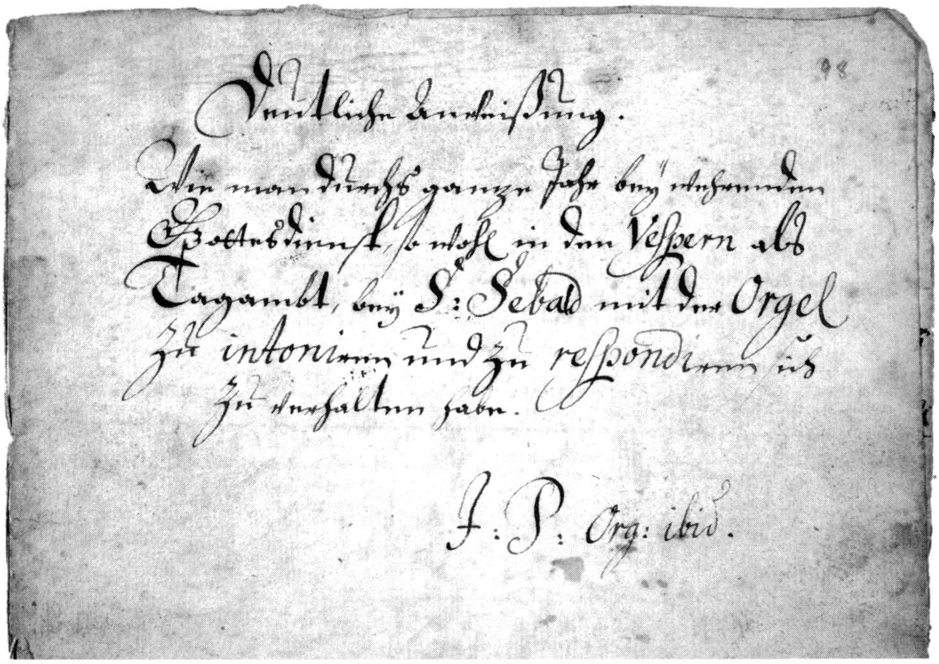

Plate 1. *Deutliche Anweisung*, title page. Bamberg, Staatsbibliothek, *Ms. J.H. Msc. Hist. 140*, Folio 98ʳ. Reproduced by permission.

The *Deutliche Anweisung* reveals in detail how one should perform on the organ during the various worship services at the city's foremost Protestant church, St. Sebald. In the process, it tells us a great deal about Pachelbel's teaching career, the liturgical practices at St. Sebald's Church, and the use of instrumental pieces within the services there.

The weekly services at St. Sebald's Church were similar to those at many other Lutheran churches in Germany during Pachelbel's time. In particular, they reflected the weekly rites in the other Lutheran churches in Nuremberg.[4] Saturdays began with a Communion Service with sermon, followed by a Choir Service. Vespers was held in the late afternoon. Sunday mornings began with the Early Communion Service, followed by the Holy Communion Service with sermon (known at the time as the Early Sermon Mass) and the Office Service, or *Tagamt*. Vespers was celebrated in the afternoon. In the *Deutliche Anweisung*, Pachelbel provides guides to the music of the Saturday Choir Service and the Sunday Office Service and Vespers Service.

The basic difference in the seven services, aside from the inclusion of Holy Communion or a sermon, appears to be in the number of deacons assigned to each and the music provided by the deacons, choir, and organist. The services at St. Sebald's appear to fall into two categories, depending on the number of personnel involved. The primary services were the Saturday Communion Service and Vespers Service and the Sunday Early Communion Service and Holy Communion Service with sermon. Each of these called for the participation of at least four clerics, a host of deacons (assistant clergy), and a choir. The secondary services—the Saturday Choir Service, the Sunday Office Service, and the Sunday Vespers—required only a principal cleric and two deacons. In addition, student singers commonly replaced the full choir.

The secondary services would have been ideal occasions for Pachelbel to use student apprentices. These rites already called for student singers in place of the choir, and the smaller number of clergy and the presumably smaller number of congregants would have put less pressure on an inexperienced organist. Indeed, the contents of the *Deutliche Anweisung* seem particularly suited to the participation of deputized organists. For the Saturdays, Sundays, and feast days in question, Pachelbel provides instructions for playing the secondary services only (Table 1). In these, the organ provides the primary musical content, with students or deacons chanting the liturgy.

The primary services at St. Sebald's, by contrast, not only required larger numbers of clergy and deacons but also included concerted choral music. It is likely that Pachelbel himself played for the primary services, since the music was more complex and called for the skill of a fully professional musician.

The *Deutliche Anweisung*, then, is a handbook for the music of the three secondary services. In it Pachelbel focuses on Advent, Christmas, New Year's, and Easter. For the services given, he includes notes on versicle texts, tablature notation of chants, key indications for intonation, and remarks on the order of service. For the Saturday Choir Service and Sunday Office Service for Advent (Plate 2), for instance, Pachelbel gives specific text incipits for the versicles and notes their accompanying chants in tablature notation. The incipits correspond very closely to those found in published service orders of the time:

> *In Adventu Domini* [On the Day of Advent]
> *Nach der Predigt am Sonnabend* [After the sermon on Saturday]
> *In diebus illis* (versicle; tablature)
> *Gloria patri* (doxology; tablature)
> C: (C major—the key in which the organist should intone)
> *Darauf singen die Schüler den Versicul, und darnach dem Priester etliche Worte, ab dann wird auff daß Magnificat praeambulirt* [Thereafter the students sing the versicle, and then the priest says several words, after which will be played a prelude to the Magnificat]
>
> *Sontage nach der Predigt in Tagambt.* [Sundays after the sermon of the Daily Service]
> *In diebus illis* (versicle; tablature)
> *Kÿrie* (tablature)

Christe (tablature)

Kyrie ut supra (tablature)

Gloria in excelsis Deo (tablature)

Gratias (tablature)

Quoniam (tablature)

Nach der Lesung des Capitels ist der Tractus außer C [After the reading of the Lesson, the Tract shall be sung in C major]

Ostende (tablature)

Two other details provided by Pachelbel add significantly to our understanding of the music for the secondary services. First, he gives six modes for the intonations that we can assume were the most common: G and D minor and C, D, F, and G major. Second, in keeping with the Nuremberg practice of using free organ pieces in the Vespers service, Pachelbel indicates that in many cases a prelude or toccata should be played before the Magnificat of the Sunday Vespers service. For the Second Sunday of Advent, for example, he states that "after the *Sicut erat* a short toccata is played and after the *Deo Gratias* it shall proceed in the same manner as on the previous Saturday."[5]

Pachelbel's specific reference to the organ toccata and organ prelude confirms and strengthens the connection of these pieces with liturgical intonations. It is thus understandable that these genres, together with chorale preludes, formed the core repertory of organ instruction. In orders of service from the late seventeenth century, one rarely finds anything more than the generic phrase "organista modulatur" as an indication that the organist should play a piece to intone a mode or to introduce an antiphon, a psalm, or the Magnificat. The *Deutliche Anweisung* highlights the prelude and the toccata and indicates where they were to be used in worship services.

In the *Deutliche Anweisung* Pachelbel is clearly using the terms *praeambulum* and *toccata* to indicate pieces of an introductory nature. He often uses the verbs *praeambuliren* and *toccatiren*, and in one instance *geschlage*, to denote that the organ should be played. The fact that he employs the terms interchangeably reflects the imprecise designation of genres that was common at the time. For example, although the toccata has come to be defined as a virtuosic composition, very free in form, featuring sections of brilliant passage work, with or without imitative or fugal interludes,[6] in seventeenth-century practice a large number of pieces fit this description—not just toccatas but also fugues, fantasies, chaconnes, and preludes.

The *Deutliche Anweisung* gives corroborative evidence of Pachelbel's choice of the prelude and toccata to introduce the Magnificat. These two types of pieces were obviously important from a liturgical standpoint, and it stands to reason that Pachelbel would have been certain to cover them in his teaching. A significant source for the kinds of preludes and toccatas that would have been used for the liturgical practices

Table 1. *Deutliche Anweisung*: Contents

Folio	Liturgical Day	Service
98r	Title page	
98v	(empty)	
99r	Sundays of Advent	Saturday after the sermon
		Sunday, Office Service
99v	Sundays of Advent, cont.	Sunday Vespers
	First Sunday of Advent	Saturday after the sermon
		Sunday, Office Service
100r	First Sunday of Advent, cont.	Sunday Vespers
	Second Sunday of Advent	Saturday after the sermon
		Sunday, Office Service
100v	Second Sunday of Advent, cont.	Sunday Vespers
	Third Sunday of Advent	Saturday after the sermon
		Sunday, Office Service
101r	Third Sunday of Advent, cont.	Sunday Vespers
	Fourth Sunday of Advent	Saturday after the sermon
		Sunday, Office Service
101v	Fourth Sunday of Advent, cont.	Sunday Vespers
	Christmas	Office Service
	After Christmas	Vespers
102r	Sunday[s] after the New Year	Saturday Vespers, after the sermon
	Sundays [after the New Year]	Office Service
		Sunday Vespers
102v	Sundays [after the New Year], cont.	Sunday Vespers
	Easter	Office Service
103r	Easter, cont.	Office Service
	Second day of Easter	Office Service
	First Sunday of Easter	[Office Service]
103v	Second Sunday of Easter	[Office Service]
	Third Sunday of Easter	[Office Service]
	Fourth Sunday of Easter	[Office Service]
104r	Fifth Sunday of Easter	[Office Service]
	Exaudi Sunday	Office Service
		Sunday Vespers
104v–105v	(empty)	

outlined in the *Deutliche Anweisung* is a tablature book belonging to the Thuringian organist Johann Valentin Eckelt.[7] Eckelt's manuscript, dating from 1692, has been recognized as one of the most important Central German collections of organ music of the late seventeenth century. It is of particular interest here because Eckelt was one of Pachelbel's last students in Erfurt. An annotation in the manuscript indicates that

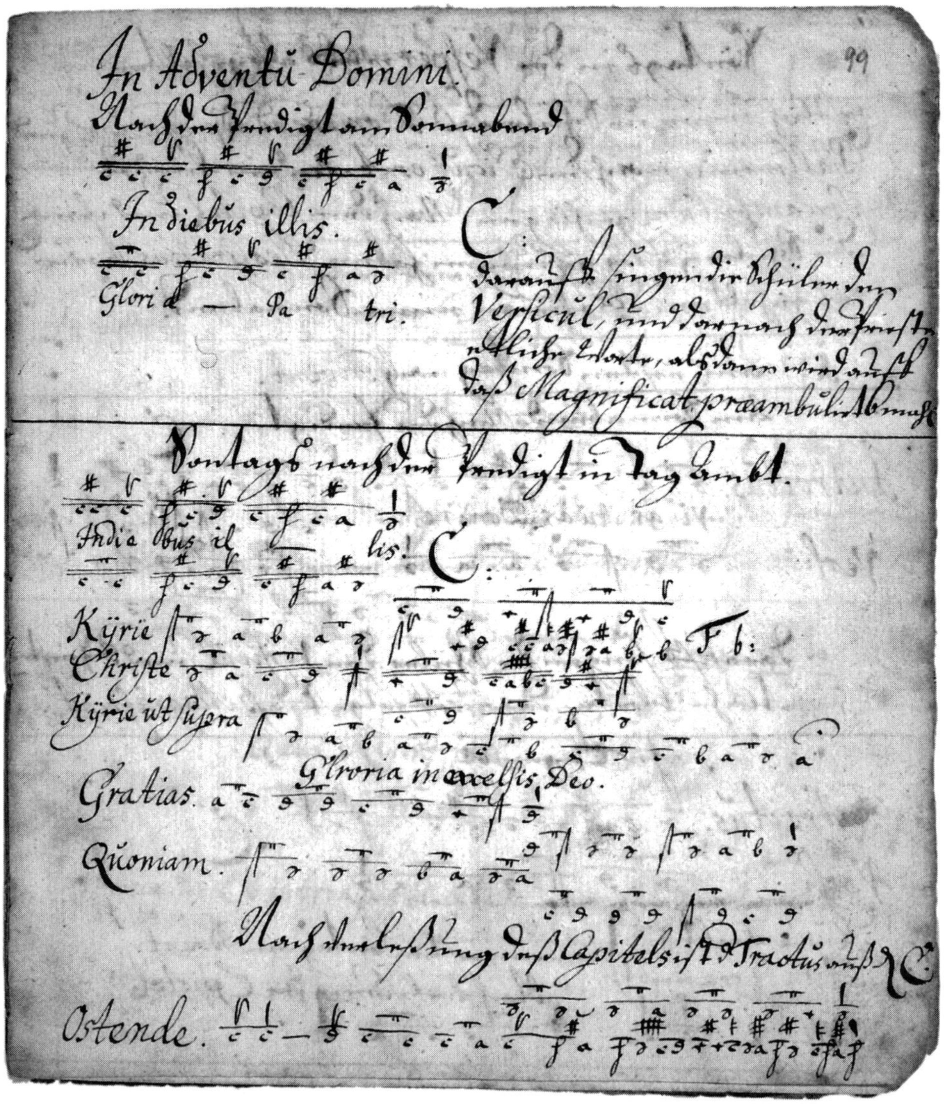

Plate 2. Folio 99ʳ of *Deutliche Anweisung*, giving versicles and chants in tablature for the Saturday Choir Service (top) and the Sunday Office Service (bottom) in Advent. Bamberg, Staatsbibliothek, *Ms. J.H. Msc. Hist. 140*. Reproduced by permission.

Eckelt studied with Pachelbel for several months in the spring of 1690, from Easter to St. John's Day. Christoph Wolff, who has studied the collection in depth,[8] has made an inventory of the contents of the manuscript's first eleven folios (Table 2).[9] These folios are particularly important because they are in Pachelbel's hand and include several of his own pieces as well as works by Froberger. Eckelt notes that he

Table 2. Johann Valentin Eckelt's Tablature Book: Contents of Folios 1–11

No.	Folio	Contents	Comments
	1^r	Title page: Johan Valentin Eckold/ 1692./Wernigerode am Harz./ Fantasien/Fugen und/Capricciosen	
	1^v	Empty	
1	2^r	Incomplete composition in C major	Close of a chorale prelude?
2	2^v	*Praeludium* [in G minor] *Joh: Bach:** [=Johann Pachelbel]	DTB IV/1, Part 1, No. 4
3	3^r–3^v	*Fuga.* [in G major]	DTB IV/1, Part 1, No. 42
4	4^r	*Toccata* [in D minor] *Joh. Bach:**	DTB IV/1, Part 1, No. 8
5	4^v–6^r	*Ricercar* [in D minor] *del Sig: J: J: Froberger*	DTÖ X/2, 82-83
6	6^v–7^r	*Fuga* [in C major] *Joh: Bach:**	DTB IV/1, Part 1, No. 31
7	7^v–9^r	*Praeludium* [in E minor] *Joh: Bach:**	DTB IV/1, Part 1, No. 25
8	9^v	*Canzon* [in A minor] *Sig: Froberg.*	DTÖ IV/1, 159-161
	11^r	"so weit bey Pachelbeln gelernet in Erffurt Anno 1690 von ostern an biß nach Johanni darnach ist er weg gezogen nach stuckhart daselbst er ietzunt Hofforgan."	[The above were studied with Pachelbel in Erfurt in 1690, from Easter until St. John's Day, after which he left for Stuttgart, where he is presently Court Organist]

*Added later by Eckelt.

bought the right to copy several of Pachelbel's works. This hints that the transmission of compositions from mentor to student may have involved a fee, thus providing the teacher with additional income.[10]

The pieces in Eckelt's manuscript also appear in the collection of another Pachelbel student, Johann Christoph Bach (1673–1727) of Gehren,[11] which supports the idea that Pachelbel earmarked specific works for pedagogical purposes that were copied repeatedly by his pupils. Lamentably, two treatises by Eckelt from the 1720s, his *Unterricht eine Fuge zu formiren* and *Unterricht, was ein Organist wissen soll*, have not survived. They might have shed additional light on his training with Pachelbel.

Viewed as a whole, Eckelt's manuscript mirrors Pachelbel's indications in the *Deutliche Anweisung* that toccatas and preludes are to be played before the Magnificat. The collection contains twenty-seven pieces by Pachelbel in all, most of them preludes, fugues, toccatas, and fantasias. All these could have been played as part of the liturgy. The first works in Pachelbel's hand include preludes in G and E minor, toccatas in D and G minor, and fugues in C and D major and E and G minor. The Toccata in

D Minor (Folio 4^r), which also appears in Johann Christoph Bach's collection, could have served as an intonational prelude, as proposed in the *Deutliche Anweisung.*

The paucity of teaching manuals such as Pachelbel's *Deutliche Anweissung* makes it difficult to study the teaching traditions of the Baroque Era. To broaden our understanding of Pachelbel's teaching methods, we can look at Sweelinck, who was renowned as an organist, composer, and pedagogue. In fact, he might be viewed as the father of German master teachers, attracting students from throughout Germany, including Andreas Düben, Samuel and Gottfried Scheidt, Paul Siefert, Jacob Praetorius, and Heinrich Scheidemann. At one point, the organists of Hamburg's four principal churches were all Sweelinck students. Students were often sent by their city councils to study with Sweelinck, and the costs for such study included room and board in his home as well as musical instruction.[12]

We can infer basic similarities between Pachelbel's and Sweelinck's teaching methods. Like most professional musicians of the seventeenth century, Pachelbel surely took on students as apprentices, to whom he taught the basics of performance and composition. The students, for their part, copied music and assisted during performances. Following Sweelinck's practice, Pachelbel may have taken certain of his apprentices into his house, offering them room and board as part of their instruction. Johann Conrad Rosenbusch began his studies with Pachelbel in Erfurt in 1685 as an eleven-year-old. Five years later, when Pachelbel moved to Stuttgart, Rosenbusch went with him. One may reasonably assume that Rosenbusch was living with Pachelbel's family during this time. We also know that Duke Eberhard Ludwig of Stuttgart sent one of his musicians, Johann Georg Christian Störl, to Nuremberg to study clavier and composition with Pachelbel and paid the expenses.[13] This mirrors the city council subventions of Sweelinck's students.

In Baroque Germany, the biographies of many professional musicians show a similar pattern of study: a promising student seeks out a master musician or is sent to study with him. Georg Caspar Wecker of Nuremberg served as teacher for many of Pachelbel's peers, including Christian Friedrich Witt, who became Capellmeister in Gotha and, in turn, a well-known teacher.[14] Another contemporary, Johann Theile of Naumburg, taught in Hamburg, Wolfenbüttel, and Merseburg. One of Theile's Wolfenbüttel pupils, Georg Oesterreich, "moved into the Capellmeister's house and lodged with [Theile], who instructed him . . . quite untiringly and faithfully in composition."[15] It appears to have been common practice, then, for students to live with their teachers, receiving room and board as part of the pedagogical package. Perhaps the most famous pedagogues in Pachelbel's time were Friedrich Wilhelm Zachow and Dieterich Buxtehude. Zachow, organist at St. Mary's Church in Halle for most of his career, taught George Frideric Handel, Gottfried Kirchhoff, Johann Gotthilf Krieger, and Johann Gotthilf Ziegler, among others. Buxtehude, organist of St. Mary's

Church in Lübeck, taught Nicolaus Bruhns and others. One of Buxtehude's students, Georg Dietrich Leiding, made a trip to Hamburg and Lübeck in 1684 to study with the "two extraordinarily famous organists, Reinken and Buxtehude."[16] This journey foreshadows Johann Sebastian Bach's own pilgrimages to observe both Reinken and Buxtehude several years later. Bach, for his part, attracted more than eighty students during his long and fruitful career as a teacher, and many of his pupils appear to have lived in his house. Moreover, a number followed him as he changed professional stations.[17]

By 1695 Pachelbel was well known in Germany, having filled municipal and church positions in Vienna, Eisenach, Erfurt, Stuttgart, and Gotha. He firmly established his reputation as a composer through the publication of three collections of keyboard music, and with his appointment in Nuremberg and the appearance of his fourth collection of printed works, the *Hexachordum Apollinis* of 1699, the composer reached the apex of his career. He dedicated the *Hexachordum* to two master musicians of "universal renown": Dieterich Buxtehude of Lübeck and Ferdinand Tobias Richter of Vienna. For Pachelbel, these virtuosos embodied the best in performance and pedagogy in the North and the South. With this dedication he was placing himself squarely in their company as a master representative of Central German keyboard artists. Thirty years later, Martin Fuhrmann, a critic who had studied with a student of Buxtehude, Friedrich Gottlieb Klingenberg, could write of the three great Bs in German music: Buxtehude, Bach, and Bachelbel.[18]

Pachelbel attracted students in Erfurt and Nuremberg who went on to distinguish themselves in music circles in Thuringia and elsewhere. The most notable of these were Pachelbel's sons Wilhelm Hieronymus and Karl Theodor; Johann Christoph Bach (not the Gehren Johann Christoph, but the elder brother of Johann Sebastian, who lived in Ohrdruf); and Buttstett. In the century and a half that spans Sweelinck to Johann Sebastian Bach, Pachelbel represents the most prominent and sought-after teacher in Central Germany in the seventeenth century.

The *Deutliche Anweisung* provides a glimpse of some of Pachelbel's teaching methods and consequently illuminates his role as master teacher. Of special significance are the instructions in intonational and responsorial practices, as well as the directions for the use of free organ pieces to introduce the Magnificat. Pachelbel's own compositions were probably used to fulfill these liturgical needs, and it is clear that these were the pieces he chose to pass on to his students. The *Deutliche Anweisung* is significant for illuminating Pachelbel's teaching practices. At the same time, it is also an important supplement to understanding the liturgical conventions at St. Sebald's Church in Nuremberg and the relation of certain musical genres to the local liturgy. The *Deutliche Anweisung* and the subsequent successful careers of Pachelbel's many students reveal his impact as pedagogue on the musical landscape of his time in

Central Germany and beyond, cementing his reputation as master teacher in the musical line that extends from Sweelinck to Bach.

Notes

1. Heinrich Buttstett, *Ut, re, mi, fa, la, tota musica et harmonia aeterna* (Erfurt: J.H. Kloss, 1716), 87. In the section on composing in a cantabile style, Buttstett stated: "dass man cantabel setzen soll. Diese Regel habe ich nun bald für 40 Jahren von meinem Lehrmeister, dem Berühmten Pachelbeln . . . empfangen." [One should compose in a cantabile style. I was taught this rule more than 40 years ago now by my teacher, the famous Pachelbel.]

2. The initials "J.P." verify Pachelbel's authorship. The designation "Org: ibid" (Organist of the same—i.e., St. Sebald's Church) suggests that he wrote the manual during his tenure at St. Sebald's, where he served from 1695 until his death in 1706.

3. Bamberg, Staatsbibliothek, *Ms. J.H. Msc. Hist. 140.*

4. For the background of liturgical music in Nuremberg, see Bartlett Russell Butler, *Liturgical Music in Sixteenth-Century Nürnberg: A Socio-Musical Study* (PhD diss., University of Illinois/Urbana-Champaign, 1970).

5. *Deutliche Anweisung*, fol. 99^r: "Nach dem Sicut erat kurz toccatirt und nach dem Deo Gratias wirds gehalten wie am vorhergehenden Sonnabend."

6. Arthur J. Ness, "Toccata," in *The New Harvard Dictionary of Music*, ed. Don Randel (Cambridge, Mass.: Harvard University Press, 1986), 859.

7. Crakow, Biblioteka Jagiellońska, *Mus. ms. 40035.*

8. Christoph Wolff, "Johann Valentin Eckelts Tabulaturbuch von 1692," in *Festschrift Martin Ruhnke zum 65. Geburtstag* (Neuhausen-Stuttgart: Hänssler, 1986), 374–86; Christoph Wolff, "Bach and Johann Adam Reinken: A Context for the Early Works," in Wolff, *Bach: Essays on His Life and Music* (Cambridge, Mass.: Harvard University Press, 1991), 60–61.

9. Wolff, "Johann Valentin Eckelts Tabulaturbuch," 382.

10. A number of copies of Bach's works, in the hand of his wife Anna Magdalena, ended up in the possession of students and colleagues, hinting that Bach, too, may have sold his works, copied out by his wife or assistants, to interested buyers for a fee. Anna Magdalena's copy of the Unaccompanied Cello Suites (*P 268*), for instance, was apparently prepared for Heinrich Ludwig Schwanberg, a Bach pupil active as a chamber musician in Braunschweig-Wolfenbüttel, during Schwanberg's stay in Leipzig in the fall of 1727. See NBA VI/2 (*Sechs Suiten für Violoncello solo*), KB, 11–12.

11. New Haven, Yale University, Irving S. Gilmore Music Library, *LM 4983.*

12. Max Seiffert, "J.P. Sweelinck und seine direkten deutschen Schüler," *Vierteljahrsschrift für Musikwissenschaft* 7 (1891), 145–260.

13. Johann Mattheson, *Grundlage einer Ehren-Pforte* (Hamburg: In Verlegung des Verfassers, 1740; reprint, Berlin: Leo Liepmannssohn, 1910), 351.

14. Even in early times, it was suggested that Pachelbel himself studied with Wecker. See Johann Doppelmayr, "Pachelbel," in *Historische Nachricht von dem Nürnbergischen Mathematicis und Künstlern* . . . [Nürnberg: P.C. Monath, 1730], 258, for instance. However, there is no direct evidence for this.

Johann Mattheson, for example, went to great pains to prove that Pachelbel could not have studied with Wecker. See Mattheson, "Pachelbel," in *Grundlage einer Ehren-Pforte*, 244.

15. Mattheson, *Grundlage einer Ehren-Pforte*, 365. See also Jocelyn Mackey, "Johann Theile," in *The New Grove Dictionary of Music and Musicians*, 2d ed., ed. Stanley Sadie (London: Macmillan, 2001), vol. 25, 345–46.

16. Kerala Snyder, *Dieterich Buxtehude: Organist in Lübeck* (New York: Schirmer, 1987), 130.

17. See Christoph Wolff, *Johann Sebastian Bach: The Learned Musician* (New York: Norton, 2000), 327–31; George B. Stauffer, "J.S. Bach as Organ Pedagogue," in *The Organist as Scholar: Essays in Honor of Russell Saunders*, ed. Kerala Snyder (New York: Pendragon Press, 1995), 25–44.

18. Martin Fuhrmann, *Die an der Kirchen Gottes gebauete Satans-Capelle* (Berlin: Marco Hilario Frischmuth, 1729), 55.

From the House of Aaron to the House of Johann Sebastian

Old Testament Roots for the Bach Family Tree

Mary Dalton Greer

And you shall hallow the fiftieth year . . . It shall be a jubilee for you: you shall return, every one of you, to your property and every one of you to your family.

—Leviticus 25:10[1]

In 1735 Johann Sebastian Bach turned fifty. During the course of that year he drew up a family tree delineating six generations of male members of the Bach family and prepared an annotated family genealogy to accompany the family tree.[2] In addition, at around the same time he began to assemble the musical compositions of his most gifted forebears into a collection: the so-called Old Bach Archive. All three endeavors attest to his deep connection to the Bach clan, nearly all of whom were musicians, and his commitment to preserving their musical legacy.

The reason for Bach's systematic documentation of his family heritage beginning in 1735 has never been satisfactorily explained. Christoph Wolff has pointed out that "Bach amassed the Archive at about the time that he witnessed, with pride, his older sons leaving the parental home and taking up careers as professional musicians in their own right."[3] To be sure, Wilhelm Friedemann and Carl Philipp Emanuel assumed their first official positions in the mid-1730s, but over a span of five years. Friedemann accepted the post of organist of St. Sophia's Church in Dresden in 1733, and Carl Philipp Emanuel entered into the service of Frederick II, the future King of Prussia, in Berlin in 1738. Until now, no compelling documentary evidence has been presented to suggest why Bach undertook these projects in 1735.

The wording of several of the entries in the genealogy and the fact that Bach, a close reader of Old Testament scriptures, commenced these ambitious family-history projects in his fiftieth year point to another explanation. His heightened interest in preserving his family's history in 1735 may have been prompted, at least in part, by the injunction in the twenty-fifth chapter of Leviticus to hallow one's fiftieth year as

15

a jubilee year and to return to one's family and property. Bach may have carried out this command figuratively by preparing the family tree and genealogy and by compiling the Old Bach Archive.

The premise that a command issued to the Israelites thousands of years earlier inspired Bach to compile his family's genealogy and assemble the compositions of his distinguished musical forebears when he turned fifty is not as improbable as it might appear. Indeed, Christoph Wolff notes that, because Levitical rules regarding ritual purification still held sway in Lutheran churches during Johann Sebastian's lifetime, his mother was excluded from his christening ceremony on March 23, 1685.[4]

There is ample evidence that Bach was familiar with the Old Testament book of Leviticus. He must have owned at least one copy of Luther's German Bible, though it has disappeared without a trace.[5] The inventory of his estate reveals that his theological library included at least two important commentaries on Luther's translation: Abraham Calov's learned *Die deutsche Bibel* and Johannes Olearius's erudite *Biblische Erklärung*.[6] Both publications incorporated nearly all of Luther's translation, together with glosses by Luther and the authors. Bach's copy of Calov's Bible survives, and it reveals that he corrected, underlined, or added marginal notations to eleven passages in Leviticus.[7] In the eighteenth line of Calov's commentary on Chapter 25:9, which concerns the sounding of the trumpet in the jubilee year, Bach inserts the letter "s" in red ink to correct the word *himmliche* in the phrase "himmlische Jubel Jahr" (heavenly Jubilee year).[8]

Bach's annotations in his Calov Bible also indicate that he read the First Book of Chronicles with great interest. His markings demonstrate his deep affinity for the Levite musicians and his especially strong identification with Asaph, King David's Capellmeister. Bach's view of his musical calling and his membership in a large, musically gifted family appear to have been shaped at the most fundamental level by his reading of Old Testament passages pertaining to the families of musicians who were called to serve in the Temple. The biblical texts provide crucial insights into Bach's choice of words in numerous documents and into the motivating forces behind certain undertakings that are not readily explained otherwise.

That Bach drew parallels between his own family and career and those of the Levite musicians can be discerned in several ways. First, he highlighted numerous passages in his copy of the Calov Bible that pertain to the divinely called Levite musicians and to the role of music in the worship service.[9] Second, he aspired to "well-appointed" church music during much of his life. Third, he consistently preferred the titles of "Capellmeister" and "*Director Musices*"—terms that are applied to Levitical musicians in Biblical commentaries known to Bach—to that of "Cantor of St. Thomas School." Fourth, Bach composed a setting of Psalm 115:12-15 (Cantata 196, *Der Herr denket an uns*) around the time of his own wedding to another member of the extended Bach family, Maria Barbara Bach. The Psalm text refers to the House of Aaron—that is, to the Israelite priests and Levites.[10] If Bach regarded members of the Bach clan as latter-day Levites, a musical setting of this text would have been highly appropriate for the wedding of two members of the Bach family.

Let us explore the biblical citations, the genealogy, and the four points just outlined.

The Jubilee Year

Olearius assigns the twenty-fifth chapter of Leviticus the heading "Jubilee, the Year of Rejoicing" ("JUBILÆUS, Das Jubel=Jahr").[11] Calov titles the second section (vv. 8-55) of the same chapter, "About the Jubilee and Free Years" ("Vom Jubel=und Frey=Jahren").[12]

In the Calov Bible, Leviticus 25:8-13 and the accompanying commentary by Luther and Calov read as follows:

> v. 8. You shall count off seven weeks of years, seven times seven years, so that the period of seven weeks of years gives forty-nine years. v. 9. Then you shall have the trumpet sounded loud throughout all your land. (*The joyful jubilee year was announced by the trumpets and this jubilee year was a beautiful model for . . . the eternal heavenly Jubilee Year . . . in which . . . all the elect shall be gathered together and also everyone of the faithful shall return to their own and remain together under their head, Christ, throughout eternity.*) v. 10. And you shall hallow the fiftieth year and you shall proclaim liberty throughout the land to all its inhabitants . . . (*in which . . . everyone can claim his inheritance*). It shall be a jubilee for you: you shall return, every one of you, to your property and every one of you to your family . . . v. 12. For it is a jubilee; it shall be holy to you . . . v. 13. In this year of jubilee you shall return, every one of you, to your property.[13]

If, as the markings in his personal copy of the Calov Bible suggest, Bach identified especially strongly with the Levite musicians, this passage provides a rationale for his systematic documentation of his family's roots and musical legacy beginning in his fiftieth year.

Further supporting this idea is the nature of the family tree and genealogy themselves. The fact that they include only male members on his father's side of the family demonstrates that Bach's purpose was not to record his children's genetic ancestors, but rather to trace a patrilineal descent like those found in the Old Testament. Moreover, by entitling the genealogy "Origin of the Bach Family of Musicians" ("Ursprung der musicalisch-Bachischen Familie") rather than simply, "Origin of the Bach Family," he signals that the Bach clan is a musical dynasty. Indeed, in his entries in the genealogy he focuses on the professional achievements of his relatives rather than their personal lives. Every entry contains a remark by Bach on the nature of each family member's talent and professional position.

In addition, it is evident that Bach conveyed to his children that most family members were church musicians and that this was a significant characteristic of the Bach clan. In describing the annual reunions of the Bach family, Johann Nicolaus Forkel, drawing on information provided by the two oldest Bach sons, Wilhelm Friedemann and Carl Philipp Emanuel, wrote:

> As the company wholly consisted of cantors, organists, and town musicians, who had all to do with the Church, and as it was besides a general custom at the time to begin everything with Religion, the first thing they did, when they were assembled, was to sing a chorale.[14]

The Genealogy

Bach chose to begin the narrative of the Bach family of musicians with his great-great-grandfather, Veit Bach. Bach's entry for Veit begins: "No. 1. Veit Bach, a white-bread baker in Hungary, had to flee Hungary in the sixteenth century on account of his Lutheran religion . . . He moved to Germany, and, finding adequate security for the Lutheran religion in Thuringia, settled at Wechmar, near Gotha."[15] The wording of this entry evokes the exodus recalled in Leviticus 25:38: "I am the Lord your God, who brought you out of the land of Egypt, to give you the land of Canaan, to be your God."[16] By highlighting the fact that Veit fled from Hungary, where he faced religious persecution, to the security of Thuringia, where generations of his descendants continued to live and thrive, Bach created a parallel—conscious or not—between Hungary and Egypt on the one hand and Thuringia and Canaan on the other.[17] Furthermore, the fact that Bach explicitly mentions the disposition of Veit's property is evocative of Genesis 13:1, which describes Abram's departure from Egypt: "And so Abram went up from Egypt, he and his wife, and all that he had . . ."[18]

Just as Asaph and the other Levite musicians were appointed by King David acting under the guidance of the Holy Spirit,[19] Bach's choice of wording in both the genealogy and in a letter to his childhood friend Georg Erdmann indicates that he felt Providence had played a key role in his personal and professional life. In his own entry in the genealogy, he states that he was "Capellmeister and Director of the Chamber Music at the Court of the Serene Prince of Anhalt-Cöthen, Anno 1717" and was "called hence, Anno 1723, to become Music Director and Cantor at the St. Thomas School, in Leipzig, where, in accordance with God's Holy Will, he still lives and at the same time holds the honorary position of Capellmeister of Weissenfels and Cöthen."[20] Bach's use of the word "called" ("vocirt"), particularly in conjunction with his subsequent reference to God's Holy Will, suggests that he felt he was summoned to his position as Music Director and Cantor of the St. Thomas School not only by the Leipzig officials, but by a Higher Authority. In a letter to Erdmann dated October 28, 1730, in which he seeks Erdmann's help in finding another position, Bach invokes God four times (the emphasis, shown through underlining, is mine):

> <u>it pleased God</u> that I should be called hither to be *Director Musices* and Cantor at the St. Thomas School. Though at first, indeed, it did not seem at all proper to me to change my position of Capellmeister for that of Cantor. Wherefore, then, I postponed my decision for a quarter of a year . . . but . . . I cast my lot, <u>in the name of the Lord</u>, and made the journey to Leipzig . . . and then made the change of position. Here, <u>by God's will</u>, I am still in service. But, [as the pay is inadequate and the Leipzig authorities irksome and not musically inclined] I shall be forced, <u>with God's help</u>, to seek my fortune elsewhere.[21]

By contrast, Johann Gottfried Walther avoided any hint of a divine hand in his description of Bach's professional advancements in the *Musicalisches Lexicon* of 1732.[22]

Furthermore, the fact that Johann Sebastian lists himself as entry no. 24 in the genealogy was apparently not mere coincidence, but rather influenced by the symbolic significance of the number 24 in the Bible. In their commentaries on First Chronicles 25:31, both Calov and Olearius point out that, just as there are twenty-four divisions of musicians, there are also twenty-four divisions of Levites.[23] Olearius goes on to explain the relevance of this number to other parts of the Bible. Most importantly, he explains that it was at the instigation of the Holy Spirit that this number was introduced into the Book of Revelation:

> The twenty-fourth. The Greeks call these twenty-four divisions who were to serve in the temple Ephemerias. Luke 1:5. Whereby we are to recall that the Holy Spirit also introduces this number in the Revelation of John chap. 4:4, in which twenty-four chairs, on which twenty-four elders are seated, are mentioned. Whereby we are also to recall 1) The twenty-four canonic authors of the Old Testament . . . 2) The twelve sons of Jacob and the twelve apostles who together, in symmetry, yield this number of 24. III. As also the divisions of the Levites, which the Most High representing all the people has chosen for his service 1. Chron. 24:18. NB are made up of twenty-four divisions. For his Faithful are all priests before God / Rev. 1. and his heavenly singers and musicians, in proper order 1. Chron. 25:31[24] and the principal lesson of the same.

Given that Bach was well-versed in biblical symbolism and owned the Olearius commentary, it may not be coincidental at all that he listed himself as "No. 24" in the genealogy.

Bach's reference to Veit Bach fleeing from Hungary due to his Lutheran religion and his mention of God's Holy Will in his own entry indicate that he believed that he and the other members of the Bach family shared a special destiny. In the letter to Erdmann cited above, Bach concludes a long description of his professional endeavors with an update on his family: "Now I must add a little about my domestic situation . . . [My children] are all born musicians, and I can assure you that I can already form an ensemble both *vocaliter* and *instrumentaliter* within my family."[25] His choice of words bespeaks the understandable pride of a *pater familias* who is pleased that his children are following in his footsteps. At the same time, it reflects his belief that not only his ancestors but also his own children were blessed by Providence with exceptional musical gifts.

The wording of Bach's obituary indicates that he succeeded in conveying to his children the belief that the Bach family's extraordinary musical talent had been bestowed by a force greater than themselves. This, in turn, was integral to their conception of themselves and their view of the extended Bach family. Indeed, Bach's son C.P.E. and student Johann Friedrich Agricola pay tribute to the musical talent of the Bach clan in the opening paragraph of the obituary:

> Johann Sebastian Bach belongs to a family that seems to have received a love and aptitude for music as a gift of Nature to all its members in common. So much is certain, that Veit Bach, the founder of the family, and all his descendents, even to the present seventh generation, have been devoted to music, and all save perhaps a very few have made it their profession.[26]

By the time Bach's obituary was written—that is, by 1750—German society was moving toward a more secular Zeitgeist. Thus, in the obituary the extraordinary musical talent of the Bach family is described as a "gift of nature" rather than a gift of God. Nevertheless, the concept of a fundamental force at work is the same.

The True Foundation

The Old Testament roots of Bach's concern with well-ordered music also deserve mention. A number of passages that Bach highlighted in his Calov Bible pertain specifically to the role of music in the worship service and to the division of the musicians. Alongside the summary of Chapter 25 of First Chronicles he noted: "NB This chapter is the true foundation of all church music pleasing to God. etc."[27] As Robin A. Leaver has observed, Bach also underlined the summary of the chapter: "(I.) Of the Singers and Instrumentalists. (II.) Appointment of the Singers by Lot," as well as Calov's comment on the first verse: "[the musicians are to] express the Word of God in spiritual songs and psalms, sing them in the temple, and at the same time to play with instruments."[28]

In the Calov Bible, First Chronicles 25:1 reads:

> And David with all the field captains set apart for offices among the children of Asaph, Heman, and Jeduthun, the prophets (*who were to form the Word of God in spiritual hymns and psalms and sing them in the temple, at the same time playing instruments*) with

harps, psalteries, and cymbals and they were numbered (*and arranged in order*) for work according to their office (*to execute the same in a certain order. For God is a God of order . . .*).[29]

Leaver connects Bach's markings with passages in two oft-cited letters in which Bach expresses the necessity of well-ordered church music.[30] The first of these, dated June 25, 1708, is Bach's request to the Council of the St. Blasius Church in Mühlhausen for permission to leave his position as organist:

> Even though I should always have liked to work toward the goal, namely, a well-regulated church music, to the Glory of God and in conformance with your wishes . . . Now, God has brought it to pass that an unexpected change should offer itself to me, in which I see the possibility of . . . the achievement of my goal of a well-regulated church music.[31]

The second document is Bach's "Short But Most Necessary Draft" of August 23, 1730, in which he outlines for the Leipzig Town Council the forces he needs for a "well-appointed church music."[32] In a marginal note to First Chronicles 28:21, Bach expresses his belief that God worked through David to establish well-appointed music. Above the verse, in which David says to his son Solomon, "Here are the divisions of the priests and the Levites for all the service of the house of God," Bach wrote: "NB A splendid example that, besides other forms of worship, music, too, was especially ordered by God's spirit through David."[33]

Christoph Trautmann and Robin A. Leaver concur that Bach's annotations in the Calov Bible indicate that he understood his profession as a church musician to be a divine calling.[34] Trautmann writes:

> Bach was deeply conscious of his own office as a church musician, ordained for him by God through David. Accordingly, the office was in his view not merely the name of a calling or the description of a sphere of activity, but on the basis of Biblical authority he identified himself as a called and ordained servant of the church.[35]

Both Leaver and Trautmann note the importance of Bach's annotation next to the summary of First Chronicles 25, mentioned above. However, Bach's observation refers to the entire chapter—"Dieses Capitel"—not just the first verse. His comment not only provides insights into his concept of church music that will find favor with the Lord, but also into his view of himself as a fellow member of a divinely-ordained musical dynasty. Verses 1-31 of First Chronicles 25, together with Calov's commentary, read:

> v. 1. And David with all the field captains set apart for offices among the children of Asaph, Heman, and Jeduthun, the prophets (*who were to form God's Word in spiritual songs and psalms and sing them in the temple, at the same time playing instruments*) with

harps, psalteries, and cymbals and they were numbered (*and arranged in order*) for work according to their office (*to execute the same in a certain order. For God is a God of order. 1 Corinthians XIV. 33*). v. 2. Among the children of Asaph were: Zaccur, Joseph, Nethaniah, and Asarelah . . . children of Asaph under Asaph (*he was their father, who was to instruct them, and also their guardian and Song-master*), who prophesied for the king (*about spiritual matters from God's Word, or also taught through the inspiration of God's spirit, and sang and played about it before the king . . .*). v. 3. Of Jeduthun: The children of Jeduthun were Gedaliah, Zeri . . . , Jeshaiah, Shimei, Hashabiah, and Mattithiah . . . the six, under their father Jeduthun, with harps, who prophesied in order to thank and praise the Lord. v. 4. Of Heman: The children of Heman were Bukkiah, Mattaniah, Uzziel . . . Shebuel . . . and Jerimoth, Hananiah, Hanani, Elia-thath, Giddalti, and Romamti-ezer, Joshbekashah, Mallothi, Hothir, and Mahazioth. v. 5. These were all children of Heman, the seer (*the prophet v.1.*) of the king, in the Word of God, to lift up the horn (*to exalt Christ, about whom he prophesied Ps. 89:25. Luke 1:69. which did not occur only with words, but also with music making and singing*). For God had given Heman fourteen sons and three daughters. v. 6. These were all under their fathers Asaph, Jeduthun, and Heman, to sing [make music] in the house of the Lord with cymbals, psalteries, and harps, according to their service in the house of God at the king's. (*as the king had created the order*) v. 7. And their number, together with their brothers (*relatives*) who were trained in the song of the Lord, was in total two hundred eighty-eight masters. (*the instructors and students together made 4,000. S. c. 23:5.*) The Second Part. | Casting of Lots for the Singers. v. 8. And they cast lots for their duties, the smallest as well as the greatest, teacher and pupil alike. (*how they should be subordinate to one another, and one should be under another.*) v. 9. The first lot fell under Asaph to Joseph (*together with his sons and brothers, or relatives, they were twelve, for it explicitly states so for the others*), the second to Gedaliah, together with his brothers and sons, they were twelve.

[Vv. 10-30 continue with the recitation of the disposition of the lots to the twenty-four sons of Asaph, of Heman, and of Jeduthun. Each verse concludes with the phrase, "together with his sons and his brothers, they were twelve."]

v. 31. The twenty-fourth, to Romamti-ezer, together with his sons and brothers (*or blood relatives as in all the preceding*) they were twelve. (*There were likewise as many divisions of singers and instrumentalists as of the priests c. 24:18 and of the Levites, who waited upon and helped the priests. Bes. c. 24:31.*)[36]

It is significant that Bach singles out this particular chapter, for First Chronicles 25 not only describes the musical proficiencies of the various temple musicians but also, like Bach's annotated genealogy, describes how the musicians are related to one another. His remark on this chapter not only provides insights into his conception of church music that will find favor with the Lord, but also underscores his belief that his calling as a musician and his membership in a large musical family had a prece-dent in the Levite clans of musicians described in the Old Testament.[37]

Bach and Asaph as Capellmeisters

Other annotations in the Calov Bible suggest that Bach identified strongly with King David's Capellmeister, Asaph, and the two other leading Levite musicians, Heman and Jeduthun. First Chronicles 25, cited earlier, the very chapter that Bach identifies as the true foundation of church music, directly concerns these three musicians and their descendants. Moreover, Bach underlined the names "Asaph," "Heman," and "Jeduthun" in red ink in the preface to the Psalter in the Calov Bible: "the prophet Asaph, King David's Capellmeister," "Heman is called a seer, that is, a prophet of the king 'according to the promise of God to exalt him' (1 Chron. 25:5; 2 Chron. 35:15)," and "Jeduthun, is called a seer of King Josiah."[38] At the beginning of Psalms 50 and 73, Calov describes Asaph as "the inspired prophet and song master" and "the inspired Capellmeister of David,"[39] characterizations that surely resonated with Bach. "That Bach should underline the statement that Asaph was the *Capellmeister* to the court of King David," Leaver writes, "is hardly surprising since it was a title he himself had carried for a good many years."[40] I believe that Bach's affinity for Asaph went beyond historical curiosity, however. For Bach, Asaph represented an inspired composer-performer appointed by King David[41] through God's direction.

In this context it is noteworthy that Olearius mentions the titles of "Capellmeister" and "Directore Chori Musici"—positions Bach held for many years—twice in his commentary on First Chronicles. In his discussion of First Chronicles 6:33 Olearius refers to "the most distinguished *Directori musici* and *Capellmeister*," and in explaining First Chronicles 15:22, he mentions "the *Director chori* and *Capell-meister*."[42] As we have seen, Bach's close reading of First Chronicles is amply documented by the markings in his personal copy of the Calov Bible. Although Bach's personal copy of Olearius's *Biblische Erklärung* has not come to light, there is evidence that he scrutinized the text with at least as much care as that of the Calov Bible.[43]

Like Asaph, Bach was a Capellmeister, composer, and the leading member of a large musical clan. Bach appears to have particularly valued his titles of Capellmeister and Royal Court Composer, both of which had direct counterparts in the two epithets associated with Asaph in the Old Testament: "King David's Capellmeister" and "prophet."[44] When Bach moved to Leipzig in 1723 to serve as St. Thomas Cantor and Director of Music, he retained the honorary title of Capellmeister to the Court of Anhalt-Cöthen.[45] Five years later, following the death of Prince Leopold, his former patron in Cöthen, Bach requested and obtained a similar honorary appointment at the court of Duke Christian of Saxe-Weissenfels.[46]

In July 1733 Bach petitioned Friedrich August II, who had just become Elector of Saxony upon the death of his father, for a title in the Court Capelle in Dresden.[47] Upon the death of Duke Christian of Saxe-Weissenfels on June 28, 1736, Bach stood to lose the title of Capellmeister, which he had held continuously since 1717. Indeed, it may have been the death of Duke Christian, in combination with the hope that the honorary title of Royal Court Composer might strengthen his position in his dispute with Johann August Ernesti, Rector of St. Thomas's, that spurred Bach to renew his application to be named Royal Court Composer in Dresden.[48] Bach apparently set enormous store in having the honorary title Electoral Saxon and Royal Polish Court Compositeur bestowed upon him. As Wolff writes:

> The award in 1736 of the prestigious title Electoral Saxon and Royal Polish Court *Compositeur*, which carried no specific obligations but gave Bach the stamp of royal approval with the privileges of courtly affiliation and protection, pleased him to a degree that cannot be overestimated.[49]

Bach's pursuit of the positions of honorary Capellmeister and Royal Court Composer may indeed have been prompted by a desire to enhance his prestige and to gain a certain amount of royal protection. On a more fundamental level, however, it is also possible that acquiring these titles confirmed for Bach that he was a true successor to Asaph, King David's divinely ordained Capellmeister and prophet.

A Wedding in the House of Aaron

Although scholars agree that *Der Herr denket an uns*, BWV 196, is an early wedding cantata dating from the Mühlhausen years, there is no general consensus about the precise occasion for which the work was written.[50] The cantata is a setting of Psalm 115:12-15, which reads:

> v. 12. The Lord has been mindful of us; he will bless us; he will bless the house of Israel, he will bless the house of Aaron.
> v. 13. He will bless those who fear the Lord, both small and great.
> v. 14. May the Lord give you increase, both you and your children.
> v. 15. May you be blessed by the Lord, who made heaven and earth.[51]

Citing the reference to the House of Aaron (which connoted priests and ministers) in verse 12 of the Psalm, Philipp Spitta proposed that Cantata 196 was composed for the wedding of the widowed pastor, Johann Lorenz Stauber, to Regina Wedemann, the aunt of Bach's wife Maria Barbara.[52] However, since Bach strongly identified with the Levite musicians—who, as we shall see, were also considered members of the House of Aaron—he may have written the cantata on the occasion of his own wedding to his second cousin, Maria Barbara Bach. Indeed, Christoph Wolff has observed that the intimate scoring of *Der Herr denket an uns* (four-part vocal ensemble, strings, and continuo) was eminently suitable for the small Dornheim church in which Johann Sebastian and Maria Barbara were married.[53] As far as we know, the wedding that took place on October 17, 1707, is the only instance in which two members of the

Bach clan married one another. It would be hard to imagine a more appropriate text for the nuptial celebration of two members of the Bach family, nearly all of whom were employed as church musicians.

Psalm 115, the basis of Cantata 196, most probably held special significance for Bach because it refers to the House of Aaron in Verse 12. Luther's summary of Psalm 115 is the only Psalm commentary in the Calov Bible that contains the phrase "we singers" ("wir Sänger"). Near the end of the gloss cited by Calov, Luther writes: "as we are called God's servants, offerers, singers, fasters, and doers of good works."[54] That Luther explicitly mentions singers—in the broad sense, musicians—in connection with the House of Aaron surely resonated with Bach and demonstrates that the text of Psalm 115 was eminently applicable to the musical Bach clan.[55] Another Bible published in Altenburg and Jena five years earlier[56] contains a nearly identical summary of the Psalm, suggesting that even if Bach did not have access to the Calov Bible as early as 1707, Luther's summary of the Psalm with its reference to "Sänger" would have been available to him in other sources.

Furthermore, in several editions of Luther's German translation of the Bible published between 1676 and 1747, Psalm 115 bears the heading, "Gott allein die Ehre!" ("To God alone the Glory!")—the German equivalent of Bach's lifelong colophon, "Soli Deo Gloria." [57] This fact, in conjunction with the reference to "we . . . singers" in Luther's gloss, lends support to the premise that this Psalm held special significance for Bach.

In two other editions of the German Bible published during Bach's lifetime, the following prayer based on Psalm 115 appears immediately after the Psalm text: "Prayer. Great Blessings-God! thou alone art worthy of Glory . . ."[58] In his commentary on Psalm 115 in the third volume of the *Biblische Erklärung*, Olearius reiterates that glory is due to God alone no fewer than four times:

> It is to the name of the Lord / to whom alone all glory is due . . . Glory be to God alone, to God the highest glory. Not to us, thou alone art worthy of Glory . . . so that we give Him alone the glory . . . About the Glory which is due to God alone.[59]

In light of Bach's identification with the Levite musicians—members of the House of Aaron—later in his life, Bach could have found no text better suited than Psalm 115 for his marriage to another member of the Bach clan.

Conclusion

We must weigh the surviving evidence and judge whether it is a coincidence that Bach compiled a family tree and genealogy of the Bach family of musicians in his jubilee year; highlighted numerous passages in his Calov Bible that allude to the role of music in the worship service and to the Levite musicians Asaph, Heman, and Jeduthun;

pursued titles consistent with those of King David's Capellmeister Asaph; strove to achieve well-regulated church music; and composed a setting of Psalm 115:12-15 that refers to the House of Aaron at the time of his own wedding to his cousin Maria Barbara Bach. I suggest that these actions were shaped by his reading of passages in Leviticus and First Chronicles, together with the related commentaries of Martin Luther, Abraham Calov, and Johannes Olearius. The title, style, and content of Bach's genealogy, the depth of his concern for the role of music in worship and its proper organization, and the biblically resonant wording of his letters regarding well-appointed music and its establishment by divine authority through David all lead one to conclude that Bach felt a special affinity with the divinely ordained House of Aaron.

Notes

1. Verses 11-13 read: "That fiftieth year shall be a jubilee for you . . . For it is a jubilee; it shall be holy to you . . . In this year of jubilee you shall return, every one of you, to your property." All biblical citations in English are from the *New Revised Standard Version* (Cambridge: Cambridge University Press, 1989).

2. It is within the genealogy that the starting date of 1735 is confirmed. In entry 18, for Johann Bernhard Bach, Johann Sebastian states that Bernhard "is still living at the present time (that is, 1735)." See NBR, 289 and also 281–82 (on the background of the family tree and genealogy).

3. Christoph Wolff, *Johann Sebastian Bach: The Learned Musician* (New York: W.W. Norton, 2000), 420.

4. Wolff, *Johann Sebastian Bach*, 14. The rule he refers to is found in Leviticus 12:2.

5. Presumably it was inherited by his widow.

6. See Robin A. Leaver, *Bach's Theological Library: A Critical Bibliography* (Neuhausen-Stuttgart: Hänssler-Verlag, 1983).

7. Howard H. Cox, ed., *The Calov Bible of J.S. Bach* (Ann Arbor: UMI Research Press, 1985), facsimiles 59–66 and p. 408–9; Thomas Rossin, *The Calov Bible of Johann Sebastian Bach* (PhD diss., University of Minnesota, 1992), 100–3.

8. Rossin, 102–3. Cox does not include this corrected passage in his facsimile edition of the Calov Bible.

9. The organization of music in the Temple and the division of the musicians, including the Capellmeister Asaph, is the principal theme of the following passages in First Chronicles: 6:31-53, 15:16-28, 16:4-10, the preface to Chapter 25, 25:1, and 28:21. Bach marked the latter three passages in his copy of the Calov Bible. See Cox, *The Calov Bible*, facsimiles 109–11 and pp. 417–18. Both Olearius and Calov employed a numbering system for First Chronicles that resulted in the present-day numbers being labeled one number smaller. For instance, the modern Chapter 16 appears as Chapter 17, and the present-day Chaper 25 appears as Chapter 26. For purposes of discussion in this essay, the modern chapter numbering is used without comment.

10. Although members of the "House of Aaron" (priests) technically differ from the Levites (the priests' assistants, including the temple musicians), Calov's gloss on Psalm 118:3 reveals that, at least

in certain instances, the term "House of Aaron" was loosely applied to refer to both priests and Levites. Psalm 118:3, together with Calov's explanation, reads: "The House of Aaron says (*the Priests and Levites, to whom it actually fell to enter into the worship service to praise God the Lord and to bring him the sacrifices, through whose offerings the reconciliation of the Lord Christ was also established / Heb. IX.*) his goodness endures forever." The original text reads: "Es sage das Hauß Aaron / (*die Priester und Leviten / denen der Gottesdienst / GOtt den HErrn zu loben / anzutreten / und ihm die Opffer zu bringen / eigentlich zukam durch derer Opffer die Versöhnung des HErrn Christi auch fürgestellet ward / Ebr. IX.*) seine Güte wäret ewiglich." Calov, *Die heilige Bibel*, vol. 1/II, col. 737.

11. Johannes Olearius, *Biblische Erklärung* (Leipzig: Johann Christoph Tarnoven, 1678–1681), vol. 1, 637.

12. Abraham Calov, *Die heilige Bibel nach S. Herrn D. Martini Lutheri* (Wittenberg: Christian Schrödter, 1681–1682), vol. 1/I, col. 737.

13. Calov, *Die heilige Bibel*, vol. 1/I, cols. 737–38. Unless otherwise noted, the translations used here are the author's. The original text reads: "v. 8. Und du solt zehlen solcher Feyer=Jahr sieben / daß sieben Jahr siebenmal gezehlet werden / und die Zeit der sieben Feyer=Jahr machen neun und viertzig Jahr. v. 9. Da solt du die Posaunen lassen blasen durch alle euer Land . . . (*Durch die Posaunen ward das fröhliche Jubel=Jahr ausgeblasen . . . Und war dieses Jubel Jahr ein schönes Fürbild des grossen Jubel Jahrs / welches der HErr Messias durch sein Leiden und Sterben uns erworben hat / zur Vergebung der Sünden / und Erlangung unser Freyheit / und seligen Erbschafft . . . dadurch auch das ewige himmlische Jubel Jahr abgebildet / in welches zur völlige Freyheit der Kinder Gottes / und Erlangung des Himmlischen Erbes . . . alle Auserwehlten versamlet werden sollen . . . da auch ein ieder / der Gläubigen zu den Seinigen kommen / und sie ewig zusammen unter ihrem Haupt Christo seyn werden.*) v. 10. Und ihr solt das funfftzigste Jahr heiligen / und solt es ein Erlas=Jahr heissen im Lande / allen / die darinnen wohnen/ (*als in welchem . . . ein ieder zu seiner Erbschafft wieder gelangen konte/*) denn es ist euer Hall=Jahr / da sol ein ieglichen bey euch zu seiner Haabe / und zu seinem Geschlecht kommen . . . v. 11. Denn das funfftzigste Jahr ist euer Hall=Jahr . . . v. 12. Denn das Hall=Jahr sol unter euch heilig seyn . . . v. 13. Das ist das Hall=Jahr / da iederman wieder zu dem seinen kommen sol."

14. NBR, 424.

15. NBR, 283; BDOK I, no. 184: "No. 1. Vitus Bach, ein Weißbecker in Ungern, hat im 16ten Seculo der lutherischen Religion halben aus Ungern entweichen müßen. Ist dannenhero, nachdem er seine Güter, so viel es sich hat wollen thun laßen, zu Gelde gemacht, in Teütschland gezogen . . ."

16. It is in the twenty-fifth chapter of Leviticus that the Israelites are directed to observe their jubilee year.

17. In his Bach biography of 1802 (*Über Johann Sebastian Bachs Leben, Kunst und Kunstwerke* [Leipzig: Hoffmeister und Kühnel]), Forkel described the proliferation of Veit's descendants in Bible-like terms: "[Veit] communicated this inclination for music to his two sons, they again to their children, till by degrees there arose a very numerous family, all the branches of which were not only musical, but made music their chief business and soon had in their possession most of the offices of cantors, organists, and town musicians in Thuringia." NBR, 423.

18. Bach's marginal notation alongside this passage in his Calov Bible indicates that he read this verse. The original text reads: "v. 1. ALso zog Abram herauf aus Egypten . . . mit seinem Weibe / und mit allen / das er hatte . . ." Calov, *Die heilige Bibel*, vol. 1/I, col. 99. Cox, *The Calov Bible*, facsimile 13.

19. In a marginal note to First Chronicles 28:21, Bach explicitly expressed his belief that God worked through David to establish well-appointed music. Cox, *The Calov Bible*, facsimile 11 and p. 418.

20. NBR, 290; BDOK I, no. 184: "(6) Capellmeister u *Director* derer Cammer *Musiquen* am Hochfürstlich Anhalt Köthischen Hoffe. *An.* 1717. (7) Wurde von dar *An.* 1723. als *Director Chori Musici* u *Cantor* an der *Thomas* Schule nacher Leipzig *vocirt*; allwo er noch bis jetzo nach Gottes H. Willen lebet, u zugleich von Haus aus als *Capellmeister* von Weißenfels u Cöthen *in function* ist."

21. NBR, 151–52; BDOK I, no. 23: "so fügte es Gott, daß zu hiesigem Directore Musices u. Cantore an der Thomas Schule vociret wurde. Ob es mir nun zwar anfänglich gar nicht anständig seyn wolte, aus einem Capellmeister ein Cantor zu werden, weßwegen auch meine resolution auf ein vierthel Jahr trainirete, jedoch wurde mir diese station dermaßen favorable beschrieben, daß endlich . . . es in des Höchsten Nahmen wagete, u. mich nacher Leipzig begabe . . . u. so dann die mutation vornahme. Hieselbst bin nun nach Gottes Willen annoch beständig. Da aber nun (1) finde, daß dieser Dienst bey weitem nicht so erklecklich als mann mir Ihn beschrieben, (2) viele accidentia dieser station entgangen, (3) ein sehr theürer Orth u. (4) eine wunderliche und der Music wenig ergebene Obrigkeit ist, mithin fast in stetem Verdruß, Neid und Verfolgung leben muß, als werde genöthiget werden mit des Höchsten Beystand meine Fortun anderweitig zu suchen."

22. Johann Gottfried Walther, *Musicalisches Lexicon* (Leipzig: Wolffgang Deer, 1732; reprint Kassel: Bärenreiter, 1986), 64.

23. Since Bach singled out First Chronicles 25 as "the [very] foundation of all church music pleasing to God" in his Calov Bible, it is highly likely that he read the corresponding chapter in Olearius's *Biblische Erklärung*.

24. Olearius, *Biblische Erklärung*, vol. 2, 533: "Das vier und zwantzigste. Diese vier und zwantzig Classes im Eintheilung derer / so im Tempel aufzuwarten hatten / nennen die Griechen Ephemerias. Luc. 1/5. Wobey wir uns zu erinnern / daß der Heilige Geist diese Zahl auch anführet in der Offenbarung Johannis Cap. 4/4. wo vier und zwantzig Stühle / auff welchen vier und zwantzig Eltesten gesessen / erwehnet werden / wobey wir uns billig zu erinnern I. Der vier und zwantzig Canonischen Schreiber Altes Testament . . . II. Die zwölff Söhne Jacobs / und die zwölff Aposteln ebenmäßig diese Zahl XXIV geben. III. Wie auch die Ordnung der Leviten / welche der Allerhöchste an statt deß gantzen Volckes zu seinem Dienst erwehlet hatte / 1. B. Chron. 24/18. NB. in vier und zwantzig Abtheilungen bestanden. Denn seine Gläubigen sind alle Priester für GOtt / Offenbar. 1. und seine himmlischen Sänger und Musicanten / in richtiger Ordnung / 1. Chron. 25.31. und Haupt=Lehre daselbst."

25. NBR, 152.

26. NBR, 297. The obituary was written in 1750 and published in 1754. In the chapter on "The Bach Family" in his Bach biography of 1802, Forkel observed: "If ever there was a family in which an extraordinary disposition for the same art seemed to be hereditary, it was certainly the family of Bach; through six successive generations there were scarcely two or three members of it who had not received from nature the gifts of a very distinguished talent for music and who did not make the practice of this art the main occupation of their lives." NBR, 422.

27. Cited in Robin A. Leaver, *J.S. Bach and Scripture: Glosses from the Calov Bible Commentary* (St. Louis: Concordia, 1985), 93; Cox, *The Calov Bible*, facsimile 110 and p. 418: "NB Dieses Capitel ist das wahre Fundament aller gottgefälliger Kirchen Music. usw." Bach's comment appears in vol. 1/I, col. 2048 of Calov's *Die heilige Bibel*.

28. Leaver, *J.S. Bach and Scripture*, 93.

29. Calov, *Die heilige Bibel*, vol. 1/I, cols. 2047–49.

30. Leaver, *J.S. Bach and Scripture*, 93.

31. NBR, 56–57; BDOK I, no. 1: "Wenn auch ich stets den Endzweck, nemlich eine regulirte kirchen music zu Gotttes Ehren, und Ihren Willen nach, gerne aufführen mögen... Alß hat es Gott gefüget, daß eine Enderung mir unvermuthet zu handen kommen, darinne ich mich in einer hinlänglicheren subsistence und Erhaltung meines endzweckes wegen der wohlzufaßenden kirchenmusic ... ersehe."

32. NBR, 145–51. The German text appears in BDOK I, no. 22.

33. Leaver, *J.S. Bach and Scripture*, 95–96. Also cited by Cox, *The Calov Bible*, facsimile 111 and p. 418.

34. Leaver, *J.S. Bach and Scripture*, 93.

35. Christoph Trautmann, "J.S. Bach: New Light on His Faith," *Concordia Theological Monthly* 42 (1971), 94.

36. Calov, *Die heilige Bibel*, vol. 1/I, cols. 2047–52: "Der Erste Theil. | Die Sänger / und Instrumentisten. v.1. UNd David samt den Feldhauptleuten sondert ab zu Aemptern unter den Kindern Assaph / Heman und Jedithun die Propheten (*welche solten GOttes Wort in geistliche Lieder und Psalmen fassen / dieselbe im Tempel singen / und zugleich darein mit Instrumenten spielen*) mit Harffen / Psaltern und Cymbeln / und sie wurden gezehlet (*und verordnet*) zum Werck nach ihrem Ampt. (*dasselbe in gewisser Ordnung zu verrichten. Denn GOtt ist ein GOtt der Ordnung 1. Cor. XIV. 33.*) v. 2. Unter den Kindern Assaph war / Sacur / Joseph / Nethanja / Asarela . . . Kinder Assaph unter Assaph / (*der war ihr Vater / der sie unterwiese / und eben auch ihr Auffsäher und Sangmeister*) der da weissaget bey dem Könige. (*von geistlichen Sachen aus GOttes Wort / oder auch aus Eingebung des Geistes GOttes lehrete / und für dem Könige davon sang / und spielete 2. Sam. XIX. 35.*) v. 3. Von Jedithun: Die Kinder Jedithun waren Gedalja / Zori . . . / Jesaja / Hasabja / Mathithia / (*und Simri v. 17.*) die sechse unter ihrem Vater Jedithun / mit Harffen / die da weissageten zu dancken / und zu loben den HErrn. v. 4. Von Heman: Die Kinder Heman waren / Bukja / Mathanja / Usiel . . . / Sebuel . . . / Jeremoth / Hananja / Hanani / Eliatha / Gidalthi / Romamthi=Eser / Jasbekasa / Mallothi / Hothir / und Mahesioth. v. 5. Diese waren alle Kinder Heman / des Schauers (*des Propheten v.1.*) des Königes in den Worten GOttes / das Horn (*Christum / von dem er weissagete / zu erheben Ps. XXCIX. 25. Luc. 1. 69. welches nicht allein mit Worten / sondern auch mit Musiciren und Gesängen geschach*) zu erheben. Denn GOtt hatte Heman vierzehn Söne und drey Tochter gegeben. v. 6. Diese waren alle unter ihren Vätern Assaph / Jedithun / und Heman / zu singen im Hause des HErrn mit Cymbeln / Psaltern und Harffen / nach dem Ampt im Hause Gottes bey dem Könige. (*wie der König die Ordnung gemacht hatte*) v. 7. Und es war ihr Zahl / samt ihren Brüdern (*Verwandten*) die im Gesang des HErrn gelehret waren / allesamt Meister zwey hundert und acht und achzig. (*die Lehrmeister und Schüler machten zusammen 4000. S. c. XXIII. 5.*) Der Ander Theil. | Losung wegen der Sänger. v. 8. Und sie wurffen Loß über ihr Ampt zugleich / dem kleinesten wie dem grossesten / dem Lehrer wie dem Schüler. (*wie sie sich zusammen solten subordiniren / und einer dem andern untergeben werden.*) v. 9. Und das erste Loß fiel unter Assaph auf Joseph / (*sampt seinen Sönen und Brüdern / oder Verwandten / der waren zwölffe / weil es von andern ausdrücklich also stehet*) das ander auf Gedalia / sammt seinen Brüdern und Sönen / der waren zwölffe . . . v. 31. Das vier und zwanzigste auff RomamthiEser / sambt seinen Sönen / und Brüdern (*oder*

Bluts Freunden / wie in allen vorigen) der waren zwölffe. (*Es waren eben so viel Ordnungen der Sänger / und Instrumentisten / als der Priesterc. XXIV.18. und als der Leviten / so den Priestern auffwarteten und halffen. Bes. c. XXIV.31.*)"

37. First Chronicles 15:16 would have resonated with Bach, too: "David also commanded the chiefs of the Levites to appoint their kindred as the singers to play on musical instruments, on harps and lyres and cymbals, to raise loud sounds of joy."

38. Calov, *Die heilige Bibel*, vol. I/II, col. 222. Cited by Cox, *The Calov Bible*, facsimile 122 and p. 420. See also Leaver, *J.S. Bach and Scripture*, 187.

39. Calov, *Die heilige Bibel*, vol. I/II, cols. 441 and 545.

40. Leaver, *J.S. Bach and Scripture*, 101.

41. First Chronicles 16:7 reads: "Then on that day David first appointed the singing of praises to the Lord by Asaph and his kindred."

42. Olearius, *Biblische Erklärung*, vol. 2, 482 and 507: "Die vornehmsten directores der Music / und Capell=Meister / und Sänger" and "Der Director chori und Capell=Meister."

43. See Mary Greer, "Embracing Faith: The Duet as Metaphor in Selected Sacred Cantatas by J.S. Bach," *Bach: Journal of the Riemenschneider Bach Institute* 34 (2003), 1–71.

44. In his gloss on First Chronicles 25:1, Olearius explains that, in this context—namely, a chapter devoted to "The Singers" ("*CANTORES, Die Sänger*")—the term "prophets" implies that Asaph, Heman, and Jeduthun were gifted composers. In the *Biblische Erklärung*, First Chronicles 25:1, together with Olearius's explanation, reads: "And David with all the field captains set apart for offices among the children of Asaph, Heman, and Jeduthun, the prophets, with harps, psalteries, and cymbals, and they were numbered for work according to their office . . . The Prophets. *who repeated God's Word with singing, as likewise the prophets with preaching. They were also good composers, who gave direction, how and where one should raise one's voice . . . These musicians were called prophets and seers, however, because they had to recite the prophetic psalms aloud . . . and sing. The masters of music or Capellmeister . . . who had more to do with prophetic promises than others . . .*" ("1. Und David sammt den Feld=Haupt=Leuten sonderte ab zu Aemmtern unter den Kindern Assaph / Heman und Jedithun die Propheten / mit Harffen / Psaltern und Cymbeln / und sie wurden gezehlet zum Werck nach ihrem Ammte. | . . . Die Propheten. *die GOttes Wort wiederholeten mit Singen / gleichwie sonst die Propheten mit Predigen. Sie waren auch gute Componisten / welche Anleitung gaben / wie und wo man die Stimme erheben solte / NB. 1.Chron.16/22. Und von Assaph Psalm. 73/1 . . . Diese Musicanten aber wurden Propheten und Schauer v.5. genant / weil sie die Prophetischen Psalmen öffentlich musten wiederholen / NB. v.2.3. und singen / NB. 2.B.Sam.19/35. also v.2.3. die Meister im Gesang / v.7. oder Capell=Meister / NB. 1.B.Chron.16/22. welche sich auch umb die Prophetischen Verheissungen / mehr bekümmerten als andere. v.5*" [underlining mine]. Olearius, *Biblische Erklärung*, vol. 2, 531.

45. Before this Bach had held the position of Capellmeister at the court of Anhalt-Cöthen for six years, from 1717 to 1723.

46. Prince Leopold of Anhalt-Cöthen died on November 19, 1728. In a testimonial Bach wrote on behalf of his student Christoph Gottlob Wecker, dated March 20, 1729, three days before the official memorial for Prince Leopold, Bach signed his name "Capellmeister to the Prince of Saxe-Weissenfels as well as to the Prince of Anhalt-Cöthen, Director Chori Musices Lipsiensis and Cantor at St.

Thomas's here." NBR, 132; BDOK I, no. 60. The chronology of these events is set forth in Wolff, *Johann Sebastian Bach*, 530.

47. On July 27, 1733, Bach petitioned the new Elector of Saxony for a title in his Highness's Court Capelle ("ein Prædicat von Dero Hoff-Capelle") in the letter he sent with the Kyrie and Gloria of the Mass in B Minor. NBR, 158; BDOK I, no. 27. Bach finally received the prestigious title of "Compositeur to the Royal Court Orchestra" in November 1736. NBR, 188; BDOK II, no. 388.

48. Although Bach's second petition to the king has not survived, evidence of its existence, and the fact that it was written before September 27, 1736, is presented in BDOK I, no. 36.

49. Wolff, *Johann Sebastian Bach*, 420.

50. See BC, vol. 3, 866. On the context of Cantata 196, see especially Konrad Küster, "Der Herr denket an uns (BWV 196). Eine frühe Bach-Kantate und ihr Kontext," *Musik und Kirche* 66 (1996), 84–96.

51. The original German text reads: "v. 12. Der Herr denket an uns und segnet uns. Er segnet das Haus Israel, er segnet das Haus Aaron. v. 13. Er segnet, die den Herrn fürchten, beide, Kleine und Große. v. 14. Der Herr segne euch je mehr und mehr, euch und eure Kinder. v. 15. Ihr seid die Gesegneten des Herrn, der Himmel und Erde gemacht hat."

52. Philipp Spitta, *Johann Sebastian Bach* (Leipzig: Breitkopf & Härtel, 1870–1880). English translation: Clara Bell and J.A. Fuller-Maitland (London: Novello, 1889; reprint New York: Dover, 1951), vol. 1, 370.

53. Wolff, *Johann Sebastian Bach*, 91–92.

54. Calov, *Die heilige Bibel*, vol. 1/II, cols. 725–6: "da wir GOttes Diener / Opfferer / Sänger / Fasten-Lehrer und Wöhlthäter heissen . . ."

55. By contrast, in the summary of Psalm 68 in the Calov Bible, the only other Psalm summary that contains a reference to "Sänger," Luther employs the third person: "Once again he calls them singers" ("wiederumb nennet er sie Sänger"). Calov, *Die heilige Bibel*, vol. 1/II, cols. 505–6.

56. *Biblia, das ist Die gantze Heilige Schrift Altes und Neues Testaments teutsch D. Martin Luther. Mit den Summarien M. Viti Dieterichs; und mit den Vorreden Francisci Vierlings* . . . (Altenburg: Wäysen-Haus and Jena: Samuel Adolph Müller, 1676), 863.

57. In *Die Heilige Schrift Altes und Neues Testaments nach dem Grund-Text aufs Neue übersehen und übersetzet . . . Johann Heinman Haug* (Berlenberg : [s.n.], 1726–1742), vol. 3 (1730), 494, the heading to Psalm 115 reads: "God alone is to be glorified, who can and will bless us" ("Gott ist allein zu ehren / der uns segenen kan und will"). In the *Evangelische Deutsche Original=Bibel. Das ist: Die gantze heilige Schrift Altes und Neues Testaments, dergestalt eingerichtet, daß der hebraische oder griechische Grundtext und die deutsche Ubersetzung D. Martin Luthers neben einander erscheinen. Nebst einer Vorrede Johann Muthmanns, der Sachsen-Salfeldischen Superintendentur Abjuncti und Pastoris z Pößneck* (Züllichau, in Verlegung des Waysenhauses, bey Gottlob Benjamin Frommann, 1741), 613, the heading reads: "To God alone the glory! That he bestow blessings on us." ("GOtt allein die ehr! [sic] daß er segen uns bescher."). In *Biblia parallelo-harmonico-exegetica, das ist. Die . . . Heilige Schrift: Alten und Neuen Testaments / nach den accuratesten Exemplarien der deutschen Übersetzung des seligen D. Martin Luthers; mit dessen Vorreden und Handglossen . . . ; herausgegeben von D. Christian Friedrich Wilischen . . .* (Freyberg: Druckts Christoph Mattäi, 1739–1764), vol. 3 (1747), 5773, the heading reads: "The 115th

Psalm. In which David bestows on God alone all glory and all praise" ("Der CXV. Psalm. Darinnen David I. GOtt allein alle Ehre und allen Ruhm beygeleget wissen will").

58. *Biblia, das ist, Die gantze Heilige Schrift Alten und Neuen Testaments : nach der Ubersetzung und mit den Vorreden und Randglossen D. Martin Luthers . . . ausgefertiget unter der Aufsicht und Direction Christoph Matthäi Pfaffen* (Tübingen: bey Johann Georg und Christian Gottfried Cotta, 1729 and 1730), 596. The original text reads: "Gebete. / GRosser Segens-GOTT! / es gebühret dir ja allein die Ehre . . ."

59. Olearius, *Biblische Erklärung*, vol. 3 (1679), 619, 620, and 623. The original text reads: "Der Nahme deß HErrn ists / dem allein alle Ehre gebühret . . . Gloria sit soli, gloria summa Deo. / Nicht uns / dir allein gebühret die Ehre . . . damit wir Ihm allein die Ehre geben . . . Von der Ehre die GOtt allein gebühret."

Bach's Vocal Music

Combinatorial Modeling in the Chorus Movement of Cantata 24, *Ein ungefärbt Gemüte*

Alexander J. Fisher

In his volume *Johann Sebastian Bach: The Learned Musician*, Christoph Wolff admirably summarizes Bach's principal goals as he embarked on the regular composition of cantatas shortly after his arrival in Leipzig on May 22, 1723:

> What clearly emerges . . . are two aims: first, to provide himself with a working repertoire of substantial size that he would be able to draw on later; to set certain goals for the individual cycles that would enable him to explore the flexible cantata typology as widely as possible, to leave his own distinct mark, and—as in other areas of compositional activity—to push the genre beyond its current limits.[1]

The twin demands of pragmatism and intellectual exploration decisively shaped the composer's output as he settled into a position that was far different, and in many ways more demanding, than the post he had held in Cöthen.

In recent decades, the pioneering work of Georg von Dadelsen and Alfred Dürr on the chronology of Bach's Leipzig cantata performances has led to a better understanding of Bach's compositional process, as well as the nature of his responsibilities as Cantor of St. Thomas.[2] Bach began his regular duties on May 30, 1723, the First Sunday after Trinity, and thereafter proceeded to provide concerted church music on a weekly basis—a task he fulfilled by composing new works as well as reviving pieces originally written during his previous positions in Mühlhausen, Weimar, and Cöthen. Because Bach performed a relatively large number of preexisting Weimar works in his first yearly cycle of church cantatas, it is not inappropriate to ask whether the revived Weimar pieces exerted a special influence on his new compositions.[3] As the chronology of Dürr and Dadelsen attests, Bach elected to revive Cantata 21, *Ich hatte viel Bekümmernis*, for the Third Sunday after Trinity. One week later, on the Fourth Sunday after Trinity, he provided a new work, Cantata 24, *Ein ungefärbt Gemüte*, which he paired with another Weimar piece, Cantata 185, *Barmherziges Herz der ewigen Liebe*.

A comparison of the revived cantata *Ich hatte viel Bekümmernis* with the newly composed cantata *Ein ungefärbt Gemüte* reveals an unusual modeling procedure on the part of Bach, a procedure that to my knowledge has not been recognized previously.

In his initial months as St. Thomas Cantor, Bach faced the task of providing large-scale concerted music on a weekly basis. Although he had composed and performed cantatas in his earlier posts (he was compelled to write one cantata per month for the Weimar court chapel in the previous decade, from 1714 to 1716, for example), the sheer quantity of music expected from Bach in Leipzig must have posed a formidable challenge. Table 1 shows a calendar of his first cantata performances in Leipzig in 1723, from the First Sunday after Trinity (May 30) to the Tenth Sunday after Trinity (August 1). The table also gives the number of movements in each work, since this information is relevant to the present discussion.

A glance at the movement structure for Cantatas 75, 76, and 21 suggests that Bach intended, at least initially, to provide large, two-part cantatas on a weekly basis, following the pattern of his audition performance, which appears to have included two works, Cantata 22, *Jesus nahm zu sich die Zwölfe*, of five movements, and Cantata 23,

Table 1. Calendar of J.S. Bach's Leipzig Cantata Performances
May 30–August 1, 1723

Date	Occasion	Work	Movements
May 30	1st Sunday after Trinity	Cantata 75, *Die Elenden sollen essen*	14 (7 + 7)
June 6	2d Sunday after Trinity	Cantata 76, *Die Himmel erzählen die Ehre Gottes*	14 (7 + 7)
June 13	3d Sunday after Trinity	Cantata 21, *Ich hatte viel Bekümmernis**	11 (6 + 5)
June 20	4th Sunday after Trinity	Cantata 24, *Ein ungefärbt Gemüte*	6
		Cantata 185, *Barmherziges Herze der ewigen Liebe**	6
June 24	Feast of St. John	Cantata 167, *Ihr Menschen, rühmet Gottes Liebe*	5
June 27	5th Sunday after Trinity	Unidentified work	—
July 2	Visitation	Cantata 147, *Herz und Mund und Tat und Leben**	10 (6 + 4)
July 4	6th Sunday after Trinity	Unidentified work	—
July 11	7th Sunday after Trinity	Cantata 186, *Ärgre dich, o Seele, nicht**	11 (6 + 5)
July 18	8th Sunday after Trinity	Cantata 136, *Erforsche mich, Gott*	6
[July 18 (?)	Funeral	Motet, *Jesu, meine Freude* (BWV 227)	11]
July 25	9th Sunday after Trinity	Cantata 105, *Herr, gehe nicht ins Gericht*	6
August 1	10th Sunday after Trinity	Cantata 46, *Schauet doch und sehet*	6

*Revival of Weimar cantata

Du wahrer Gott und Davids Sohn, of four movements.[4] Because Bach had several weeks prior to May 30 in which to prepare Cantata 75, he was probably able to handle the scale of the work. However, as Stephen Crist has shown, the autograph score of Cantata 76, which was performed the following Sunday, was more hastily written, suggesting that Bach may have had difficulty providing new works of such scope on shorter notice.[5] Bach relieved some of the pressure by choosing a piece composed previously (Cantata 21) for the Third Sunday after Trinity. The selection of this work seems to have been appropriate on account of its organization into two parts, as well as its designation by Bach as *Per ogni Tempo*—for any time of the year.[6] As Crist has pointed out, Bach compromised the following week by writing a shorter work, Cantata 24, and pairing it with an equally concise Weimar work, Cantata 185, thus providing roughly the same amount of music as he had for the preceding three weeks.[7] It is significant that for subsequent Sundays Bach seems to have abandoned the idea of writing new works of the magnitude of Cantatas 75 and 76, electing instead to provide works of more modest proportions, such as Cantata 167 (five movements), Cantata 136 (six movements), and Cantata 105 (six movements).[8] Moreover, by July Bach had settled upon a relatively consistent movement structure for newly composed works: Cantatas 136, 105, and 46, performed in consecutive weeks, all display a six-movement format: chorus-recitative-aria-recitative-aria-chorale. This scheme contrasts with the more flexible structures of the Weimar revivals and the first Leipzig cantatas of May and June.

Cantata 24, then, was written during a period of accommodation—a time during which Bach sought to reconcile the characteristics of his previous cantata output with the rigorous demands of his new position. I will return to this point in a moment, but first it is necessary to review briefly some important details about Cantata 24 itself and the nature of its sources. According to Kirsten Beißwenger, the editor of *Ein ungefärbt Gemüte* for the *Neue Bach-Ausgabe*, there are two principal sources for the work: an autograph score, *P 44*, and a set of original performance parts, *St 19*, which appear to have been copied from the autograph score by Johann Andreas Kuhnau, one of Bach's principal copyists at the time.[9] Both the score and the parts are in relatively good condition and nearly entirely legible.

Cantata 24 consists of six movements:

1. Aria (alto): "Ein ungefärbt Gemüte"
2. Recitative (tenor): "Die Redlichkeit ist eine von den Gottesgaben"
3. Chorus: "Alles nun, das ihr wollet, das euch die Leute tun sollen, das tut ihr ihnen"
4. Recitative (bass): "Die Heuchelei ist eine Brut"
5. Aria (tenor): "Treu und Wahrheit sei der Grund"
6. Chorale: "O Gott, du frommer Gott"

The text for *Ein ungefärbt Gemüte* was written by Erdmann Neumeister and disseminated through libretto collections printed in 1714 and 1716. The text develops the theme of the Gospel for the fourth Sunday after Trinity, Luke 6:36-42, which describes the Sermon on the Mount. The text of the third-movement chorus, "Alles nun, das ihr wollet, das euch die Leute tun sollen, das tut ihr ihnen," the focus of this study, is the well-known Golden Rule: "Do unto others as you would have done unto you" (Matthew 7:12). Although this extremely short passage admits of no obvious structural or semantic divisions, Bach nevertheless divides his setting into two distinct parts. The first section of the chorus, mm. 1–36, features fully scored, mostly homophonic writing for tutti chorus and orchestra. The second section, mm. 37–104, is marked *Vivace e allegro* and begins as a double fugue, first for solo voices and then for tutti chorus with instruments.[10] The text is not divided between the first and second portions of the movement; rather, the entire text is used in both.

In the chorus of Cantata 24, Bach seems to employ a previously unrecognized compositional technique that I call "combinatorial modeling." In composing this chorus, Bach drew into a single movement material from no fewer than four different movements of the work from the previous week, Cantata 21, *Ich hatte viel Bekümmernis*. The borrowings involve motivic as well as harmonic elements, which were appropriated from the Weimar cantata and fused into a coherent musical texture in the new chorus.

As early as the 1870s, Philipp Spitta recognized a possible connection between Cantata 24 and Cantata 21, although he did not know that the two works were performed in consecutive weeks in 1723:

> The third-movement chorus on the Biblical passage "Alles nun, das ihr wollet . . . " is, in its double fugue in the second part, a busy, energetic and urgently declaimed piece; the short periods with which the chorus and instruments respond to one another, however, remind one of the style of the older church cantatas, and measures 11–18, in particular, of measures 11–25 of the second chorus from Bach's earlier cantata "Ich hatte viel Bekümmernis."[11]

As can readily be seen by a comparison of the vocal and continuo parts of the two passages (Examples 1 and 2), both feature disjunct motivic material treated contrapuntally in the vocal parts. In movement 6 of Cantata 21, the music, set to the text "und bist so unruhig," creates an effective contrast with the homophonic setting of "Was betrübst du dich, meine Seele" that directly precedes it. For "und bist so unruhig," Bach writes motivic figures involving ascending and descending leaps of thirds, fourths, and fifths, followed by more consistently descending scalar passages at m. 18, leading to the dramatic quarter-rest pause before the homophonic statement of "in mir?" at mm. 26–27.

Example 1. Chorus "Was betrübst du dich, meine Seele," Cantata 21, movement 6, mm. 10–27.

Example 1. *Continued*

In "Alles nun, das ihr wollet" of Cantata 24, the vocal material from m. 11 is organized in a slightly more rigid manner: the ascending leaps of a fourth are invariably followed by descending leaps of thirds. However, the overall similarity to the corresponding music from movement 6 of Cantata 21 is striking. The resemblance to the earlier cantata is strengthened by the descending scalar passages beginning in the soprano in m. 16 of the Cantata 24 chorus, as well as by the clear caesura in m. 22. Spitta neglected to mention that both passages share a similar harmonic underpinning, one that outlines a circle of fifths from C major or C minor to A♭ major (Cantata 21, movement 6, mm. 11–15; Cantata 24, movement 3, mm. 13–17). Finally, in the Cantata 24 chorus the rhetorical relationship between music and text ("das tut ihr ihnen") is less lucid than in corresponding passage of the Cantata 21 chorus, raising the possibility that the music of Cantata 24 was, in fact, adapted from a preexisting work.[12]

A comparison of the continuo and instrumental parts of the same passage from the Cantata 24 chorus with mm. 38–43 of movement 2 of Cantata 21, the chorus "Ich hatte viel Bekümmernis," suggests that Bach brought together material from two

Example 2. Chorus "Alles nun das ihr wollet, das tut ihnen," Cantata 24, movement 3, mm. 10–27.

41

Example 2. *Continued*

Example 2. *Continued*

different sources as he composed the new chorus movement (Example 3). In the "Ich hatte viel Bekümmernis" chorus, the sudden *moto perpetuo* beginning in m. 39 effectively portrays the text "deine Tröstungen erquicken meine Seele" and forms a striking contrast with the laborious, dissonance-laden music used for the previous words "Ich hatte viel Bekümmernis in meinem Herzen."

From m. 11 onward, the continuo line in the Cantata 24 chorus bears motivic as well as harmonic similarities to m. 39 of the Cantata 21 chorus. First, although the running continuo figures begin in different metrical positions in the two movements, they both involve an initial leap of a fourth followed by conjunct runs of sixteenth notes. Transposed to the same key, in fact, the first five notes of the continuo are identical in the two passages. Furthermore, sixteenth-note runs are punctuated at intervals by pairs of eighth notes (mm. 13, 14, 16, and 18 in Cantata 24; mm. 40 and 43 in Cantata 21). Finally, the passage from movement 2 of Cantata 21 also outlines a circle-of-fifths progression: transposed to G minor (Dorian), the key of the Cantata 24 chorus, the harmony would proceed G→C→F→B♭→E♭ in mm. 39–40. This is very close to the parallel progression in the Cantata 24 chorus. In the vocal parts of the Cantata 24 movement, there is no obvious textual justification for the abrupt

Example 3. Chorus "Ich hatte viel Bekümmernis," Cantata 21, movement 2, mm. 38–43.

entry of *moto perpetuo* figuration in m. 11, which suggests once again that this music may not be new composition but rather old material adapted from another source. Thus Bach managed to combine, albeit with significant alterations, aspects of the vocal material from movement 6 of Cantata 21 with instrument material from movement 2 of the same work. The circle-of-fifths harmonic scheme common to both passages allowed him to bring these elements together in a single location.

Another striking example of combinatorial modeling occurs at the beginning of the double fugue in the Cantata 24 movement, at m. 37 (Example 4). The chorus, which has been singing tutti from the beginning, comes to a halt in m. 35, while the orchestral accompaniment continues for another measure. The double fugue, marked *Vivace e allegro*, features a radical reduction in texture: with the exception of continuo, the instruments fall silent for twenty-two measures and the chorus is reduced to four

Example 4. Chorus "Alles nun das ihr wollet, das tut ihnen," Cantata 24, movement 3, mm. 37–47.

solo voices only.[13] It is highly significant that the vocal parts return to singing tutti in a staggered fashion—the bass in m. 54, the tenor in m. 59, the alto in m. 64, and the soprano in m. 69. The orchestra reenters at m. 59, simultaneously with the tutti indication for the tenors. Thus, the overall design of the movement features a tutti opening, a reduction to solo voices, and a gradual augmentation of forces working back to the initial tutti texture. This provides the movement with a well-rounded dynamic profile.

The practice of dividing the choir into soloists and ripienists was not without precedent for Bach. In fact, it is discernible in each of the cantatas he performed in Leipzig prior to Cantata 24. It appears in his audition pieces: the opening chorus "Jesus nahm zu sich die Zwölfe" from Cantata 22 features solo choral entries followed by staggered tutti indications, while the chorus "Aller Augen warten, Herr" from Cantata 23 displays alternating sections of tutti chorus and solo tenor and bass.[14] Once established as Cantor of St. Thomas, Bach continued the practice in the opening chorus of Cantata 75, "Die Elenden sollen essen," in which a tutti chorus in a relatively homophonic texture is followed by a meter change and fugue for solo voices. The full chorus then repeats the fugue to end the movement.[15]

In Cantata 76, for the following Sunday, the opening choral movement, "Die Himmel erzählen die Ehre Gottes," features a passage for solo bass followed by tutti chorus. A fugue for solo voices then ensues in which the voices gradually return to tutti in a staggered fashion. Cantata 21, for the Third Sunday after Trinity, contains solo-tutti choral divisions in movements 6, 9, and 11.[16] Of most immediate interest is the final chorus, "Das Lamm, das erwürget ist." Here a grandly homophonic, fully scored introduction is followed by a permutation fugue for solo voices, beginning in the bass and marked *Allegro*. As in the chorus movement of Cantata 24, the solo voices return to tutti in a staggered manner, and in precisely the same ascending order: bass→tenor→alto→soprano. The orchestra, initially silent, enters with the tutti basses and is present for the remainder of the movement. Both the Cantata 24 chorus and movement 11 of Cantata 21, then, demonstrate Bach's concern not only with dividing his chorus into solo and tutti but also with gradually adding vocal and instrumental forces over time in the course of a large-scale choral movement.

It remains unclear whether Bach continued to divide the chorus into solo and ripieno singers and used the staggered entry of the ripieno singers in fugues, once written indications disappear from the performance parts after the presentation of Cantata 24 on June 20, 1723. Gerhard Herz and Joshua Rifkin present contrasting views on the matter. Herz argues that such divisions had been long-standing practice in Leipzig, and that Bach needed to be explicit about their execution for only a short time after his arrival:

> With this embarrassment of riches [that is, a sizable chorus] documented for his first month in Leipzig Bach showed nothing more nor less than that in this respect he followed a performance tradition his predecessors, Thomas Cantors Sebastian Knüpfer, Johann Schelle, and Johann Kuhnau, had observed. It is possible that the solo-tutti concept was so firmly established and so commonly understood in Leipzig that Bach found it necessary to spell it out only in his test pieces and his first four cantatas performed there.[17]

The solo-ripieno division, Herz concludes, may be applied profitably in later vocal works as well, for which there are no written indications. Although Rifkin concedes that Bach used soloists and ripienists in the first month of his tenure in Leipzig, he

Example 5. Chorus "Das Lamm, das erwürget ist," Cantata 21, movement 11, bass, mm. 12–15.

insists that the source materials themselves provide no justification for positing the presence of ripieno singers after the performance of Cantata 24.[18] The question of whether Bach might have expected suitable ripienists to be consistently available for his cantatas after this time is beyond the scope of this chapter.

Apart from the overall resemblance in design and vocal texture between the chorus of Cantata 24 and movement 11 of Cantata 21, further connections between the two movements emerge when one examines details of the music. The initial fugue subject in the bass voice of the Cantata 21 chorus (Example 5), for instance, shows features appearing in the bass fugue subject of the Cantata 24 chorus (Example 4, m. 38). Despite the metrical differences between the two figures (the first begins on the strong first beat of the measure, the second starts on the weaker second half of the first beat), they both share three sets of leaping figures separated by eighth rests, followed by a smoother, mainly stepwise descending motive uninterrupted by rests. It should be noticed, again, that there is a marked difference between the two figures in their rhetorical relationship to the text. In Cantata 21, the trumpet-like, leaping motives arpeggiating a C-major triad express the triumphal sentiment of the words "Lob, und Ehre, und Preis, und Gewalt." In Cantata 24, by contrast, there seems to be no direct expressive relationship between the same motive and the text "das tut ihr ihnen." This suggests once again the possibility that the music of Cantata 24 was adapted from a preexisting source.

The principal subject of the double fugue in Cantata 24 (Example 4, tenor, m. 37) may also have been derived from Cantata 21, but from a different movement of that work altogether. The ninth movement of Cantata 21, the chorale fantasy "Sei nun wieder zufrieden" for chorus and instruments *colla parte*, shares with the chorus of Cantata 24 its 3/4 meter and G-dorian key signature (G minor, with one flat). A comparison of the opening melodic figure of the chorale fantasy (Example 6, soprano) with the main theme of the double fugue of Cantata 24 (Example 4, tenor) demonstrates the possible connection between the two. Both melodic lines begin on the second beat of a 3/4 measure, descending from the fifth to the second scale degree. While the continuo holds the pitch g throughout measure 1 of the Cantata 21 movement, descending to the dominant only by m. 3, the continuo underpinning for the

Example 6. Chorus "Sei nun wieder zufrieden," Cantata 21, movement 9, mm. 1–5.

tenor entry in m. 37 of the Cantata 24 chorus begins on the dominant and ascends to the tonic on beat 1 of m. 38.

The resemblance between the two passages is strengthened when one takes the harmony of m. 40 of Cantata 21 into account. The first ending leads back to the repeat sign in m. 2. In contrast to m. 1, m. 40 outlines a dominant chord in the continuo, beginning on d and ascending through e, f♯, and back to the g on beat 1 of m. 2 (Example 7).

At this point a word of caution is necessary. With the exception of the second fugue subject of the Cantata 24 chorus (which begins in the bass, in m. 38), which I believe is exceptionally closely related to the corresponding fugue subject from Cantata 21, movement 11 (Examples 4 and 5), many of the modeling relationships I have suggested seem less tenable if viewed in isolation. For instance, the broken vocal texture of Cantata 24 (Example 2, m. 11), moving harmonically in a circle of fifths, might not necessarily be seen as related to the music of "und bist so unruhig" from movement 6 of Cantata 21 (Example 1). Similarly, the running continuo line at the same spot in Cantata 24 could be seen as a stereotypical construction, not necessarily derived from the continuo in Cantata 21, movement 2 (Example 3, m. 39). However, given that none of these modeling relationships can be proven definitely through an examination of the extant source materials, the simultaneous presence of these potential affinities in two cantatas performed closely in time bolsters considerably what might otherwise be regarded as a circumstantial case.[19]

It is curious, perhaps, that Bach's procedure of combinatorial modeling—or modeling of any kind, in fact—appears to have played a role only in the composition of the chorus from Cantata 24 and not in the other movements of the work. The chorus is the most substantial movement of the cantata, posing the greatest compositional challenge to a composer just settling into his office.[20] Cantata 21, still fresh in Bach's

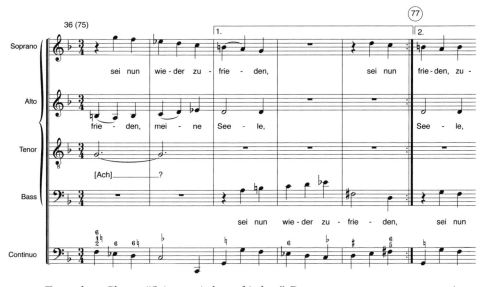

Example 7. Chorus "Sei nun wieder zufrieden," Cantata 21, movement 9, mm. 36–40, 77.

memory from its performance the previous Sunday, could have served as a ready source for raw musical material that could be adapted and combined at will. Another vexing question concerns the degree to which Bach may have been conscious—or unconscious—of the role of Cantata 21 in the composition of the new chorus for Cantata 24. On the one hand, the correspondence between the musical material of the two cantatas is far from exact and often seems to have the character of reminiscence rather than of direct copying or adaptation. On the other hand, the facility with which Bach united similar, disparate elements in one place suggests a certain amount of careful deliberation.

Although the manuscript sources neither support nor contradict my thesis of combinatorial modeling, they do seem to rule out the possibility that the chorus of Cantata 24 was copied in its entirety in Weimar from a source contemporary with Cantata 21. The music is relatively free of corrections and adjustments, but sufficient compositional work is present in *P 44* to conclude that the chorus was, in fact, newly written for the Fourth Sunday after Trinity, 1723.[21] For the present, the answer to the question of whether Bach adapted material from Cantata 21 must rest on internal evidence. No matter what the outcome, the detailed comparison of new Leipzig cantatas with older works performed at roughly the same time clearly yields further insights into Bach's compositional process as he embarked upon his new career as Cantor of St. Thomas.

Notes

1. Christoph Wolff, *Johann Sebastian Bach: The Learned Musician* (New York: W.W. Norton, 2000), 269. The present chapter originated as a seminar paper for a course on Bach's cantatas that Professor Wolff offered at Harvard University in the spring of 1997. For his comments on this paper, and his mentorship during my graduate studies, I am extremely grateful.

2. See particularly Georg von Dadelsen, *Beiträge zur Chronologie der Werke Johann Sebastian Bachs*, Tübinger Bach-Studien, Heft 4/5 (Trossingen: Hohner-Verlag, 1958); Alfred Dürr, *Zur Chronologie der Leipziger Vokalwerke J.S. Bachs*, 2d ed. (Kassel: Bärenreiter, 1976).

3. In Bach's first yearly cycle of weekly cantatas, the following works probably represent Weimar revivals or adaptations: Cantata 21 (June 13, 1723), Cantata 155 (January 16, 1724), Cantata 185 (June 20, 1723), Cantata 18 (February 13, 1724), Cantata 147 (July 2, 1723), Cantata 182 (March 25, 1723), Cantata 186 (July 11, 1723), Cantata 199 (August 8, 1723), Cantata 31 (April 9, 1724?), Cantata 162 (October 10, 1723), Cantata 163 (October 31, 1723?), Cantata 12 (April 30, 1724), Cantata 194 (November 2, 1723), Cantata 172 (May 28, 1724), Cantata 70 (November 21, 1723), Cantata 61 (November 28, 1723), Cantata 63 (December 25, 1723), Cantata 165 (June 4, 1724), and Cantata 154 (January 9, 1724). This information is drawn from Dürr, *Zur Chronologie*, 57–71, and Dadelsen, *Beiträge zur Chronologie*, 123–25. Although the chronologies of Dürr and Dadelsen are not completely identical, they demonstrate the frequency with which Bach revived his pre-Leipzig works in his first year as St. Thomas Cantor.

4. Christoph Wolff firmly establishes the performance of Cantata 23 on this date in "Bachs Leipziger Kantoratsprobe und die Aufführungsgeschichte der Kantate *Du wahrer Gott und Davids Sohn BWV 23*," BJ 64 (1978), 78–94. See also Wolff, *Johann Sebastian Bach*, 221–25.

5. Stephen A. Crist, "Bach's Debut in Leipzig: Observations on the Genesis of Cantatas 75 and 76," *Early Music* 13 (1985), 212–26. Crist's suggestion that Cantata 75 was written prior to Bach's arrival in Leipzig is based on the fact that the watermark of the autograph score is unique among Bach's cantata manuscripts. The paper may well have originated in Cöthen, although it is impossible to demonstrate precisely when Bach composed the work, as Crist admits (p. 213).

6. The original wrapper of the parts (*St 354*) contains the following title: "Per ogni Tempo | Concerto. | a 13. | 3 Trombe è | Tamburi. | 1 Oboe. | 2 Violini è | una Viola | Fagotto è | Violoncello. | 4 Voci, con | Continuo | da | GS Bach."

7. Crist, "Bach's Debut in Leipzig," 215.

8. However, the Weimar cantatas revived during this period are typically larger works, such as Cantata 147 (July 2, 1723; 10 movements), Cantata 186 (July 11, 1723; 11 movements), and BWV 199 (August 8, 1723; 8 movements).

9. See NBA I/17 (*Kantaten zum 4. Sonntag nach Trinitatis*), KB, 73. A third extant source for Cantata 24, *P 1159*, was copied in the nineteenth century and is of little relevance for editing the work or the purposes of this chapter.

10. Werner Neumann noted that in this double fugue Bach characteristically divides the text between the two subjects. Thus, the words "alles nun, das ihr wollet, das euch die Leute tun sollen" are assigned to the principal theme, the descending stepwise figure beginning in the tenor at m. 37, while the words "das tut ihr ihnen" are set to the accompanying theme, characterized by leaping fourths, which starts in the bass in m. 38 (see Example 4). Similar examples may be found in Canta-

tas 6, 17, 40, 47, 50, 64, 65, 67, 71, 136, and 179; the "Sicut locutus est" from the *Magnificat*; and various *turba* choruses from the St. John Passion and the St. Matthew Passion. See Werner Neumann, *J.S. Bachs Chorfuge: Ein Beitrag zur Kompositionstechnik Bachs*, 2d ed. (Leipzig: Breitkopf & Härtel, 1950), 91.

11. Philipp Spitta, *Johann Sebastian Bach* (Leipzig: Breitkopf & Härtel, 1873–1880), vol. 2, 188–89. The translation is mine.

12. See the discussion in notes 19 and 21.

13. Bach added solo-tutti indications in the vocal parts ("solo" indication in the soprano part, m. 43; "tutti" indications in the bass, tenor, alto, and soprano parts, in mm. 54, 59, 64, and 69, respectively) after they had been copied from the score, *P 44*, most probably for the first performance of the work on June 20, 1723. Indications for choral ripienists and soloists are entirely absent from the *P 44* score (see NBA I/17, KB, 77 and 89). It was not unusual for Bach to add performance refinements to the parts in the process of preparing and proofing them.

14. It is significant that the audition pieces for the cantor position by Christoph Graupner, performed on January 17, 1723, also feature a chorus with solo and tutti components. I am indebted to Christoph Wolff for drawing this to my attention.

15. The procedure here is similar to that seen in the fugue "daß er meines Angesichtes Hülfe, und mein Gott ist" from Cantata BWV 21, movement 6 (beginning at m. 43).

16. As I am concerned here only with Bach's performance practice in the first several weeks of his Leipzig tenure, I will not address in detail the possibility that Cantata 21 was originally conceived in Weimar entirely for solo voices, as suggested by Joshua Rifkin in his essay "From Weimar to Leipzig: Concertists and Ripienists in Bach's *Ich hatte viel Bekümmernis*," *Early Music* 24 (1996), 583–603. Paul Brainard has shown, in any case, that the tutti-solo indications in Cantata 21 were added after the vocal parts were copied (*St 354*), implying that the cantata was originally conceived without a division of the chorus into soloists and ripienists. See Brainard, "Cantata 21 Revisited," in *Studies in Renaissance and Baroque Music in Honor of Arthur Mendel*, ed. Robert L. Marshall (Kassel: Bärenreiter, 1974), 232–35. Regardless of the pre-Leipzig practices concerning Cantata 21, it is indisputable that Bach performed the work with a differentiated chorus in June 1723.

17. Gerhard Herz, "Concertists and Ripienists: An Old Performance Problem Revisited," *American Choral Review* 29 (1987), 43.

18. Rifkin, "From Weimar to Leipzig," 594.

19. The autograph score of Cantata 24, *P 44*, does not contain any significant compositional alterations. This suggests that Bach may have been "copying" in some way from Cantata 21, or from a work that was written at the same time as Cantata 21 (see n. 21).

20. The modeling procedure illustrated here may lend some weight to Werner Breig's speculation that Bach's abandonment of fully orchestrated chorale settings shortly after his arrival in Leipzig stemmed from "the desire for a certain relief from the pressures of composing and rehearsing the new weekly cantatas." See Breig, "Das Finalproblem in Bachs frühen Leipziger Kirchenkantaten," in *Festschrift Arno Forchert zum 60. Geburtstag am 29. Dezember 1985* (Kassel: Bärenreiter, 1986), 107. The preference for leaner scoring, however, in no way detracts from the richness of compositional invention. Wolff, in *Johann Sebastian Bach*, 269–75, notes the impressive variety and scope of these initial Leipzig cantatas, the rhetorical power of their opening choruses, and their development of

interpretive imagery. He also speculates on the possibility of a full "double cycle" of cantatas in the first year, with either a single large cantata or two smaller cantatas performed every Sunday. If this, in fact, was the case, then many cantatas from the first annual cycle are now lost.

21. Robin A. Leaver has proposed, in private correspondence, that Cantata 24 could also represent the reworking of a cantata composed close in time to Cantata 21, either in Weimar or perhaps even in Cöthen, for the Hamburg audition of 1720 (at which Cantata 21 appears to have been performed). George B. Stauffer has pointed out, also in private correspondence, that the Dorian G-minor key signature used in Cantata 24 is characteristic of Bach's Weimar works (see the *Orgelbüchlein* chorales, for instance) but not typical of cantatas newly composed in Leipzig (see Cantatas 105, 46, 48, or 89, for example).

Choral Unison in J.S. Bach's Vocal Music

Daniel R. Melamed

O ne of the most striking textures in J.S. Bach's ensemble vocal music is unison choral writing, in which four (or more) parts join in singing the same melodic line.[1] Passages scored this way (Table 1) stand out from their musical surroundings, and we might well ask why Bach turned to this device when he did. There is no single answer, but we can identify several motivations for his use of this distinctly un-polyphonic kind of writing, including signification of quotation, reference to the sound of instruments or voices, and allusion to liturgical music. Some instances are connected with instrumental material that itself employs unison writing.

Perhaps the clearest examples are those in which octave writing for voices represents the quotation of human speech. In Cantata 198, *Laß, Fürstin, Laß noch einen Strahl* ("Trauer-Ode"), two lines at the end of the concluding movement, the chorus "Doch Königin! Du stirbest nicht," are presented in this way (here and elsewhere in quoted texts words set in unison or octaves are highlighted in boldface):

> Doch Königin! Du stirbest nicht,
>
> Man weiß, was man an Dir besessen;
>
> Die Nachwelt wird Dich nicht vergessen,
>
> Biß dieser Weltbau einst zerbricht.
>
> Ihr Dichter, schreibt! wir wollens lesen:
>
> **Sie ist der Tugend Eigenthum,**
>
> **Der Unterthanen Lust und Ruhm,**
>
> Der Königinnen Preis gewesen.

This concluding stanza of Johann Christoph Gottsched's text calls on poets to write in honor of the deceased, Electress Christiane Eberhardine, and the last three lines (typographically distinctive in the original printed text) present these words as if they were read aloud. Bach sets the first two of the lines in octaves as *Choreinbau*[2] based on the head of the ritornello. He returns to four-part writing for the final line,

Table 1. Unison and Octave Passages in J.S. Bach's Vocal Music

Work	Movement	Text set in unison or octaves	Description
Cantata 65	1	"und des Herren Lob verkün-[digen]"	octave passage at end
Cantata 71	6	"Du wollest dem Feinde nicht geben die Seele deiner Turteltauben"	unison passage at end
Cantata 149	1	"die Rechte des Herrn behält den Sieg"	octave passage
Cantata 190	1	"Herr Gott, dich loben wir" "Herr Gott, wir danken dir"	octave passage octave passage
Cantata 198	10	"Sie ist der Tugend Eigenthum, der Unterthanen Lust und Ruhm"	octave passage
Cantata 214	1	"Tönet, ihr Paucken! Erschallet, Trompeten"	octave opening
Cantata 215	1	"Preise dein Glücke"	octave opening
Lost cantata, BWV Anh. 11/1	1	"Es lebe der König"	octave opening?
Motet, *Jesu meine Freude*, BWV 227	5	"Trotz den alten Drachen" "Ich steh hier und singe"	octave passage octave passage
B-Minor Mass, BWV 232	23	"Osanna, osanna" "Osanna in excelsis"	octave opening octave passages
St. Matthew Passion, BWV 244	58d	"Ich bin Gottes Sohn"	octave passage at end
St. Mark Passion, BWV 247	132	"Mein Leben kommt aus deinem Tod/ Hier hab ich meine Sünden-Noth"	octave passage?
Christmas Oratorio, BWV 248	Cantata 1/1	"Jauchzet! frohlocket! auf! preiset die Tage"	octave opening
Related Works Cantata 26	1	"Ach, wie flüchtig, ach wie nichtig" and other phrases	octave passages ATB; S cantus firmus
Cantata 80	5	"Und wenn die Welt voll Teufel wär . . ."	octaves throughout?

presumably to make a strong cadence, but the meaning of the octave writing as an illustration of quotation is evident.

This passage was presumably parodied in the concluding chorus "Bey deinem Grab und Leichen-Stein" of the lost St. Mark Passion, BWV 247, though the lack of musical sources prevents us from being absolutely certain:

> Bey deinem Grab und Leichen-Stein
>
> Will ich mich stets, mein Jesu, weiden,
>
> Und über dein verdienstlich Leiden,
>
> Von Hertzen froh und danckbar seyn.
>
> Schau, diese Grabschrift solt du haben:
>
> **Mein Leben kommt aus deinem Tod,**
>
> **Hier hab ich meine Sünden-Noth**
>
> Und Jesum selbst in mich begraben.

Here the lines probably marked by octave writing set the words of a gravestone inscription for Jesus. Arguably only the first of the three concluding lines ("Mein Leben kommt aus deinem Tod") represents the epitaph, with the last two lines back in the frame of the poem. Either way, octave writing again marks a quotation, perhaps also to be imagined as read aloud.

The most famous instance of octaves representing quotation in Bach's music appears in the St. Matthew Passion, BWV 244, at the end of the Gospel chorus "Andern hat er geholfen" (movement 58d):

> Andern hat er geholfen und kann sich selber nicht helfen. Ist er der König Israel, so steige er nun vom Kreuz, so wollen wir ihm glauben. Er hat Gott vertrauet, der erlöse ihn nun, lüstet's ihn; denn er hat gesagt: **Ich bin Gottes Sohn.**

The last four words, presented in stark octaves by the combined voices and instruments of the two choruses, are a quotation of Jesus' own statement.[3] Given the importance in oratorio Passions of the direct speech of Jesus (usually underlined in the St. Matthew Passion by orchestrally accompanied recitative), Bach needed some way to emphasize these indirectly reported words. He turned to octave writing.[4]

Octave writing may play a role as a signifier of human speech in verse 3 (movement 5) of the motet *Jesu, meine Freude*, BWV 227. The section in question presents the third stanza of the hymn *Jesu, meine Freude* in a free paraphrase of the melody:

> **Trotz dem alten Drachen,**
>
> Trotz des Todes Rachen,
>
> Trotz der Furcht darzu;

Tobe, Welt, und springe,

Ich steh hier und singe

In gar sichrer Ruh.

Gottes Macht hält mich in acht;

Erd und Abgrund muß verstummen,

Ob sie noch so brummen.

Two text phrases—"Trotz dem alten Drachen" and "Ich steh hier und singe"—are sung in octaves, each as an intensified repetition of an earlier harmonized statement. (We can note that these phrases occur in the parallel A sections of this AAB chorale, but in different places in the poetry.) Bach turns to octave writing partly for emphasis, of course; given the text, it is easy to hear this texture as a musical symbol of Lutheran resolve ("Hier steh ich . . . "). Nevertheless, the second phrase also refers to singing—that is, to audible music-making by human voices—and to this extent it is related to the use of octave writing for quoted words.

Two passages suggest the use of unison or octaves as an invocation of liturgical singing. In the opening movement of the incompletely transmitted New Year's work, Cantata 190, *Singet dem Herrn ein neues Lied*, octave passages present the first two lines of the German *Te Deum* as a concluding punctuation to Psalm verses:

Singet dem Herrn ein neues Lied! Die Gemeine der Heiligen soll ihn loben! Lobet ihn mit Pauken und Reigen, lobet ihn mit Saiten und Pfeifen! **Herr Gott, dich loben wir!**
Alles, was Odem hat, lobe den Herrn! **Herr Gott, wir danken dir!** Alleluja!

The phrases of this hymn (taken up again in the second movement of the cantata), in their stark octave presentation, invoke liturgical chant singing.

The only true unison choral passage in Bach's vocal music is similarly motivated; it appears in the sixth movement of Cantata 71, *Gott ist mein König*, written for the Mühlhausen Town Council:

Du wollest dem Feinde nicht geben die Seele deiner Turteltauben.

This movement is a setting of a Psalm verse, one of several in the libretto; the texture is homophonic and melodically dominated. The final statement among the many repetitions of this short text is intoned, mostly on one note with an inflection at the end. The tune closely resembles the first Psalm tone, and indeed this appears to have been the rationale for Bach's strategy. The movement represents an unusual setting of a biblical text, and his invocation of psalmody is a reminder of its status as a Psalm verse.[5]

Several octave choral passages stem from unison or octave material in instrumental ritornellos. The vocal opening of the first movement of Cantata 214, *Tönet, ihr Pauken, erschallet, Trompeten*, echoes the solo timpani part that begins the ritornello:

> **Tönet ihr Paucken! Erschallet Trompeten!**
>
> Klingender Saiten erfüllet die Luft!
>
> Singet itzt Lieder ihr muntren Poeten!
>
>   Königen lebe! wird fröhlich geruft.
>
>   Königen lebe! diß wünschet der Sachse.
>
>   Königen lebe und blühe und wachse.
>
>   Da capo

Bach presents the first two text phrases in choral octaves, mimicking the references in the text to drums and trumpets, respectively. (In the setting itself, Bach holds back the entrance of the trumpets until the next phrase, using triadic vocal writing to invoke them first.) It is also worth noting that this octave passage sets a text about musical sounds, representing a connection with other uses of this texture.

The relationship between text and music is much less specific in the reuse of this material as the opening movement of the first cantata of the Christmas Oratorio, BWV 248:

> **Jauchzet! frohlocket! auf! preiset die Tage,**
>
> Rühmet, was heute der Höchste gethan,
>
> Lasset das Zagen, verbannet die Klage,
>
> Stimmet voll Jauchzen und Frölichkeit an:
>
> Dienet dem Höchsten mit herrlichen Chören
>
> Laßt uns den Nahmen des Höchsten verehren.
>
>   Da Capo

Here the octave writing simply underlines a text of general rejoicing, vocally echoing the unharmonized opening of the ritornello.

Octave vocal writing is also related to ritornello material in a complex of three movements tied to one another by parody. The opening chorus of Cantata 215, *Preise dein Glücke, Gesegnetes Sachsen*, also begins (both in its ritornello and in its first vocal statement) with plain octaves:

> **Preise dein Glücke,** Gesegnetes Sachsen,
>
>   Weil Gott den Thron deines Königs erhält.

> Fröhliches Land,
>
> Dancke dem Himmel, und küsse die Hand,
>
> Die Deine Wohlfahrt noch täglich läst wachsen,
>
> Und deine Bürger in Sicherheit stellt.
>
> Da Capo

As in the opening chorus of Cantata 214, the octave vocal writing stems from the texture of the opening ritornello. Bach repeats this figure throughout the movement, quoting it in the accompanying vocal ensemble (sometimes the first, sometimes the second chorus). Octave scoring appears to be motivated here less by the text than by the design of the ritornello with its unharmonized opening. This would also seem to be true of the lost model from which the movement is evidently derived, "Es lebe der König, der Vater im Lande," BWV Anh. I 11/1, perhaps also a spoken toast:

> **Es lebe der König,** der Vater im Lande,
>
> Der weise, der milde, der tapfer August!
>
> Er ist unser Schmuck und Ruhm,
>
> Er ist unser Eigenthum,
>
> Er ist Selbst des Himmels Lust,
>
> Der weise der milde, der tapfer August!
>
> Da Capo

Bare octaves also underscore an exclamation in the most famous use of this music, the "Osanna" of the B-Minor Mass, BWV 232. Here the text is limited to a single phrase:

> **Osanna in excelsis**

In this incarnation, the piece is shorn of its opening ritornello, as are a number of parodied movements in the Mass. This means that octave vocal writing—opening without continuo—begins the piece; the unison ritornello from which this vocal texture derives appears only at the end, and the unannounced opening renders the vocal octaves even more striking. The choice of this music, with its octave writing, may not have been textually motivated. However, as in our first examples, the phrase "Osanna in excelsis" may be understood as a quotation to the extent that the passage as a whole was taken to be a reference to the entry of Jesus into Jerusalem described in Matthew 21:6, where these are the words of the onlookers. And of course most of the "Sanctus" text (though not these words in particular) presents the words of the seraphim quoted in Isaiah 6:1. Thus, the relationship between choral octaves and quotation may not be completely absent here.

Another passage in which octave vocal writing is derived from ritornello material is found in the opening movement of Cantata 65, *Sie werden aus Saba alle kommen*, the last vocal phrase of which is mostly unharmonized:

> Sie werden aus Saba alle kommen, Gold und Weihrauch bringen **und des Herren Lob verkün-**digen.

Here the octave texture stems not from the opening, but from the epilogue of the ritornello, which is unharmonized except for the concluding cadence. The closing ritornello, using the full instrumental ensemble and voices in *Choreinbau*, presents the original form of the epilogue for the first time since the opening. One might also see the use of octaves here as loosely motivated by the text, which refers to the (audible?) spreading of God's praise.

In another work, an octave choral passage originates from instrumental material but not directly from the ritornello. In a passage from the opening movement of Cantata 149, *Man singet mit Freuden vom Sieg*, the voices present one isolated text phrase in octaves:

> Man singet mit Freuden vom Sieg in den Hütten der Gerechten: Die Rechte des Herrn behält den Sieg, die Rechte des Herrn ist erhöhet, **die Rechte des Herrn behält den Sieg!**

The passage occurs in mm. 113–116, in the B section of this da capo chorus, and it represents an unharmonized statement of the phrase that concludes both verses of the Psalm text (Psalm 118: 15-16). It is not clear what might have motivated Bach's use of this texture here, but an answer probably lies in the model for this parodied movement, the concluding chorus of Cantata 208:

> Ihr lieblichste Blicke, ihr freudige Stunden,
>
> Euch bleibe das Glücke auf ewig verbunden!
>
> Euch kröne der Himmel mit süßester Lust!
>
> Fürst Christian lebe! Ihm bleibe bewusst,
>
> Was Herzen vergnüget,
>
> Was Trauren besieget!

The octave passage in the Cantata 149 chorus corresponds to mm. 102–103 of the model, in which the four voices rest. In Cantata 149, Bach fills in the empty vocal measures with new material; the fanfare-like musical lines he gives them are present at this spot in bassoon and cello in the Cantata 208 model, and this same fanfare material (derived from the opening of the ritornello) is presented later in unison by instruments several times (in mm. 109–126, for instance). Here, a unison line originally for instruments is given to choral voices in the derived version.

Two related movements deserve mention here for their use of unharmonized choral writing. One is the first movement of Cantata 26, *Ach, wie flüchtig, ach wie nichtig*, a concerted chorale setting with soprano cantus firmus. Alto, tenor, and bass provide faster-moving supporting material, and each of the chorale phrases (or half-phrases) ends with the unharmonized ATB statement of a figure derived from the opening of the chorale melody (mm. 18–19, 22–23, etc.). This technique, in which an unharmonized phrase recurs throughout a movement as a punctuating accompanimental figure, recalls the approach used in "Es lebe der König," "Preise dein Glücke," and "Osanna." In Cantata 26 it is realized with only four vocal lines instead of the eight available in the three polychoral works.

Finally, the famous movement "Und wenn die Welt voll Teufel wär" from Cantata 80, *Ein feste Burg ist unser Gott*, would appear to belong on our list of choral-octave pieces. However, the textual history of this movement is complex, and even if the SATB octave scoring of the movement does derive from J.S. Bach (and the transmission of this movement solely in secondary copies makes this difficult to determine), the piece may well have had its origin in a more usual solo chorale setting with instruments.[6] Either way, the work ostensibly calls for unharmonized voices throughout, in contrast to the other movements discussed here. In those movements, a great part of the effect of octave or unison writing, whether meant to mark a quotation, illustrate musical sounds, invoke liturgical singing, or refer to textures in the ritornello of a movement, comes from the shift from choral harmony to the sharply etched uniting of voices in a single melodic line.

Notes

1. Strictly speaking, we are dealing with octave passages, not unisons, because there is only one true unison passage in the Bach repertory, that in Cantata 71.

2. The term *Choreinbau*, coined by Werner Neumann in his classic study *J.S. Bachs Chorfuge: ein Beitrag zur Kompositionstechnik* (3d ed.) (Leipzig: Breitkopf & Härtel, 1953), denotes the repetition of the opening ritornello, or part of it, during the course of a choral movement, with vocal parts "built into" the instrumental material.

3. Eric Chafe, in *Tonal Allegory in the Vocal Music of J.S. Bach* (Berkeley: University of California Press, 1991), 381–84, has pointed out the harmonic significance of this passage.

4. By contrast, the inauthentic words reported by the two false witnesses ("Er hat gesagt: Ich kann den Tempel Gottes abbrechen . . . ") in movement 33 of the St. Matthew Passion are presented in polyphony.

5. This point is discussed in more detail in Daniel R. Melamed, "Der Text der Kantate 'Gott ist mein König' (BWV 71)," in *Über Leben, Kunst und Kunstwerke: Aspekte musikalischer Biographie. Johann Sebastian Bach in Zentrum*, ed. Christoph Wolff (Leipzig: Evangelische Verlagsanstalt, 1999), 160–72.

6. I discuss this topic in more detail in "The evolution of 'Und wenn die Welt voll Teufel wär' BWV 80/5," in *The Century of Bach and Mozart*, ed. Thomas Kelly and Sean Gallagher (Cambridge, Mass.: Harvard University Department of Music, 2008), 189–205.

You Say *Sabachthani* and I Say *Asabthani*

A St. Matthew Passion Puzzle

Michael Ochs

To the memory of Siegfried Ochs (1858–1929)

In Johann Sebastian Bach's St. Matthew Passion, the final words uttered by Jesus read, in published librettos and scores:[1]

Jesus: "Eli, Eli, lama asabthani?"
Evangelist: Das ist: "Mein Gott, mein Gott, warum hast du mich verlassen?"

However, nearly all of the myriad translations of this passage into English read:

Jesus: "Eli, Eli, lama *sabachthani*?" [emphasis added]
Evangelist: That is, "My God, my God, Why hast Thou forsaken me?"[2]

This conflict raises numerous questions, among them: Did Bach write *asabthani* or *sabachthani*? What textual source did he use? Why do English versions of the Passion text read differently from Bach's? How does the phrase read in the Gospel of Matthew? Is one of the versions "wrong," and if so, which one? In what language is the foreign phrase? What, according to scholars, did Jesus actually say? Finally, which word should be used for translations and performances of the St. Matthew Passion in English?

The answer to the question of what Bach wrote is simple: Both his autograph for the work and a copy, made around 1756 by Johann Christoph Farlau, probably from Bach's composing score, clearly read *asabthani*.[3] The librettist for Bach's St. Matthew Passion was Picander, pseudonym of Christian Friedrich Henrici. Although the printed libretto supplies all of the newly written poetry set by Bach as arias, ensembles, and choruses, it does not provide the entire narrative thread, that is, the recitatives; instead, it specifically indicates which sentences from the Gospel of Matthew belong where in the text.[4] The standard translation of the New Testament used by Protestants throughout German-speaking lands dates back to that published by Martin Luther in 1522,[5] and indeed, Luther's text in all versions down to the present reads *asabthani*. It is, for example, the textual basis of the Bible commentary published by Abraham Calov, which Bach owned and annotated.[6] At first blush, one might guess that the overwhelming number of translations into English (and into other modern languages) cite the passage correctly and, unlikely as it would be, that the Luther Bible errs. As we will see, though, that is not the case.

To fully understand the mysteries surrounding this important quotation, we need to examine the early history of the text as it appears in Matthew (27:46) and in the Gospel of Mark (15:34), which most scholars agree predates Matthew[7] (the Gospels of Luke and John do not include the quotation). The authoritative version of the New Testament comes down to us in the form of Greek scriptures dating from AD ca. 50–ca. 200, with the four Gospels dating from the first forty to fifty years of that period.[8] However, the exact origin of this traditional Greek text is uncertain, although scholars generally agree that parts of it, at least, were compiled from earlier manuscripts, including a hypothetical Greek source labeled "Q" (from the German *Quelle*, source). Some of these sources are thought to have contained sayings attributed to Jesus, and some were written in the Syriac dialect of Aramaic, the vernacular language of Palestine at the time of Jesus. Like Q (if indeed it was a specific document), these sources have not survived, but through reconstructions based on the traditional Greek gospel texts and more recent archaeological discoveries, they are thought as well to have contained sayings of Jesus. A manuscript containing a Coptic translation of an earlier Greek manuscript, the noncanonical gnostic Gospel of Thomas, proved to doubters that such collections of sayings had existed.[9]

The reading *sabachthani* in English translations of the text in both Mark and Matthew appears, notably, in the King James Version, produced by a group of scholars and published in 1611. Although it was not nearly the first, it has been by far the most influential English version of the Bible.[10] It is safe to say that virtually all translations into English, both before and after the King James Version, both Protestant and Catholic, agree that the last word of the biblical quote we are considering is *sabachthani*. Indeed, a spot check reveals that nearly all translations into languages other than German reproduce the word as *sabachthani* in one or another transliteration—as does, for example, St. Jerome's Latin Vulgate of AD 404, a primary source for a millennium of translations. Like the King James Version scholars, who claimed to have translated the text "out of the original tongues," Luther claimed to have worked from the original Hebrew and Aramaic (for the Hebrew Scriptures) and the traditional Greek (for the New Testament). Thus, supposedly based on the same sources, Luther and the writers of the King James Version came to separate conclusions, leading to the thought that Luther either was using a different or defective source or had some other reason for writing *asabthani*.

In fact, Luther would doubtless have recognized the words attributed to Jesus as a passage from Psalm 22:1, but not quite as the Psalm reads in the Hebrew Scriptures, in which the sentence appears as Psalm 22:2. He would have known or learned that the word *sabachthani* is an approximation of the Aramaic word שבקתני (*šabaqtani*, you have forsaken me). The entire phrase in Psalm 22:2 of the Hebrew Scriptures reads אלי אלי למה עזבתני (*Eli, Eli, lama azavtani*, in modern English transliteration), in which the final word derives from the three-letter root עזב, whose basic meaning is *leave*, or *forsake*, and with the endings ת (you have) and י‎נ (me) becomes עזבתני (in German transliteration of Luther's era, *asabthani*, you have forsaken me). Thus the two words we know as *asabthani* (from Hebrew) and *sabachthani* (from Aramaic) have the same meaning. It is clear, then, that Luther consciously chose to have Jesus speak his final words in Hebrew, in contradistinction to all the early sources that were known in his time.[11]

In the traditional Greek version of Matthew, the quote reads ηλι ηλι λεμα σαβαχθανι (*eli, eli, lema sabachthani*), whose meaning is given as θεε μου θεε μου, ινατι με εγκατελιπες (*thee mou thee mou, inati me egkatelipes* [my God my God, why have you forsaken me]). In the Gospel of Mark, the traditional Greek text reads ελωι, ελωι, λαμα σαβαχθανί (*eloi, eloi, lama sabachthani*), varying slightly, though significantly, from the version in Matthew. Matthew's substitution of ηλι for ελωι, while not changing the meaning (*my God*), introduces a Hebrew word into what otherwise looks like an Aramaic quote.[12] Thus Mark appears to present the entire phrase in Aramaic, whereas Matthew, by some accounts, mixes Aramaic (*sabachthani*) with Hebrew (*eli eli*).[13] Now we must ask why Mark (and Matthew) would have Jesus apparently misquote the Psalms by crying out the words wholly or even partly in Aramaic.

As the vernacular spoken by Jesus, Aramaic was, so to speak, his mother tongue and the language in which he preached, Hebrew by that time having been limited to use in scriptures, prayer, and religious studies. One can argue that because the Aramaic version found in Mark is older, probably all in one language, and in the vernacular of the time, it suggests itself as the words more likely to have been cried out by Jesus, who would surely have known the phrase in both languages. But, although the apostles Mark and Matthew both describe the crucifixion, neither was present, and we have no first-hand accounts of it. That Jesus uttered the phrase at all, however, seems beyond dispute, because the content contradicts the Gospel writers' mission to convince people that Jesus was a manifestation of God. Having this manifest God cry out, "My God, my God, why hast thou forsaken me?" does not help their cause, and the phrase would not have been taken up by the Gospel writers had the story been anything but credible to them.

Before the advent of various modern-language translations in the Middle Ages, Roman Catholic Europeans (as opposed to Eastern Church Catholics) wishing to read the Bible had, first, to be able to read at all, and second, to know Latin or Greek. These two prerequisites prevented all but a small percentage of Western Church members from reading the text. Among the educated few who could read these languages were clergy, who conducted church services in Latin. Indeed, the reading in the Vulgate is *sabacthani*, in consonance (spelling aside) with the Greek versions. Thus, people in the German-language areas of medieval Europe and, presumably, everywhere else where the Vulgate held sway, knew only that form of the word. It is therefore all the more notable that Luther chose to go back to the reading in the Hebrew scriptures for this all-important passage, the only one in the Book of Matthew where the traditional Greek text quotes Jesus in a Semitic language.

We know from Luther's own writings that he did not take the task of translation lightly,[14] so we can be sure that his version was not just a slip of the pen. Several theories may be advanced for Luther's decision to disregard so openly a millennium of Christian tradition. For theological reasons, he modified the text; for example, he translated the words of Paul in the Epistle to the Romans, 3:28, as "So halten wir nun dafür daß der Mensch gerecht wird ohne des Gesetzes Werke, allein durch den Glauben" (Thus we hold that man becomes righteous without the works of the law, by faith alone), thereby inflaming the anger of the "papists," who argued that the word *alone* does not appear in the Vulgate. Luther then mocked Catholic theologians for judging his translation blasphemous, calling them donkeys and worse.[15] He felt deeply that the Roman Church had long departed from what he regarded as true Christianity. Still, anger at the Church would hardly have given him cause to make changes that have a theological basis. Moreover, his hatred of Jews and Judaism was so thoroughgoing[16]—seemingly exceeding even his hatred of papists and the papacy—that one is led to wonder at his preference for putting Hebrew, the holy, scriptural language of the Jews, into Jesus' mouth a moment before his death on the cross. Hebrew would, after all, remind the reader of Jesus' Jewish identity. Only one conclusion can be drawn: Luther must, in his heart, have truly believed that Jesus would not, under these circumstances, have cried out in his vernacular Aramaic; rather, being a learned Jew, would have quoted a verse from scripture—the only scripture he knew—in its original language.

So we are left with the question of how the English translation and other vernacular versions of Bach's text should read. The case in favor of *sabachthani* is strong: it is the reading found in virtually all the early texts in Greek, Latin, and Syriac; it appears in all the texts sanctioned by the Western Church, including the King James Version and its progeny; and it is the term that is familiar to English speakers. However, the case for choosing *asabthani* is even stronger. First, although one could say that Bach would surely have used *sabachthani* had he been setting the text in any other language, he was not writing in another language but in German, using the text he knew. Second, the Hebrew wording was carefully and deliberately chosen by Martin Luther, who in a way could be called a co-librettist of the St. Matthew Passion. Luther was, for better or worse, making a theological point in going back to the Hebrew of the Psalms when contemplating Jesus' dying words on the cross. Although Bach's role in transmitting Luther's theology may have been unwitting, the fact remains that by using a term Luther had consciously rejected, translators are not being true to *their* role of presenting an English text that represents the German as closely as possible. But leaving those two reasons aside, *asabthani* is the word that Bach employed. Given that it is not subject to translation, and barring an overwhelmingly cogent reason, it should be left as the composer intended.

Notes

1. For example, NBA II/5 (*Matthäus-Passion. Markus-Passion*), 252. Handel's St. Matthew Passion of 1719, on a text by Barthold Heinrich Brockes, has the variant spelling *asaphtani*.

2. For an exception, see Z. Philip Ambrose, "J.S. Bach: Texts of the Complete Vocal Works, with English Translation and Commentary" at http://www.uvm.edu/~classics/faculty/bach (accessed September 29, 2005), where the passage "Eli, Eli . . . " as it appears in Bach is unchanged in the translation.

3. A facsimile of the autograph can be found in Bach's *Passio Domini Nostri J. C. Secundum Evangelistam Matthaeum* (Leipzig: Insel-Verlag, 1922) and of the Farlau copy in NBA II/5a.

4. Picander's libretto was printed in 1729 in a collection of the writer's works, *Ernst-Scherzhaffte und Satÿrische Gedichte* (Leipzig: Boëtius, 1727–1729), vol. 2, 101–12.

5. *Das newe Testament deutzsch*, ed. and trans. Martin Luther (Wittenberg: Melchior Lotther d. J., 1522).

6. *Die heilige Bibel, nach D. Martini Lutheri: Deutscher Dolmetschung und Erklärung vermöge des Heil. Geistes im Grund-Text*, ed. Abraham Calov (Wittenberg: Christian Schrödten, 1681–1682).

7. On this issue, however, as on almost every other issue relating to the early history of Bible texts, opinion among scholars is divided, sometimes more-or-less evenly, making it difficult to arrive at firm conclusions. For example, though most scholars agree that the Gospel of Mark predates that of Matthew, "a surprising number of [the same] scholars support Matthean originality" on the question of Jesus' last words. See Raymond E. Brown, *The Death of the Messiah, from Gethsemane to the Grave: A Commentary on the Passion Narratives in the Four Gospels* (New York: Doubleday, 1994), vol. 2, 1052, n. 2. Brown, in the same book (pp. 1050–58), offers an excellent summary and discussion of the various controversies surrounding the quote in question.

8. The authoritative Christian version of the Old Testament, also in Greek, is based in part on the Septuagint, a Greek translation of the Hebrew Scriptures (which, despite the appellation, include two books in Aramaic) completed by Jews for Jewish readers and worshipers whose first language was Greek. Thought to date from ca. 200–ca. 100 BC, the Septuagint was, according to legend, prepared by some seventy scholars—thus the name Septuagint.

9. One view, based solely on internal evidence in the Greek gospels, holds that they originally appeared in Aramaic but that copies of the text were systematically destroyed. See Elaine Pagels, *The Gnostic Gospels* (New York: Random House, 1979), introduction.

10. An Anglo-Saxon translation of the New Testament appeared as early as AD 995, but what is assumed to be the first translation into modern English of a complete Bible was produced ca. 1384 by John Wycliffe, working from the Latin Vulgate. William Tyndale published an English translation of the New Testament in 1525–1526, based on a Greek text that had recently been published by Erasmus. Most of the language in the King James Version is drawn from Tyndale's poetic English.

11. The Greek text of the *Codex Bezae* (Cambridge University Library), probably dating from the early fifth century, reads ηλι ηλι λαμα ζαφθανι (*eli eli lama zaphthani*) in both Mark and Matthew, seemingly reproducing the Hebrew text of Psalm 22 (apart from the omission of one syllable).

12. This statement, like a number of others in this study, can be challenged. First, the Aramaic form אלוי (*eloi* [my God]) is also a version of a late Hebrew form, אלהי (*elohai* [my God]); second, אלי (*eli* [my God]) can be found in the Targum, an Aramaic translation of the Hebrew Bible. See *The Anchor Bible Matthew*, ed. and trans. W. F. Albright and C. S. Mann (Garden City, NY: Doubleday, 1971); Max Wilcox, "eli, eli, lama sabachthani," in *The Anchor Bible Dictionary*, ed. David Noel Freedman (New York: Doubleday, 1992), vol. 2, 457.

13. The word למה (*lama* [why]) poses significant problems: in the identity of its language (Hebrew or Aramaic), its vowels (*lema* in some sources, *lama* or *lamma* in others), and its meaning (*why* in the sense of *for what reason* versus *why* in the sense of *for what purpose*). The standard Greek and Latin texts have *lama* in Mark and *lema* in Matthew, although there is little unanimity among early texts, modern texts, and transliterations about what the first syllable should be. However, since the German and English versions of the St. Matthew Passion text agree on the transliteration (*lama*) and meaning (*for what reason*), these problems are left aside in this study. The chief difficulties, though certainly not the only ones, in transliterating Hebrew and Aramaic occur because in the period covered, only the consonants were written and the vowels were "understood," like accidentals in Renaissance *musica ficta*.

14. In regard to his Bible translation, Luther wrote in 1530, "Es ist mein Testament und meine Dolmetschung und soll mein bleiben und sein. Hab ich drinnen etwa gefehlt (das mir doch nicht bewußt, und freilich ungern einen Buchstaben mutwilliglich wollt unrecht verdolmetschen), darüber will ich die Papisten nicht zu Richtern leiden" (It is my testament and my translation, and it will stay and be mine. If I have made mistakes in it [though I am not aware of any, and I would certainly not want to purposely mistranslate a single letter], I would not want the papists to be my judges about that). See *"Ein Sendbrief D. M. Luthers: Von Dolmetzschen und Fürbit der heiligenn"* (An Open Letter on Translating and the Intercession of the Saints), in *D. Martin Luthers Werke* (Weimar: Böhlau, 1883–), vol. 30, part 2, 633. This and all subsequent translations are mine.

15. "Denn sie haben noch zur Zeit zu lange Ohren dazu, und ihr Ika Ika ist zu schwach, mein verdolmetschen zu urteilen" (Because at present their ears are still too long and their hee-haw hee-haw too weak to judge my translating). See Luther, *"Ein Sendbrief,"* 633.

16. A 1543 essay of Luther's "Von den Juden und ihren Lügen" (Concerning the Jews and Their Lies), makes ten recommendations for dealing with Jews, among them: "Erstlich, dass man ihre Synagogen und Schulen mit Feuer anstecke . . . Zum anderen, dass man auch ihre Häuser desglei-

chen zerbreche und zerstöre . . . Zum dritten, dass man ihnen nehme all ihre Betbüchlein und Talmudisten, darin solche Abgötterei, Lügen, Fluch und Lästerung gelehrt wird." (First, that one sets their synagogues and schools on fire . . . Also, one must similarly smash and destroy their houses . . . Third, that one take away all their prayer books and Talmudic texts, in which their idolatry, lies, cursing, and blasphemy are taught.)

Sein Segen fliesst daher wie ein Strom, BWV Anh. I 14

A Source for Parodied Arias in the B-Minor Mass?

William H. Scheide

Based on the latest diplomatic source studies, all but perhaps two of the twenty-seven movements in Bach's B-Minor Mass can now be considered to be parodies,[1] and virtually all of the nine arias fall into this category. So far, however, a concrete model has been pinpointed for only one of the arias: the "Agnus Dei," an aria for alto, violins, and continuo that shares its music with the aria "Ach, bleibe doch, mein liebstes Leben" from the Ascension Oratorio, BWV 11. Both appear to be derived from the aria "Entfernet euch, ihr kalten Herzen" from the lost wedding cantata *Auf! Süss entzückende Gewalt*, BWV Anh. I 196.[2] In this chapter, I focus on another of Bach's wedding cantatas, *Sein Segen fliesst daher wie ein Strom*, BWV Anh. I 14,[3] as a possible source of parodies for some of the remaining eight arias in the B-Minor Mass for which no model has yet been found. Although the music of *Sein Segen fliesst* is lost, its text, by an unknown librettist, has survived.[4] The arias of the cantata (Table 1) all contain allusions to flowing water, which seems to be explained by the fact that the groom at the ceremony is referred to in the libretto as "Floß-Verwalter," or Director of Barge Traffic on the rivers of Saxony.

I would like to begin by pointing to the extremely inappropriate setting of the word "sedes" in mm. 75–78 of the "Qui sedes" of the B-Minor Mass as a continuous stream of forty-eight sixteenth notes. Clearly, some other text originally inspired this music. The text of "Laudamus te" is also of interest in this context. It presents four verbs, and all four occur in each of the three sections of this modified (ABA') da capo aria. In my opinion, so unusual and curious a feature confirms that the Latin text of the Mass has been adapted to a preexistent model. However, there is an important distinction between the recognition that a chorus or aria is an arrangement modeled on a lost original and the reconstruction of that lost original. I do not believe that such a reconstruction would necessarily be fruitful, since it would very likely be highly speculative and, in many details, open to question. Instead, it may be sufficient, at least occasionally, to discover a particular musical feature in the parody movement

Table 1. Text of the Arias in *Sein Segen fliesst daher wie ein Strom*, BWV Anh. I 14

VOR DER TRAUUNG (Before the wedding rite)

1. ARIA

Sein Segen fliesst daher wie ein Strom	His blessing flows hither like a torrent
und tränket die Erde wie eine Sündflut.	and drowns the earth like a great flood.[a]

3. ARIA

Wohl dir, da zur erwünschten Stunde,	Happy are you when at the wished hour,
Von des Altars geweihten Grunde,	From the altar's consecrated base,
Ein unergründlich Wasser schiesst.	An unfathomable water shoots forth
So lass dein Halleluja schallen,	So let your halleluja resound,
Wenn diese Ströme zu dir wallen,	When these streams surge up to you,
Durch die der Segen reichlich fliesst.	Through which the blessing richly flows.[b]

Da Capo

NACH DER TRAUUNG (After the wedding rite)

4. ARIOSO

Ein Mara weicht von dir,	A Mara[c] withdraws from you
mit allen Bitterkeiten	with all its bitternesses,
Dir ist der Anmut Milch	For you is destined the milk
und Honig zugedacht,	and honey of sweetness,
Denn Mosis Segens-Wort	For Moses's word of blessing
kann einen Strom bereiten,	can prepare a stream,
Denn selbst der Lebens-Baum	Which the tree of life itself
dir heute lieblich macht.	makes lovely for you today.[d]

6. ARIA

So tritt in dieses Paradies,	So step into this paradise,
Du sollt die güldnen Schätze spüren,	You shall discover the golden treasures,
So Pisons Wellen in sich führen.	For Pison's[e] waves lead to them.[f]
Sie werden durch gesegnet Steigen,	They will through blessed uprising,
Den Überfluss des Segens zeigen.	Manifest the superabundance of blessing.

Da Capo

---

a. Ecclesiasticus 39:27 (39:22 in some English Bibles). "*Sündflut*" in the German text is a reference from the story of Noah to the flood in which the world was drowned because of its sins.

b. Compare Ezekiel 47:1-23.

c. "*Mara*" is a transliteration of the Hebrew word meaning "bitterness."

d. Compare Exodus 15:23-25.

e. Pison or Pishon is a river that flows "where there is gold" (Genesis 2:11).

f. Compare Genesis 2:11.

that strikingly suggests a detail in the text of the original, the music of which has been lost.

In this context I would mention the "Quoniam tu solus sanctus." The presence of two obbligato bassoons, in addition to continuo, is unique in Bach's music. There is also the great horn solo, the only appearance of that instrument anywhere in the B-Minor Mass. Setting aside source evidence, both features point to parody. Is there any hint as to the origins of this movement?

In my opinion, the music was originally inspired by the text of the aria "Wohl dir, da zur erwünschten Stunde," the third movement of *Sein Segen fliesst*. The music of the "Quoniam," in particular that in the horn part at mm. 1–2, 20–21, 97–98, and 116–117, with its high octave leap (Example 1), presents a vivid musical representation of "the altar's consecrated base." Only slightly less convincing is the image of gushing water projected particularly in the horn and voice parts of mm. 21–28 (Example 2)[5] as a graphic depiction of the text, "an unfathomable water shoots forth."[6] Such correspondences between the music of an aria from the B-Minor Mass and an aria text in Bach's lost wedding cantata raise the question of whether there might be further parallels.

In answering this question, let us return to the "Laudamus te" and in particular to the comparison of mm. 25 and 57 (Example 3). In m. 25 the voice follows the solo violin (for the most part at the interval of a sixth) up one octave in modulating to the dominant tonality. In m. 57, the voice starts a fourth higher in parallel motion with the solo violin (again at the interval of a sixth), but this time rises only a fifth, stopping at e″ while the solo violin continues on up to a″, the highest note in any Bach violin music. I interpret the clear breaking-off of the recapitulation in the vocal part[7] and the extreme range of the solo violin as evidence that the "Laudamus te" represents a transposed arrangement of music from a lost original. It should be noted that the opening aria of the wedding cantata *Sein Segen fliesst* refers to a "torrent" (*Strom*) that "drowns the earth like a great flood" (*tränket die Erde wie eine Sündflut*). If the first statement of the word "*Strom*" is placed at the cadence in m. 19 of the "Laudamus te," one hears, as if for the first time, the inexorably rising flood water in the imitative entries of the string parts at mm. 19–21. Thus we can make a strong claim to have found the models for the music of the "Quoniam" and "Laudamus te."

Example 1. "Quoniam tu solus sanctus" from the B-Minor Mass, BWV 232, mm. 1–2.

Example 2. Hypothetical reconstruction of the aria "Wohl dir, da zur erwünschten Stunde," BWV Anh. 14/3, mm. 21–28, from the music of the "Quoniam tu solus sanctus" of the B-Minor Mass.

One wonders whether Bach's predilection for parodying music from earlier compositions, so pronounced in the *Missa* (Kyrie and Gloria) of the B-Minor Mass, was still an important compositional factor in the later sections of the work (Credo, Sanctus, and Agnus Dei). These portions were composed or assembled some fifteen years later. Concerning the aria "Et in Spiritum Sanctum," Rudolf Steglich notes "how lovely" (*lieblich*) the music is, and further, that "whoever did not already know what the text was would certainly imagine it to be in a profane love aria, possibly even a wedding aria."[8] At the very least, this directs our attention to this aria, in which the relation of text and music is unusually complicated (Table 2). The modified da capo structure is the only example known to me in which the concluding A' section sets a new text. I also see as peculiar the division of the B section into two vocal passages (7 and 9 in Table 2) each ending in the same key, F♯ minor.

Example 3. "Laudamus te" from the B-Minor Mass, BWV 232, Soprano 2, mm. 25 and 57.

One notes with interest how easy it would be to return to the opening key and music immediately after the first solo and ritornello in the B section (Example 4). This suggests to me that the second section (mm. 79–92) was not original but added to receive the new text ("qui locutus est per Prophetas"). When one considers that the vocal part here is rather high, almost never going below A and seldom above e', the final low F♯ in m. 92 might well have been intentionally inserted by Bach to highlight the extreme note in the singer's lower range. The result is that what was at first a modest and radiant aria became overloaded with textual matter as contrasting and as diverse as the three members of the Trinity, the prophets, and the Catholic church —each of which could have been granted a separate composition. But the lovely wedding text of movement 6 of *Sein Segen fliesst* corresponds as closely to the equally lovely mood and fervor of the music of "Et in Spiritum Sanctum" as does its structure; so, one is persuaded that the wedding text with its musical setting could well have been the model and inspiration for the parody.

And so we come to the final aria in the wedding cantata, the fourth movement "Ein Mara weicht von dir," labeled "Arioso" in the libretto. Its text consists of four alexandrines that divide easily into two couplets. So simple a text suggests a straightforward, nonrepeating musical setting in two halves, with appropriate phrase structures accommodating alexandrines and trimeters (half an alexandrine). The contrasting affections in the first two lines of the text ("Bitterkeiten" versus "der Anmut Milch und Honig") are also noteworthy.

A number of these elements are to be found in the "Benedictus."[9] The text divides into two clear sections separated in the music by a six-measure ritornello. Although in the Mass the same text, "Benedictus qui venit in nomine Domini," appears unchanged in both halves, the music is quite different. Although different, nothing in the second half of the text of the "Benedictus" remotely approaches the affective shift from poignant minor to bright major in mm. 19–22, which parallels effectively the change from "Bitterkeiten" to "Anmut" in lines 1 and 2 of the text of "Ein Mara weicht von dir." A curious parallel occurs in the voice parts at mm. 22–24 in D major and 41–43 in B minor (Example 5). As both words in the parallel German text are happy ("Anmut" for m. 23 and "lieblich" for m. 43), it is hard to understand why the

Table 2. Structural and Textural Comparison of "Et in Spiritum Sanctum"
and "So tritt in dieses Paradies" (hypothetical reconstruction)

Section	Measures	Key	Text/Section	
			"Et in Spiritum"	*"So tritt"*
A				
1	1–13	A→E	Ritornello	Ritornello
2	13–17	A	Et in Spiritum Sanctum, Dominum et vivificantem,	So tritt in dieses Paradies
3	17–25	A	Ritornello	Ritornello
4	25–36	A→E	Et in Spiritum Sanctum, Dominum et vivificantem,	Du sollt die güldnen Schätzen spüren
5	36–49	E	qui ex Patre Filioque procedit,	So Pisons Wellen in sich führen
6	50–61	E	Ritornello	Ritornello
B				
7	61–75	E→f♯	qui cum Patre et Filio simul adoratur et conglorificatur,	Sie werden durch gesegnet Steigen den Überfluss des Segens zeigen.
8	75–79	f♯	Ritornello	Ritornello
9	79–92	f♯	qui locutus est per Prophetas.	?
10	92–93	f♯→A	Ritornello	Ritornello
A'				
11	92–97	A	Et unam sanctam et apostolicam Ecclesiam.	So tritt in dieses Paradies
12	97–105	A	Ritornello	Ritornello
13	105–132	A	Et unam sanctam et apostolicam Ecclesiam.	So tritt in dieses Paradies Du sollt die gulden Schätzen spüren So Pisons Wellen In sich führen.
14	132–144	A	Ritornello	Ritornello

Example 4. Reconstruction of mm. 76–84 of "So tritt in dieses Paradies," BWV Anh. I 14/6, from mm. 76–79 and 98–102 of "Et in Spiritum Sanctum" of the B-Minor Mass.

first passage is in the major mode while the second is in the minor mode. Perhaps the text of the cantata aria was not original, like that of, say, the opening movement of Cantata 215, and that would account for the pervasive minor mode in mm. 32–57. Because it is impossible to know what any earlier text might have been, one cannot offer a satisfactory solution. Nevertheless, this does not alter the fact that the "Benedictus" is a parody for which the model remains unknown. This is confirmed by the long passage in the minor mode at mm. 32–57, so very inappropriate for the cheerful affect of the Mass text. The contrasting sweet-versus-sour, happy-versus-sad affects in the text of "Ein Mara weicht von dir" are close to both the musical text of the "Benedictus" and the declamation of the wedding aria.

Example 5. Reconstruction of mm. 22–24 and 41–43 of "Ein Mara weicht von dir" from the music of the "Benedictus" of the B-Minor Mass.

In conclusion, it is my opinion that the texts and music of at least three, and possibly four, movements of the lost wedding cantata *Sein Segen fliesst daher wie ein Strom*, BWV Anh. I 14, served Bach as models for arias in the B-Minor Mass. Thus, of the Mass's nine arias, only three have not been considered—the duets "Domine Deus" and "Et in unum Dominum" and the aria "Qui sedes."[10] Given the fact that virtually all the arias in the B-Minor Mass can now be shown to be parodies based on preexisting models, it is clear that Bach did not "favor" the arias over the choruses by composing proportionately more original music for them.

Notes

1. For a useful summary of the latest thinking on this score, see George B. Stauffer, *Bach: The Mass in B Minor* (New Haven, Conn.: Yale University Press, 2003), 48–50.

2. Friedrich Smend, "Bachs Himmelfahrts-Oratorium," in *Bach-Gedenkschrift 1950* (Leizpig: VEB Deutscher Verlage für Musik, 1950), 42. In addition, Yoshitake Kobayashi has presented evidence suggesting that when writing the "Benedictus" in the autograph score of the B-Minor Mass (*P 180*), Bach was tracing a sketch in paler ink that preceded the final musical text (which is in darker ink). See Yoshitake Kobayashi, "Die Universalität in Bachs h-Moll-Messe—Ein Beitrag zum Bach-Bild der letzten Lebensjahre," *Musik und Kirche* 57 (1987), 19.

3. See NBA I/33 (*Trauungskantaten*), ed. Frederick Hudson, KB, 31–33.

4. The full title reads as follows: *An dem | Verehligungs-Tage | Des | Wohl-Edlen, Vest und Wohlgelahrten | HERRN | Christoph Friedrich | Lösners, | Sr. Kön. Majest. In Pohlen und Churfürst. Durchl. | zu Sachsen Wohlbestalten Proviant- und Floß-Verwalters | in Leipzig, | Mit der | Wohl-Edlen und Tugend-belobten | JUNGFER | Johanna Elisabetha, | Des | Wohl-Edlen und Groß-Achtbaren Herrn | Gottfr. Heinrich Scherlings, | Vornehmen Kauff- und Handels-Mannes, | Jungfer Tochter, | Den 12. Febr. 1725. | Ward | Folgend Trauungs-CANTATA | aufgeführet | von | Johann Sebastian Bachen, | H. A. C. Capell-Meister, auch Directore Chori Musici Lipsiensis und Cantore | der Schulen zu St. Thomae. | Leipzig, gedruckt bey Immanuel Tietzen.* For a facsimile reproduction of the libretto, see *Sämtliche von Johann Sebastian Bach vertonte Texte*, ed. Werner Neumann (Leipzig: VEB Deutscher Verlag für Musik, 1974), 388–89.

5. For this example the music of the "Quoniam" is transposed up a fourth to G major, a more comfortable tessitura for the bass voice (at least in the A section of the da capo aria, mm. 13–45). In addition, the two bassoons of the Mass aria are replaced by two oboes da caccia. A different key, D major, may have been necessary in the Mass aria to permit a higher tessitura expressing the word "altissimus," especially in the B section (mm. 53–89). Here one may observe the highest bass notes in the aria. These and other high notes in the B and A' sections of the "Quoniam" occur on the word "altissimus." This repetition is not paralleled in the text of "Wohl dir, da zur erwünschten Stunde."

6. Such imagery is suggestive of a fire hydrant spewing forth water on a hot summer day.

7. It should be noted, however, that although the vocal part climbs to e″ on a number of occasions, it never exceeds this upper limit in the movement. Thus, the breaking of the ascent in m. 57 may be a matter of "tailoring" the vocal part to a particular singer, perhaps Faustina Bordoni at the Dresden court where the music was first performed. See Christoph Wolff, "Anmerkungen zu Bach und 'Cleofide,'" in *Johann Sebastian Bachs Spätwerk und dessen Umfeld—Bericht über das wissenschaftliche Sympo-*

sion anläßlich des 61. Bachfestes der Neuen Bachgesellschaft Duisburg 1986, ed. Christoph Wolff (Kassel: Bärenreiter, 1988), 167–69. The link between the "Laudamus te" and Bordoni was first mentioned by Robert L. Marshall in "Bach the Progressive: Observations on His Later Works," in Marshall, *The Music of Johann Sebastian Bach: The Sources, the Style, the Significance* (New York: Schirmer Books, 1989), 42.

8. Rudolph Steglich, *Wege zu Bach* (Regensburg: Bosse, 1949), 149: "Wer noch nicht weiss, was für Texte das sind, vermutet sie gewiss in einer weltlichen Liebesarie, vielleicht gar einer Hochzeitsarie."

9. It may be significant that this is the only aria in the B-Minor Mass with only one instrumental obbligato part. Such diminutive forces would be especially appropriate for a separate performance in the intimate context of, and space for, a wedding. The range of the part is suitable for either violin or transverse flute, but the latter is generally favored. Bach may have omitted to name the instrument in *P 180* because, depending on the availability of a *traverso* player, he may at times have had to use a violinist. I would opt for the flute, an instrument that Bach may not always have had at his disposal.

10. As noted earlier, the music of this aria is highly inappropriate to its text.

Bach Circle

Johann Friedrich Schweinitz, "A Disciple of the Famous Herr Bach in Leipzig"

Hans-Joachim Schulze

Absent from Hans Löffler's groundbreaking compilation of Johann Sebastian Bach's students[1] is the name of the Göttingen organist, university music director, and city cantor Johann Friedrich Schweinitz (1708–1780). Apparently Löffler had not encountered Georg Linnemann's earlier research on the music history of the city of Celle, in which Schweinitz is referred to in a testimonial by the Göttingen University professor and former rector of the Leipzig St. Thomas School Johann Matthias Gesner as "a disciple of the famous Herr Bach in Leipzig."[2] Gesner's letter of recommendation for Schweinitz came at a moment when two important musical posts in Celle were filled within a few weeks of one another—an infrequent occurrence in the seventeenth and eighteenth centuries.[3]

The position of city organist became vacant with the death of Dieterich Hinrich Christoph Vornwald on January 25, 1745. We encounter as unsuccessful competitor for the position Karl Christoph Hachmeister (1710–1777), who three years later was to take up a position as organist in Hamburg.[4] The post of city cantor in Celle also became available at the beginning of 1745, when the officeholder left to take up a position elsewhere as pastor (undoubtedly at a higher salary). Gesner's letter of recommendation for Schweinitz, dated January 18, 1745, was written with regard to this event.[5] Nothing came of this offer from Celle. Schweinitz, employed in a respectable position, turned it down, apparently because he was unwilling to submit himself to the selection process and risk a rejection that might have been damaging to his career. Instead, the new city cantor in Celle turned out to be Johann Christian Winter (1718–1802), previously adjunct organist in Wolfenbüttel and later cantor in Hanover and a member of Mizler's "Society of Musical Sciences." Winter was the son-in-law of Heinrich Bokemeyer (1679–1751) for some time and is remembered in the history of music as the temporary custodian of the "Bokemeyer Collection."[6]

There is no reason to doubt Gesner's characterization of Schweinitz as a "disciple of the famous Herr Bach in Leipzig." Schweinitz's presence in Leipzig is amply and securely confirmed by his enrollment at the university on June 23, 1732, and through his transfer to the University of Göttingen on October 13, 1735. Johann Christian Limmer (1712–1772), a younger fellow-student who had been studying in Leipzig since October 1729, kept an album that contains a Leipzig entry of August 21, 1732, inscribed "Johann: Frider: Schweinizius."[7] The entry not only offers further documentary evidence of Schweinitz's stay in the "Athens on the Pleiße," but also confirms Gesner's evaluation of Schweinitz as writing "with a fair hand which, in a *Praeceptore classico*, is no slight virtue."[8] Certainly, it is clear from that scribal sample, in conjunction with related Göttingen documents in Schweinitz's hand dated April 18, 1764, and September 27, 1771,[9] that no known contemporary copies of compositions by J.S. Bach can be attributed to Schweinitz either as scribe or owner. Nor does it offer anything further concerning Bach's method of instruction in keyboard or in composition.

However, there is a true Leipzig musical connection: Schweinitz's application, made in October 1735 just after his move to Göttingen, for permission to establish a Collegium Musicum there based on the model of similar ensembles at other universities. The Collegium was to serve as a music training ground for the students but also to open up the possibility of presenting "every Saturday or so, a performance of a well composed piece of music *in loco publico* for which each member of the audience would pay an entry fee of no more than three Groschen, as is customary in Leipzig." Its formulation gives no indication to which of the two Leipzig Collegia Musica this remark refers. Nevertheless, Schweinitz would hardly have been described as "a disciple of Herr Bach" if he had performed not in Bach's Collegium but rather in the competing ensemble directed by Johann Gottlieb Görner, organist of St. Thomas Church. Schweinitz's personal and musical experiences may have been similar to those recalled in 1784 by Jacob von Stählin (1709–1785), who participated in the Collegium in the early 1730s.[10]

Already at the beginning of 1735, nine months before Schweinitz's Göttingen initiative, Christoph Gottlieb Fröber (1704–1759) had founded a Collegium Musicum on the Leipzig model in the neighboring town of Delitzsch.[11] Evidently he was drawing on his participation from 1726 to 1731 in the Leipzig Collegium directed first by Georg Balthasar Schott (until spring 1729) and then by Johann Sebastian Bach. Another Collegium, founded by Johann Gottfried Donati (1706–1782) and also based on the Leipzig model, was established in Greiz in 1746. Since Donati left Leipzig at the beginning of 1729, the roots of his ensemble must be credited to the Schott era.[12]

Evidence of performances by Schweinitz's "Göttingisches Collegium Musicum" is provided by a series of extant printed texts to festive cantatas for various occasions, beginning with New Year's Day 1736 (the "newly founded Chorus Musicus in Göttingen" had been responsible for an inaugural concert on October 29, 1735). Schweinitz is specifically mentioned as composer in only a few cases. However, given the traditions of the time, one can assume that the works without a composer's name stem for the most part—if not completely—from his pen. This certainly holds true for those compositions resulting from commissions that were subsequently performed by the Göttingisches Collegium Musicum. To this group belong a "Cantata which was performed with music in the presence of his royal highness George II . . . in the University Church on August 1, 1748" (with the text incipit, "Besingt, ihr Musen, unsre Triebe, / Bringt unsre Freude vor den Thron!"), as well as a "Serenata which, on the same occasion in the most-desired presence of George II, was performed on August 1, 1748, by a number of Göttingen students as a most humble token of their deepest respect" (with the text incipit, "Laßt freudige Trompeten schallen, Jauchzt, Völker, jauchzt, Georg ist hier"). The congratulatory librettos, dedicated to the founder of the University of Göttingen, George II (1683–1760), Elector of Hanover and King of Great Britain and Ireland, were composed by no less a figure than Albrecht von Haller (1708–1777), the Professor of Anatomy, Botany, and Surgery at the University and a widely read poet. Haller was active in Göttingen from 1736 to 1751 and decades later considered it worthwhile to publish a reprint of the texts in his *Versuch Schweizerischer Gedichte*.[13]

When Schweinitz accepted the post of "Cantor figuralis" at the City School in Göttingen in 1743, he had to give up the position of organist at the city and university churches that he had occupied since at least 1738. His introduction as cantor on May 1, 1743, was celebrated with a *Programma* written by Johann Christoph Leonhard (ca. 1680–1753).[14] Schweinitz's connection with Leipzig is mentioned in the text but without any reference to Bach.

The trajectory of Schweinitz's career from this time on reveals many similarities to that of his mentor: Latin instruction and vocal training for the schoolboys, composition and performance of church music, organ examinations, celebratory music for the city and the university, and teaching of private students. The same is true of the problems he encountered in his various activities as cantor: in particular, difficulties of personnel, the inadequate capabilities of the city musicians, and the necessity of augmenting forces through the recruitment of *Hautboisten* (military musicians) and, above all, university students.

Moreover, Schweinitz's withdrawal from the directorship of regular concerts in 1767 and his limiting himself to a few important organizations finds its parallel in the actions of Bach as well. Schweinitz held the title of "Director Musices bey dortiger Universität," which he requested at the end of 1749, received in January 1750, and retained until the end of his life. The fact that Schweinitz functioned nominally as Director Musices even after 1767, when the concerts shifted to the directorship of the university concertmaster, Georg Philipp Kreß (1719–1779), may have led to some confusion in Göttingen. On February 4, 1779, two days after the death of Kreß, Johann Nikolaus Forkel applied for the position of Academic Music Director[15] without mentioning or noticing that the real holder of the position, Schweinitz, was still alive —though as a consequence of health problems probably unfit for service. Whether the university authorities were aware of this situation and consequently held off Forkel's appointment until the death of Johann Friedrich Schweinitz in Pyrmont on July 10, 1780, is unknown.

Whatever the case, it is noteworthy that as far as we know, Forkel nowhere refers to the fact that he succeeded in office a true pupil of Johann Sebastian Bach. Certainly when Forkel entered the University of Göttingen in 1769, Schweinitz's Leipzig student years were already more than three decades in the past, and it is likely that he did not make much ado over his years of instruction with Bach. In addition, he had not been active as an organist for a long time and had not exactly followed in his great teacher's footsteps as a composer. That the aged Schweinitz also harbored a certain antipathy toward the younger Forkel cannot be ruled out: "the orderly conduct of his [Schweinitz's] life" as attested to by Gesner in 1745 and the not exactly exemplary life led by the young Forkel belonged to two different worlds.[16]

To what extent Forkel knew or valued the compositions of Schweinitz is impossible to say. In this regard, there is no difference between Forkel and other historians down to the present day. For his highly important *Quellenlexikon* of 1900–1904, Robert Eitner was able to find only one composer by the name of Schweinitz in the sources available to him. This was one Andreas Schweinitz from Treuenbrietzen in Mark Brandenburg, a known organist and teacher of Christoph Nichelmann (1717–1762) during his youth.[17] Eitner attributed all extant Schweinitz compositions to Andreas Schweinitz without a second thought, despite the fact that nowhere is it documented that the Treuenbrietzen organist ever had anything to do with the composition of church cantatas.[18] Thus, until there is proof to the contrary, the nine extant manuscripts of cantatas in the Bibliothèque du Conservatoire Royal de Musique in Brussels at issue here will be attributed to the Director of Music in Göttingen, Johann Friedrich Schweinitz. These are given in Table 1, in order of their numbering in the printed catalog of 1898.[19]

This group of scores, prepared by several scribes (in some instances evidently copying from performance parts), may stem as a unit from the collection of the Schwerin organist and music collector, Johann Jakob Heinrich Westphal (1756–1825).[20] The fact that the collection is limited to festive cantatas might be an indication of a purposeful choice on the part of the collector. At the same time, it also raises the possibility that in Göttingen, during the period in question, concerted church music was restricted to the high feasts of the liturgical year. An exception among the Brussels group is the cantata specified for the "Raths Predigt" (No. 917), which bears an attribution—subsequently crossed out—to Telemann.

Table 1. Cantatas of Johann Friedrich Schweinitz in Brussels, Bibliothèque du Conservatoire Royal de Musique, Wotquenne Catalog Nos. 910–918[a]

Catalog number	Title	Key	Instrumentation	Manuscript attribution
910	*Jauchzet, ihr Völker der Heiland ist kommen*	D major	S,A,T,B,Tr I/II, Timp,Vn I/II,Vla,Bc	"Auf Weihnachten di Schweinitz"
911	*Ich bin der Erste und der Letzte*	D major	S,A,T,B,Tr I/II, Timp,Vn I/II,Vla,Bc	"Auf Ostern Schweinitz"
912	*Wer ist der, der so von Edom kömmt*	E♭ major	S,A,T,B,Tr I/II, Timp,Vn I/II,Vla,Bc	"Auf Ostern di Schweinitz"
913	*Auf Christi Himmelfahrt allein*	C minor	S,A,T,B,Tr I/II, Timp,Vn I/II,Vla,Bc	"Auf Himmelfahrt di Schweinitz"
914	*Das Reich Gottes ist nicht Essen und Trinken*	D major	S,A,T,B,Tr I/II, Timp,Vn I/II,Vla,Bc	"Auf Pfingsten di Schweinitz"
915	*Schaffe in mir, Gott, ein reines Herz*	F major	S,A,T,B,Hn I/II, Vn I/II,Vla,Bc	"Auf Pfingsten di Schweinitz"
916	*Gott der Vater, wohn uns bei*	D major	S,A,T,B,Hn I/II, Vn I/II,Vla,Bc	"Festo. S. S. Trinit: di Schweiniz"
917	*Auf, redliche Bürger, ermuntert die Herzen*	D major	S,A,T,B,Tr I/II, Timp,Vn I/II,Vla,Bc	"CANTATA auf die Raths Predigt di Schweinitz"
918	*Er hat seinen Engeln befohlen*	F major	S,A,T,B,Hn I/II, Vn I/II,Vla,Bc	"Festo Michaelis di Schweinitz"

a. Alfred Wotquenne, *Catalogue de la Bibliothèque du Conservatoire Royal de Musique de Bruxelles* (Brussels: J.J. Coosemans, 1898).

The opening measures of this cantata (Example 1) argue against the ascription of the work to Telemann, for they leave one with the distinct impression that the composer had attended the performance of a work by Bach, Cantata 207a, *Auf, schmetternde Töne der muntern Trompeten*, on August 3, 1735—a correspondence that strongly suggests Schweinitz as the composer.

Speaking conclusively for the attribution of the other eight cantatas to Johann Friedrich Schweinitz is the fact that a manuscript copy of an Ascension cantata by Gottfried Heinrich Stölzel has survived, whose musical text as well as title page are unquestionably in Schweinitz's hand.[21] The title page in question reads: "Festo Resur. Chr. | GOTT sey Danck, der uns den | Sieg gegeben hat etc. | â | 2 Clarini | Principal et | Timbalo | 2 Corni | 2 Violini | Viola | Canto Alto | Tenor et Basso | con | Basso continuo | obligato. | di Sig(nore) Stölzel | JFSchweiniz."[22] The close corre-

Example 1. Johann Friedrich Schweinitz, *Auf, redliche Bürger, ermuntert die Herzen*, movement 1, mm. 1–11.

spondence with the foregoing nine cantatas is remarkable in its specification for a high feast day as well as its setting for brass and string instruments without woodwinds.

Having connected nine cantatas by Schweinitz and a composition of Stölzel in this way raises the question of the extent to which Schweinitz's compositions point to an influence by "the renowned Bach." The initial impression speaks rather in favor of a kinship to Telemann, Fasch, Stölzel, and other contemporaries writing in a more fashionable style than that of Bach. Whether a thorough comparison of styles and future investigations might alter this opinion remains to be seen.

—Translated by Gregory G. Butler

Notes

1. Hans Löffler, "Die Schüler Johann Sebastian Bachs," BJ 39 (1953), 5–28. Although Löffler's essay remains the most important study of Bach's students, it is now much in need of a thorough updating.

2. Georg Linnemann, *Celler Musikgeschichte bis zum Beginn des 19. Jahrhunderts* (Celle: Schweiger & Pick, 1935), 151.

3. See Linnemann, *Celler Musikgeschichte*, 125–28 and 151–52.

4. Hachmeister has gone down in the history of Bach source transmission as the possible owner of a set of performing parts of the Concerto in C Major for Two Harpsichords, BWV 1061a, copied jointly by Johann Sebastian and Anna Magdalena Bach. In addition, Hachmeister's nephew, August Friedrich Christoph Kollmann (1756–1829), has long been recognized as a central figure in the English Bach renaissance. For details, see Hans-Joachim Schulze, *Studien zur Bach-Überlieferung im 18. Jahrhundert* (Leipzig and Dresden: Peters, 1984), 26.

5. The letter was mentioned in passing by Linnemann in 1935 but not published in full until 1989. See Daniela Garbe, "Der Director musices, Organist und Kantor Johann Friedrich Schweinitz. Ein Beitrag zur Musikgeschichte Göttingens," *Göttinger Jahrbuch* 37 (1989), 88.

6. See *Johann Gottfried Walther, Briefe*, ed. Klaus Beckmann and Hans-Joachim Schulze (Leipzig: Deutscher Verlag für Musik, 1987), 8, 253, 300.

7. This source is in private hands.

8. Garbe, "Der Director musices, Organist und Kantor Johann Friedrich Schweinitz," 88: "er schreibt eine gute hand, welches bey einem Praeceptore classico keine geringe Tugend ist."

9. See Bernd Wiechert, "Noch einmal: Johann Friedrich Schweinitz," *Göttinger Jahrbuch* 41 (1993), 133–36 (entry from April 18, 1764); Garbe, "Der Director musices, Organist und Kantor Johann Friedrich Schweinitz," 85 (entry of September 27, 1771). See also *Göttinger Jahrbuch* 39 (1991), 61–71 ("Die Inaugurationsfeier 1737").

10. Von Stählin entered the University of Leipzig on June 13, 1732, and left the *Messestadt* again in April 1735. Evidence of his activities in the Collegium Musicum, as well as his acquaintance with the Bach family, is provided by a surviving letter. See Hans-Joachim Schulze, "Vier unbekannte Quittungen J.S. Bachs und ein Briefauszug Jacob von Stählins," BJ 59 (1973), 88–90.

11. See Arno Werner, "Zur Musikgeschichte von Delitzsch," *Archiv für Musikwissenschaft* 1 (1918/19), 534–64.

12. See Hans Rudolf Jung, *Geschichte des Musiklebens der Stadt Greiz. I. Teil. Von den Anfängen bis zum Stadtbrand 1802. Schriften des Heimatmuseums Greiz* 4 (Greiz: Heimatmuseum, 1963), 144–46 and 86–95.

13. See A. von Haller, *Versuch Schweizerischer Gedichte*, 11th ed. (Carlsruhe: Christian Gottlieb Schmieder, 1778), 273–79 and 280–84. Copy preserved in Leipzig, Bach-Archiv, *Go. S. 65*.

14. Berlin, Staatsbibliothek zu Berlin, *B. Diez. 2900/12*. The full title reads: *Programma quo scholae Gottingensis quae modo Paedagogii, modo Gymnasii nomine quondam insigna est, cantores figurales, ab suo ortu, ordine recensentur, eorundemque vitis nonnulla, scholae pariter ac urbis fata, inserentur . . . ad solemnem novi cantoris Io. Friderici Schweinizii . . . officiose invitatur a Io. Christophoro Leonhard, scholae directore et scholarcha.*

15. See Günter Hart, "Georg Philipp Kreß (1719-1779)," *Die Musikforschung* 22 (1969), 328–34; Elisabeth Noack, *Musikgeschichte Darmstadts vom Mittelalter bis zur Goethezeit. Beiträge zur Mittelrheinischen Musikgeschichte* 8 (Mainz: Schott, 1967), 212 and 221–23.

16. Forkel (1749–1818) is reported to have had, as a young student, a long-standing affair with Therese Heyne née Weiß (daughter of the famous lutenist Sylvius Leopold Weiß), who was married in 1761 to Christian Gottlob Heyne (1729–1812), professor at the University of Göttingen. See Ludwig Geiger, *Therese Huber, 1764 bis 1829. Leben und Briefe einer deutschen Frau* (Stuttgart: J. G. Cotta, 1901).

17. Robert Eitner, *Biographisch-bibliographisches Quellen-Lexikon der Musiker und Musikgelehrten* (Leipzig: Breitkopf & Härtel, 1900–1904), vol. 9, 109. On Nichelmann see Friedrich Wilhelm Marpurg, *Historisch-Kritische Beyträge zur Aufnahme der Musik* (Berlin: Joh. Jacob Schützens sel. Wittwe, 1755), vol. 1, ch. 5, 432.

18. This is still the case in RISM A/II (CD-ROM ed., 2004).

19. Alfred Wotquenne, *Catalogue de la Bibliothèque du Conservatoire Royal de Musique de Bruxelles* (Brussels: J.-J. Coosemans, 1898), vol. 1, 168–69.

20. Concerning the Westphal collection, see Ulrich Leisinger and Peter Wollny, *Die Bach-Quellen der Bibliotheken in Brüssel. Katalog. Mit einer Darstellung von Überlieferungsgeschichte und Bedeutung der Sammlungen Westphal, Fétis und Wagener. Leipziger Beiträge zur Bach-Forschung* 2 (Hildesheim: Georg Olms, 1997), 25–72.

21. The writing can be confirmed as that of Johann Friedrich Schweinitz by a comparison with the Göttingen documents of 1732, 1764, and 1771, already cited in this chapter.

22. Berlin, Staatsbibliothek zu Berlin, *Mus. ms. 21412*, vol. 2, no. 4a. The manuscript was previously owned by Georg Poelchau.

Johann Christian Bach and
the Church Symphony

Jen-yen Chen

Among the members of the Bach family, Johann Christian (1735–1782) enjoyed the widest renown during the eighteenth century. Far more traveled than his father and brothers, he became the principal figure of a "Bach tradition" outside of Germany before the nineteenth century. This can be credited to his associations with important musical centers such as Milan, Naples, London, Mannheim, and Paris, and the broad dissemination of his music through prints and manuscripts. This chapter examines a single aspect of this tradition as an illustrative example of the diverse nature of Christian's sphere of influence: It investigates a group of symphonies preserved in manuscript parts at Göttweig Abbey in Lower Austria that belonged to the liturgical repertoire of this Benedictine monastery. These parts, most if not all of which date from the composer's lifetime, are unusual among eighteenth-century symphony source materials, for they record the uses of the music—that is, dates and places of performance.

The survival of this information confirms the function of the works as *sinfonie da chiesa*, or church symphonies, a little-studied yet common type of orchestral music during this period that found a place in religious services, usually as accompaniment to the Gradual portion of the Mass.[1] In the following discussion, I first offer some general remarks on the circumstances of Bach's career that fostered the ready reception of his compositions in a great variety of locales, including a Catholic monastic institution. I then detail the liturgical context and musical style of Bach's church symphonies at Göttweig, exploring along the way the intersections of sacred and secular realms and the conventional eighteenth-century categories of church, theater, and chamber styles that are underscored by this repertoire.

J.C. Bach can justifiably be regarded as an aberrant representative of the most celebrated of musical clans. Departing from what Stephen Roe calls "the Protestant, Kapellmeister tradition which had nourished the Bach family for two centuries,"[2] Christian prepared at first for a career as an Italian *maestro di capella* during a sojourn in Milan in the late 1750s, converting to Catholicism in the process. However, he eventually turned to opera and instrumental music—the genres that would occupy his compositional energies for the rest of his life. Opera brought Bach to England through a commission from the King's Theatre in London, but it was instrumental music that had a more profound impact on his growing fame. Beginning in 1764, he collaborated with Carl Friedrich Abel, a former pupil of his father in Leipzig, in directing a concert series that contributed crucially to London's burgeoning commercial musical life. The programs featured symphonies, concertos, and chamber music, together with vocal pieces. This repertory included Bach's (and Abel's) own works.

For example, according to Bach's own announcement of his opus 3 on April 3, 1765, in *The Public Advertiser*, the six symphonies in the set were "as they were performed at the Wednesday Subscription-Concert, in Soho-square."[3] Altogether, eighteen sets of publications appeared during the two decades of Christian's residence in the British capital, spanning the years 1763 to 1781.[4] Of these, fifteen were devoted to instrumental genres, two to canzonets, and one to the *opera seria La clemenza di Scipione*. The range of cities of publication offers a fair idea of the extent of Bach's reputation: London, Amsterdam, the Hague, Paris, Berlin, Offenbach, Vienna, and Riga.[5] To these must be added many other cultural centers in Italy, Austria, Switzerland, and elsewhere, where his compositions were known through manuscript copies.[6]

This impressive dissemination, which reflects the esteem accorded Bach's music during his lifetime, becomes all the more striking when set against the nineteenth century's largely negative assessments of the composer. The new aesthetics of the Romantic period, which favored the figure of the idiosyncratic, uncompromising genius, resulted in the devaluation of Bach's works, which were now regarded as conventional and unchallenging. In fact, the criticisms of the composer embraced not only his musical style but also his life itself, as is evident from the oft-quoted remark from the 1830s that Carl Philipp Emanuel Bach lived to compose while Johann Christian composed to live.[7] This notion of a less-than-total artistic commitment, tainted by extramusical factors, as a basic explanation for an unexceptional compositional achievement occurs in numerous other commentaries. Susanne Staral has made a detailed study of these, and it suffices here to state the core idea that defined Bach's image during the Romantic era: namely, that the qualities of facility, accessibility, and relaxed sensuality that marked both his life and his music were irreconcilable with creative activity of the first order.[8]

This viewpoint prevailed until the twentieth century, when a more favorable estimation began to emerge. Even so, modern scholarly interest has tended to focus narrowly on the single issue of Bach's influence on Mozart. The title of Heinz Gärtner's 1989 monograph *Johann Christian Bach, Mozarts Freund und Lehrmeister* is characteristic.[9] Vital as this relationship is for the history of music in the late eighteenth century, it fails to explain the success experienced by a composer of Bach's particular stylistic and expressive cast.

Daniel Heartz's study, *Music in European Capitals: The Galant Style, 1720–1780*, illuminates the matter in a memorably comprehensive fashion.[10] In an extended elaboration upon the thesis that the *galant* style represented the prime artistic current in Europe between 1720 and 1780, Heartz considers three "apostles" who transmitted the *galant* idiom to far-flung corners of the continent: Bach in London, Giovanni Paisiello in St. Petersburg, and Luigi Boccherini in Madrid. In the author's view, Bach was an exemplary composer of a trend that "dominat[ed] music for much of the century and defin[ed] it as a musical-historical epoch."[11] Heartz numbers among the chief characteristics of the *galant* style the simplification of the weighty contrapuntal gestures of the late Baroque and the strong inspiration of Italian opera, especially that of the Neapolitan tradition.[12]

Bach's music typifies both of these traits, and his ties with Naples—he wrote the operas *Catone in Utica* (1761) and *Alessandro nell'Indie* (1762) for the Teatro San Carlo, for instance—are of particular relevance for the present discussion. Viewing Bach within the larger cultural world of which he was a part makes possible a clearer understanding of the extent of his reputation in the late eighteenth century. Bach's musical language, with its finesse and grace, so well suited the broadest aesthetic tendencies of his day that his work could be assimilated into a great variety of contexts, ranging from major European opera theaters to a bourgeois concert enterprise in London to a Benedictine abbey in Lower Austria. Sometimes the same compositions served all three endeavors. Among these are a number of the symphonies performed at Göttweig.

In an encompassing survey of the church symphony, Neal Zaslaw notes the many locales in which performances of the genre can be documented: Vienna, Bologna, Milan, Naples, Montserrat (near Barcelona), Salzburg, Bamberg, Cologne, Heidelberg, Fulda, Schäftlarn (near Munich), Koblenz-Ehrenstein, Weyarn (near Munich), and Trier.[13] Augmenting this roster are a number of Austrian abbeys that possess substantial collections of symphonies, among them Göttweig, Kremsmünster, and Lambach.[14] According to a thematic catalog of the Göttweig collection prepared in 1830 by P. Heinrich Wondratsch,[15] orchestral music at the time included 359 "Synphoniae et Parthiae" and fifty-six "Cassatio, Divertimento et Quadro." Not all of these found a place in the monastery's liturgical observances; festive events of a more worldly nature that also took place within the institution, including namedays of abbots and visits by distinguished (and generally aristocratic) guests, frequently required music. In these cases symphonies served as a kind of *Tafelmusik*[16] and contributed to a secular dimension of Austrian monastic culture that in no way conflicted with religious faith per se. At Kremsmünster the mix of the profane and the sacred could even accommodate the performance of "Turkish" music during summer evenings.[17] *Sinfonie da chiesa* also demonstrated this same blurring of boundaries, though from within the liturgy rather than from outside it.

The precise balance of functions that symphonies fulfilled at Göttweig can no longer be determined because of the loss of manuscript covers that appear to have contained annotations of performances. However, an approximate idea is provided by the surviving record of performances of orchestral music by Joseph Haydn at the abbey during the years 1762 to 1787. His works were utilized seventy-eight times in the celebration of Mass, thirteen times as part of a special rite on Passion Sunday (always featuring, appropriately, Symphony 49, *La Passione*), and twenty-five times as *Tafelmusik*.[18] In some cases the same work served as music for both liturgical and secular occasions (Symphonies 37, 39, and 41, for instance), thereby illustrating the primacy of external function over internal style in the musical practice of the time and also, again, the blending of the sacred and the worldly.

J.C. Bach's symphonies began to enter the repertoire at Göttweig while the composer was still a young man. A total of fourteen works, eleven authentic and three doubtful, appear in the 1830 catalog (one of the genuine works is incorrectly attributed to Carl Philipp Emanuel). Today only eight of the fourteen survive in the abbey's collection, two in a fragmentary state (see Table 1). Fortunately, Wondratsch included in his catalog the dates of copying and names of copyists when these were noted in the manuscripts. As a consequence, such information is available for ten of the fourteen symphonies. The first work arrived in 1762, when Johann Christian was twenty-seven, followed by two more pieces in 1764 and 1770, respectively, and then seven in 1773. For one further work, an initial performance date of 1771 provides a *terminus post quem non*. The last recorded performance of a symphony by Bach took place in 1787; thus, we know that his music maintained a presence at Göttweig for a period of approximately a quarter-century. Joseph II's ecclesiastical reforms of the 1780s, which threatened the very existence of monasteries in the Habsburg empire, provide the best explanation for the eventual disappearance not only of Bach's symphonies but also of the *sinfonia da chiesa* in general from liturgical rites. Less persuasive is the reputed precipitous decline of Bach's popularity in the years immediately following his death in 1782, a point exaggerated in early accounts.[19]

Ten of the eleven authentic symphonies at Göttweig made their way into print during Bach's lifetime. Three appeared in opus 3 of 1765, four in opus 6 of 1770, and one in opus 8, also of 1770. Two further works, the overtures to the pasticcio operas *Il tutore e la pupilla* (1762) and *La Giulia* (1760), were published without opus numbers in 1766 and 1763, respectively. Thus, nearly all of the monastic manuscripts might have been prepared from contemporary editions. However, the copy of the Symphony in E♭ Major, op. 6, no. 3 (W C9),[20] which carries the false attribution to Carl Philipp Emanuel, predates by eight years the first publication of the work by J J. Hummel of Amsterdam. Its scribe, P. Joseph Unterberger (1731–1788), must therefore have had access to the work in manuscript form. Among the possible routes of acquisition, one originating from the south seems especially probable, given the proliferation of manuscript copies of Bach's music in Italy. Italian copies exist not only for the E♭-Major Symphony but also for eleven of the thirteen symphonies attributed to Johann Christian at Göttweig. They are presently located in archives in Bergamo, Bologna, Florence, Genoa, Mantua, Modena, Padua, Palermo, and Rome.[21] Only further investigation can determine whether any of these are likely to have served as exemplars for the Göttweig manuscripts.

Nonetheless, the possible connection between the Italian sources and the Göttweig manuscripts hints at an important reason for the wide currency enjoyed by Bach's music in Italy and Austria during the late eighteenth century. The close political and religious links between the Italian territories and the Habsburg empire, reinforced above all by a shared Catholic faith, surely fostered the acceptance of Johann Christian's works in Austria in a way that would not have been possible for other members of the Bach family, with their Central- and North-German Protestant orientation.

Performance dates have survived for only three of the Göttweig symphonies, offering a partial but nonetheless illuminating picture of the role these works played in the liturgical celebrations of the abbey. They extend over a period from 1771 to 1787 and encompass a noteworthy variety of religious feasts (Table 2).[22] Only seldom did the music figure as part of a High Mass, however. These instances are indicated by a remark of "ad Sum. Sac.", "ad Sac: Sol:", or "quid Sum: Sac:" (standing for *ad Summum Sacrum*, *ad Sacrum Solenne*, and *quid Summum Sacrum*, respectively) next to the recorded date. The Symphony in D Major, op. 3, no. 1 (W C1a), for instance, received altogether three performances at Göttweig, one each in the years 1774, 1782, and 1784. The annotations in the manuscript of this work do not specify whether all of its three movements were heard when it was performed.

When a church symphony was featured during the celebration of a Mass, normally only the opening fast movement or the slow movement or both were performed. The length and elaborateness of the specific observance played an essential role in deciding the matter.[23] Finales were rarely used as liturgical music, especially when they exhibited the characteristic idiom of a fast dance, in fast triple or compound meter, as does the third movement of Bach's D-Major Symphony. The much more extensive performance record of the Symphony in C Major (W G24) that served as the Overture to *Il tutore e la pupilla* illustrates the practice of favoring the first two movements. Between 1771 and 1784, the opening *Allegro assai* of this work was heard thirteen times, the *Andante* three times (always in conjunction with the *Allegro assai*), and the concluding *Presto* just once.

The general avoidance of overtly secular finales suggests that considerations of internal style did not exist wholly independent of those of external function in the musical culture of the period. The centuries-old controversies surrounding religious

Table 1. Symphonies of Johann Christian Bach at Göttweig Abbey

Göttweig manuscript	Work[a]	Date copied and copyist	Composition date	First edition	Comments
MS 2617	Symphony in D Major, W C9	1762; P. Joseph Unterberger	by 1762	Hummel, op. 6, no. 3 (Amsterdam, 1770)	Incorrectly attributed to C.P.E. Bach
MS 2618	Symphony in D Major, W C39	?	late 1760s[b]	—	"Symphonia concertante"
MS 2620	Symphony in G Major, W C13	?	by 1767[c]	Markordt, op. 8, no. 2 (Amsterdam, 1770)	Manuscript lost
MS 2621	Symphony in C Major, W YC14	1770, P. Odo Schachermayr	?	—	Manuscript lost; also attributed to J. Haydn and F.A. Miča
MS 2622	Symphony in B♭ Major, W C4a	1773, P. Odo Schachermayr	by 1765	J.C. Bach, op. 3, no. 4 (London, 1765)	Manuscript lost
MS 2623	Symphony in C Major, W G24	?	1762	Six Favourite Overtures, no. 4 (London, 1763)	Overture to Il tutore e la pupilla (London, 1762)
MS 2624	Symphony in B♭ Major, W C10	1773, P. Odo Schachermayr	by 1766[d]	Hummel, op. 6, no. 4 (Amsterdam, 1770)	
MS 2625	Symphony in D Major, W C1a	1773, P. Odo Schachermayr	by 1765	J.C. Bach, op. 3, no. 1 (London, 1765)	Manuscript fragmentary

MS 2626	Symphony in D Major, W G22	1773, P. Odo Schachermayr	1760	An Overture in eight parts (London, 1766)	Manuscript lost; Overture to La Giulia (1760, Milan)
MS 2627	Symphony in E♭ Major, W C11	1773, P. Odo Schachermayr	by 1766[d]	Hummel, op. 6, no. 5 (Amsterdam, 1770)	
MS 2628	Symphony in C Major, W C2a	1773, P. Odo Schachermayr	by 1765	J.C. Bach, op. 3, no. 2 (London, 1765)	Manuscript lost
MS 2629	Symphony in G Major, W C7	1773, P. Marianus Pratzner	1764[e]	Hummel, op. 6, no. 1 (Amsterdam, 1770)	Manuscript lost
MS 2972	Symphony in E♭ Major, W YC54	1764, P. Leander Staininger	—	—	Manuscript fragmentary; "Cassatio"; also attributed to J. Haydn and F.J. Aumon
MS 2973	Symphony in E♭ Major, W YC48	—	—	—	"Cassatio"; doubtful according to Warburton

a. Catalog numbers (W) from Ernest Warburton, *The Collected Works of Johann Christian Bach* 48/1 (*Thematic Catalogue*) (New York and London: Garland Publishing, 1999).

b. Warburton, *Thematic Catalogue*, 103.

c. Symphony listed in the Breitkopf catalog of 1767. See Niels Krabbe, "J.C. Bach's Symphonies and the Breitkopf Thematic Catalog," in *Festskrift Jens Peter Larsen*, ed. Nils Schiørring, Henrik Glahn, and Carsten E. Hatting (Copenhagen: Wilhelm Hansen Musik, 1972), 233–54.

d. Symphony listed in the Breitkopf catalog of 1766. Krabbe, "J.C. Bach's Symphonies," 233–54.

e. Dated in a manuscript copy at Kremsmünster Abbey (*Ms. H31/271*).

Table 2. Performances of Symphonies of Johann Christian Bach
at Göttweig Abbey, 1771–1787

Work[a]	Date	Liturgical feast	Remarks in manuscript	Movements
Symphony in C Major,	December 6, 1771	St. Nicholas (*Tafelmusik?*)	—	1
W G24 (Göttweig	December 21, 1771	St. Thomas (*Tafelmusik?*)	—	3
MS 2623)	January 20, 1772	Sts. Fabian and Sebastian	"in Furth"	1, 2
	May 16, 1772	St. John Nepomucene	—	1
	August 15, 1772	Assumption of the Virgin	—	1
	September 8, 1772	Nativity of the Virgin	"in Roggendorf"	1
	December 26, 1772	St. Stephen	"in Mauttern"	1
	February 2, 1773	Purification of the Virgin	—	1
	June 6, 1773	Trinity Sunday	"ad Sum. Sac."	1
	January 20, 1774	Sts. Fabian and Sebastian	"in Furth"	1
	November 27, 1774	First Sunday in Advent	—	1
	November 22, 1779	St. Cecilia	—	1, 2
	November 1, 1780	All Saints' Day	—	1
	January 20, 1784	Sts. Fabian and Sebastian	—	1, 2
Symphony in D Major,	June 29, 1774	Sts. Peter and Paul	"ad Sac: Sol:"	2?
op. 3, no. 1 (W C1a)	February 2, 1782	Purification of the Virgin	—	2?
(Göttweig MS 2625)	August 26, 1784	?	"in Crÿpta"	2?
Symphony in E♭ Major,	September 4, 1774	Guardian Angels	"quid Sum: Sac:"	1
op. 6, no. 5 (W C11)	March 26, 1780	Easter	—	1
(Göttweig MS 2627)	January 14, 1784	St. Peter Urseolus	—	1
	April 8, 1787	Easter	—	1

a. Catalog numbers (W) from Ernest Warburton, *The Collected Works of Johann Christian Bach* 48/1 (*Thematic Catalogue*) (New York and London: Garland Publishing, 1999).

music of a markedly profane character are of course well known, and these did not fail to touch the *sinfonia da chiesa*.[24] The eighteenth-century differentiation of church, theater, and chamber styles was far from distinct. Yet, at the same time, the blurring of boundaries did not eradicate the three categories.

An important clue to the mystery of which movements of the D-Major Symphony were performed is provided by an annotation standing above the three dates in the manuscript: "Prod: Smum," an abbreviation of *Producta ad Sanctissimum*.[25] This refers to the ritual of the Elevation of the Host, during which the body of Christ in the form of bread was placed on display upon the altar (the so-called *Expositio*). Music of a slower tempo typically accompanied this presentation, thus making the *Andante* of Bach's symphony the most likely candidate for the movement heard on these occasions. The liturgical observances in question consisted of the Feast of Saints Peter and Paul (High Mass) on June 29, 1774; the Purification of the Virgin on February 2, 1782; and a rite on August 26, 1784, that I have not been able to identify. The last event took place in the lower level of the abbey church ("in Crÿpta"), an area dedicated to the relics of Göttweig's founder, Bishop Altmann of Passau (ca. 1015–1091). Altmann's life was celebrated in a special annual commemoration service, but this occurred on the Sunday closest to August 8, the anniversary of his death. Extant rubrics from the eighteenth century for Göttweig indicate that the 26th of August was devoted to a variety of observances, including the feast of St. Bernard Ptolemy and the dedication of the cathedral at Passau (the diocese to which the monastery belonged).

The manuscript of the Symphony in E♭ Major, op. 6, no. 5 (W C11), notes four performances of the first movement between 1774 and 1787 and none of the remaining two movements. Two of the performances occurred on no less a celebration than Easter, on March 26, 1780, and April 8, 1787. The symphony's spirited and energetic opening *Allegro con brio* no doubt lent an appropriately festive tone to the most important day of the church year. The beginning of the movement, up to the arrival of the second key area, illustrates well the kind of music that twice adorned the Easter liturgy at Göttweig (Example 1).

The unison statement of an initial four-bar idea leads to a powerful crescendo articulated by a rising sequence on a motif derived rhythmically from the first measure, a tremolo in the second violins in which the first violins eventually join, and a tonic bass pedal in eighth notes. These elements build to a first climactic point in mm. 11–12. Four bars that feature a characteristically *galant* melody and reduced instrumentation then offer a brief respite before the entire orchestra resumes the bustling texture heard just before. The first definitive cadence occurs at m. 19, followed by a theme that functions as the transition to the second key area, where the first violins and the oboes play sweeping figures in thirty-second notes. Repeated cadential gestures on the dominant bring about a firm caesura in m. 25. The second theme commences in the next bar.

One might wonder how this dynamic and busy music sounded in the resonant space of the Göttweig abbey church. Neal Zaslaw has argued that slower tempos and a more restrained playing style characterized the performance of church symphonies in the eighteenth century because they better suited the typical church acoustic and also the solemn nature of a religious observance.[26] Zaslaw finds support for this view in a passage from Johann Joachim Quantz's *Versuch einer Anweisung die Flöte traversiere zu spielen* of 1752, which also calls to mind the music of Bach's E♭-Major Symphony, especially an unusual D♭ that opens the development section (Example 2):

If in a work for the church the composer has inserted some bold and bizarre ideas that are inappropriate to the place, the accompanists, and the violinists in particular,

Example 1. Johann Christian Bach: Symphony in E♭ Major, op. 6, no. 5 (W C11), *Allegro con brio*, mm. 1–29.

Example 1. *Continued*

must endeavor to mitigate, subdue, and soften them as much as possible by a modest execution.[27]

Thus, the Göttweig chapel musicians may well have moderated their playing on the two Easter occasions. Even so, a sober and restrained mood seems improbable in any performance of the symphony, and one must therefore bear in mind the multi-faceted nature of religious expression. Exuberance had a place beside solemnity, even if this exuberance could and did strike some as excessively profane. The Baroque splendor of Göttweig, apparent in its architecture, interiors (Plates 1 and 2), and elevated location 425 meters above the surrounding towns, underscores this point, which pertains generally to the culture of Catholicism in eighteenth-century Austria.

Example 2. Johann Christian Bach: Symphony in E♭ Major, op. 6, no. 5 (W C11), *Allegro con brio*, mm. 45–50.

The Symphony in C Major that formed the Overture to *Il tutore e la pupilla* enjoyed by far the most performances at Göttweig. This work found particular favor at the abbey between 1771 and 1774, when it was featured in religious or festive celebrations no fewer than eleven times. During the next decade it was heard three more times. The music accompanied a wide variety of liturgical occasions, including rites central to the church calendar: the Purification of the Virgin (February 2), the Assumption of the Virgin (August 15), the Nativity of the Virgin (September 8), and All Saints' Day (November 1). In addition, it was used for the feasts of several saints: Fabian and Sebastian (January 20), John Nepomucene (May 16), Cecilia (November 22), and Stephen (December 26).

Some of these services took place not at the abbey itself, but in the churches of the incorporated parishes of Furth, Mautern, and Roggendorff. The opening *Allegro assai* was performed most frequently, and three times it was followed by the *Andante*. The manuscript of the work records a unique instance of the use of a finale of a Bach symphony, on December 21, 1771. Since this date fell within Advent, one of the two penitential seasons of the church year when a general prohibition of instrumental music was in effect, Bach's concluding *Presto* may in fact have served as *Tafelmusik* for a nonliturgical celebration rather than for the observance of the Feast of Saint Thomas.[28] The rarity of last-movement performances supports this supposition, despite the absence next to the annotated date in the manuscript of the remark "in refectorio" or "ad prandium" that was customary when music served as *Tafelmusik*.[29] The same set of circumstances characterizes the very first documented performance

Plate 1. Choir, Abbey Church, Göttweig. Photograph by Jen-yen Chen.

Plate 2. Rear gallery, Abbey Church, Göttweig. Photograph by Jen-yen Chen.

of a Bach symphony at the monastery fifteen days earlier, when the first movement of the C-Major Symphony was played, also during Advent.

The popularity of this particular work as a *sinfonia da chiesa* at Göttweig, coupled with its origin as the overture to a pasticcio opera that premiered on November 13,

1762, at the King's Theatre in London, presents the best example of all of the reuse of secular music for sacred purposes. Another symphony in the abbey's collection (and the only work definitely written before the beginning of Bach's residence in England), the Overture to *La Giulia*, also illustrates this same facet of musical practice. Unfortunately, its manuscript has disappeared, along with any performance history it might have preserved.

The music of the Overture to *Il tutore e la pupilla* clearly evokes the world of the theater (Example 3). Its opening "hammer blows," consisting of successive tonic chords played in triple stops by the first violins and accompanied by an active texture of syncopations and repeated notes in the other strings, typifies the function of such pieces of calling the audience to order. Quick sixteenth-note gestures answer the chords; then the entire sequence is restated in the subdominant. Throughout this movement simple harmonies, short, rapid motifs, and textures consisting of tremolos and pedal notes prevail, contributing to the *buffa* atmosphere. The sole full-fledged theme begins at m. 40 and features a delicate *galant* accompaniment of triplets in the second violins and eighth notes punctuated by rests in the lower strings. Even this theme is characterized by the repetition of a short figure most often made up of a quarter-note upbeat followed by two eighth notes and a quarter note. As was true with the E♭-Major Symphony, the Overture must have called for a careful balance of lively music, a resonant acoustic, and liturgical solemnity.

A number of important eighteenth-century commentators, including Johann Mattheson, Johann Adolf Scheibe, and J.A.P. Schulz, recognized three subgenres of the symphony, corresponding to the tripartite division of music into church, chamber, and theater styles.[30] Nevertheless, modern investigators of Johann Christian Bach's symphonies have tended to divide them into only two types, theater and concert. These writers include Heinrich Peter Schökel and Fritz Tutenberg, whose studies of the repertoire[31] played an important part in restoring the composer's reputation in the early twentieth century. Beginning in the 1780s, the *sinfonia da chiesa* gradually vanished from Austrian religious and musical life, a victim first of Emperor Joseph's reforms and then of the rise of Cecilianism. It appears to have had an active existence during the preceding decades, however, one that belies the lack of scholarly attention it has garnered in modern times. Without a doubt this bias stems in part from the elevation of the symphony as the epitome of absolute music in the nineteenth century, when it was viewed primarily as concert music. The genre played a much wider role during the eighteenth century, as Zaslaw has pointed out.[32] Informed historical understanding often involves overcoming a hegemony of viewpoints stemming from modern attitudes and conceptions. This certainly applies to the music and the composer that have formed the subject of this chapter.

Example 3. Johann Christian Bach: Symphony in C Major, W G24 (Overture to *Il tutore e la pupilla*), *Allegro assai*, mm. 1–44.

Example 3. *Continued*

Notes

I wish to express my thanks to the following individuals for their kind assistance in the preparation of this article: Otto Biba (Gesellschaft der Musikfreunde, Vienna), Martin Eybl (Universität für Musik und darstellende Kunst, Vienna), P. Gregor Lechner (Göttweig), Michael Grünwald (Göttweig), and P. Franz Schuster (Göttweig).

1. Two articles of basic importance on this subject are Neal Zaslaw, "Mozart, Haydn, and the Sinfonia da Chiesa," *Journal of Musicology* 1 (1982), 95–124, which offers an excellent introduction to the genre, and Friedrich Wilhelm Riedel, "Joseph Haydns Sinfonien als liturgische Musik," in *Festschrift Hubert Unverricht zum 65. Geburtstag*, ed. Karlheinz Schlager (Tutzing: Hans Schneider, 1992), 213–22, which examines the performance of Haydn's symphonies at Göttweig.

2. Stephen Roe, "Johann Christian Bach," in *The New Grove Dictionary of Music and Musicians*, 2d ed., ed. Stanley Sadie (London and New York: Macmillan, 2001), vol. 2, 414. The biographical information presented here is drawn largely from this article.

3. Cited in Ernest Warburton, *The Collected Works of Johann Christian Bach 48/1 (Thematic Catalogue)* (New York and London: Garland Publishing, 1999), 84.

4. These publications are summarized in Charles Sanford Terry, *John Christian Bach* (London: Oxford University Press, 1929), 170–72.

5. As a consequence of this vigorous printing activity, a given work sometimes appeared in multiple editions that did not necessarily share the same opus number, thereby creating confusion for the modern scholar. For instance, the collections published in Amsterdam in 1770 by J.J. Hummel as opus 6 and by Siegfried Markordt as opus 8 contain a number of the same symphonies.

6. Warburton, in his *Thematic Catalogue*, comprehensively details these copies, which have survived in great numbers throughout Europe. See also Peter Ross and Andreas Traub, "Die Kirchenmusik von Johann Christian Bach im Kloster Einsiedeln," *Fontes artis musicae* 32 (1985), 92–102.

7. Gustav Schilling, *Encyclopädie der gesammten musikalischen Wissenschaften, oder Universal-Lexicon der Tonkunst* (Stuttgart: Franz Heinrich Köhler, 1835), vol. 1, 384. Cited in Susanne Staral, "Carl Philipp Emanuel und Johann Christian Bach—Originalgenie und Tageskomponist? Bemerkungen zur Rezeption," in *Carl Philipp Emanuel Bach: Musik für Europa*, ed. Hans-Günter Ottenberg (Frankfurt an der Oder: Konzerthalle "Carl Philipp Emanuel Bach," 1998), 498–99.

8. Staral, "Carl Philipp Emanuel und Johann Christian Bach," 496–505.

9. Heinz Gärtner, *Johann Christian Bach, Mozarts Freund und Lehrmeister* (Munich: Nymphenburger Verlagshandlung, 1989). Other literature that explores the artistic connections between the two composers includes Hermann Abert, "Joh. Christian Bachs italienische Opern und ihr Einfluss auf Mozart," *Zeitschrift für Musikwissenschaft* 1 (1919), 313–28; Stefan Kunze, "Die Vertonungen der Arie 'Non sò d'onde viene' von J. Chr. Bach und von W.A. Mozart," *Analecta Musicologica* 2 (1965), 85–111; Niels Krabbe, "Mozart's KV 107 and Johann Christian Bach's Opus V," *Dansk Arbog for Musikforskning* 6 (1968–1972), 101–12; Klaus-Jürgen Sachs, "Impuls und Ingenium: Der Kopfsatz aus Mozarts Haffner-Sinfonie KV 385 vor dem Hintergrund von Johann Christian Bachs Grand Ouverture Es-Dur op. 18/1," *Mozart-Jahrbuch* 1991, 844–51; Murl Sickbert, "The Mozarts in Milan, February 9–10, 1770: A Funeral Performance of Johann Christian Bach's Dies irae and Vespers Music?" *Mozart-Jahrbuch* 1991, 461–67; Susanne Staral, "Wolfgang Amadé Mozart, Johann Christian Bach und Mannheim," in *176 Tage: W.A. Mozart in Mannheim*, ed. Karin von Welck and Liselotte Homer-

ing (Mannheim: Reiß-Museum der Stadt Mannheim, Edition Braus, 1991), 164–73; Staral, "Mozart und Johann Christian Bach: Einige Anmerkungen zu ihrer menschlich-künstlerischen Beziehung," in *Internationaler Musikwissenschaftlicher Kongress zum Mozartjahr 1991, Baden-Wien*, ed. Ingrid Fuchs (Tutzing: Hans Schneider, 1993), 943–48.

10. Daniel Heartz, *Music in European Capitals: The Galant Style, 1720–1780* (New York: W.W. Norton, 2003).

11. Heartz, *Music in European Capitals*, 23.

12. Heartz, *Music in European Capitals*, 18–20, 23.

13. Zaslaw, "Mozart, Haydn, and the Sinfonia da Chiesa," 103–6.

14. See Rudolf Flotzinger, "Anfänge der Bach- und Händel-Rezeption in österreichischen Klöstern," in *Johann Sebastian Bach: Beiträge zur Wirkungsgeschichte*, ed. Ingrid Fuchs (Vienna: Verband der wissenschaftlichen Gesellschaften Österreichs, 1992), 52–54, 62–63.

15. Facsimile with commentary in Friedrich Wilhelm Riedel, *Der Göttweiger thematische Katalog von 1830* (Munich and Salzburg: Katzbichler, 1979). A significant number of the manuscripts listed in this catalog were lost as a result of World War II. See Riedel, "Musikpflege im Stift Göttweig unter Abt Gottfried Bessel," in *Gottfried Bessel (1672–1749). Diplomat in Kurmainz—Abt von Göttweig— Wissenschaftler und Kunstmäzen*, ed. Franz Rudolf Richard (Mainz: Gesellschaft für mittelrheinischen Kirchengeschichte, 1972), 146, n. 47.

16. Riedel, "Joseph Haydns Sinfonien," 217–18.

17. See Altmann Kellner, "Beiträge zur Musikgeschichte des Stiftes Kremsmünster," *Mitteilungen des oberösterreichischen Landesarchivs* 11 (1974), 281–344, which presents a transcription of the journal of musical events at the abbey kept by P. Beda Plank (1741–1830) between the years 1807 and 1830. The "Turkish" music served as entertainment for summer evenings mainly during the early part of this period; the last such occasion recorded in the journal occurred on August 27, 1819.

18. Riedel, "Joseph Haydns Sinfonien," 214–18.

19. Roe, "Johann Christian Bach," 417.

20. The work numbers used here are from Warburton, *Thematic Catalogue* (see n. 3).

21. Information on these sources is available in Ernest Warburton, *The Collected Works of Johann Christian Bach 48/2: Sources and Documents* (New York and London: Garland Publishing, 1999) and in the same author's *Thematic Catalogue*.

22. I have identified liturgical occasions celebrated at Göttweig by consulting the rubric *Directorium liberae et exemptae Gottwicensis ordinis sancti Patris Benedicti*, published annually at the nearby town of Krems. However, exemplars from the eighteenth century are preserved only for the following years in the abbey's archive: 1749, 1751, 1762, 1768–1770, 1774, 1778, and 1783. An additional exemplar from 1767 is located in the Austrian National Library, Vienna. Because performances of Bach's symphonies at Göttweig took place only during one of these years, 1774, I have inferred the feasts from other years on the basis of information contained in the surviving rubrics. Certain major feasts, such as the Purification of the Virgin, were regularly observed on the same day of the church calendar each year. In these cases their identification is unproblematic. Table 2 omits the Mass settings which the symphonies complemented, as this requires the perusal of some 700 Mass manuscripts at Göttweig to correlate annotated performance dates—a project I have not yet had the opportunity to carry out.

23. Riedel, "Joseph Haydns Sinfonien," 214.

24. For example, the pastoral letter of Archbishop Colloredo of Salzburg, issued on July 15, 1782, that prohibited the use in church of all instruments except the organ stated that "every good thought is driven out of the heart of the common people by the miserable fiddling . . ." Translation from Reinhard G. Pauly, "The Reforms of Church Music under Joseph II," *Musical Quarterly* 43 (1957), 381 (cited in Zaslaw, "Mozart, Haydn, and the Sinfonia da Chiesa," 108).

25. I am indebted to Otto Biba for deciphering this abbreviation and also for providing me with a detailed explanation of its meaning.

26. Zaslaw, "Mozart, Haydn, and the Sinfonia da Chiesa," 117–18.

27. Zaslaw, "Mozart, Haydn, and the Sinfonia da Chiesa," 118, n. 63.

28. See Riedel, "Joseph Haydns Sinfonien," 219, n. 11.

29. Riedel, "Joseph Haydns Sinfonien," 220, n. 24.

30. Zaslaw, "Mozart, Haydn, and the Sinfonia da Chiesa," 95–101.

31. Heinrich Peter Schökel, *Johann Christian Bach und die Instrumentalmusik seiner Zeit* (Wolfenbüttel: Georg Kallmeyer, 1926); Fritz Tutenberg, *Die Sinfonik Johann Christian Bachs* (Wolfenbüttel: Georg Kallmeyer, 1928).

32. Zaslaw, "Mozart, Haydn, and the Sinfonia da Chiesa," 95.

Bach's Instrumental Music

Scribes, Engravers, and Notational Styles

The Final Disposition of Bach's Art of Fugue

Gregory G. Butler

Notational Styles in the Original Print

To my knowledge, the first detailed examination of the engraving in the original edition of J.S. Bach's Art of Fugue was carried out by a graduate seminar conducted by Christoph Wolff at Columbia University in 1971.[1] On the basis of a detailed analysis of the engraving, a student in that seminar, Richard Koprowski, differentiated between five main notational styles, which he lettered A through F.[2] His determination of these styles was based on the notation of symbols such as half-note stems, whole rests, clefs, and common time/alla breve time signatures. It is clear that for Koprowski, these notational styles reflected the handwriting of the scribes of the *Abklatschvorlagen*,[3] or manuscript copies prepared for the engravers, and not that of the engravers of the plates themselves, for in his commentary he links notational style B closely with the scribe of the manuscript *Vorlage*, J.S. Bach.[4]

In a study on the engraving of the Art of Fugue published not long after the Columbia report, Wolfgang Wiemer acknowledged that differences in the notation of certain symbols "create the impression of two different engravers having been at work." However, he also stated categorically that any such conclusion is groundless.[5] He went on to attribute the notational discrepancies in the engraving to the involvement of a number of copyists who assisted Bach in the preparation of the *Vorlagen* for the engravers.[6] In a subsequent study, Wiemer was able to identify Johann Heinrich Schübler from Zella in the Thuringian Forest as the single artisan responsible for the engraving of the plates.[7]

Wiemer, however, overlooked the striking resemblance between the plates engraved by Johann Heinrich's brother, Johann Georg, for Bach's Musical Offering[8] and one of the two dominant notational styles that Johann Georg represents in the plates of the Art of Fugue. I submit that the same two principal engravers involved in the Musical Offering project were responsible for engraving the plates for the original edition of the Art of Fugue: Johann Georg and Johann Heinrich Schübler. In addition

Table I. Scribes, Engravers, and Notational Styles in the Original Print of the Art of Fugue

Pages	Early Phase	Middle Phase	Late Phase	BWV	Scribe[a]	Engraver[b]	Notational Style
1–2	Contrapunctus 1			1080/1	J.S.B.	J.G.S.	A
3–5	Contrapunctus 2			1080/2	J.S.B.	J.H.S.	E[1]
6–8		Contrapunctus 3		1080/3	J.S.B.	J.G.S.	B
8–12		Contrapunctus 4		1080/4	J.S.B.	J.G.S.	B
13–15	Contrapunctus 5			1080/5	J.S.B.	J.H.S.	C
16–18		Contrapunctus 6		1080/6	J.S.B.	J.H.S.	D
19–21		Contrapunctus 7		1080/7	J.S.B.	J.H.S.	D
21–25		Contrapunctus 8		1080/8	J.S.B.	J.H.S.	D
26–28	Contrapunctus 9			1080/9	J.S.B.	J.H.S.	C, E
29–31	Contrapunctus 10			1080/10	J.S.B.	J.H.S.	E, E[1]
32–36		Contrapunctus 11		1080/11	J.S.B.	J.G.S.	B
37–38		Contrapunctus 12, 2		1080/12, 2	J.S.B.	J.H.S.	D
39–40		Contrapunctus 12, 1		1080/12, 1	J.S.B.	J.G.S.	B
41–42		Contrapunctus 13, 2		1080/13, 2	J.H.S.?	J.H.S.	D
43–44		Contrapunctus 13, 1		1080/13, 1	J.S.B.	J.G.S.	B
45–47			Contrap: a 4	1080/10a	J.C.F.B.	J.H.S.	F
48–50		Canon by Augmentation		1080/14	J.S.B.	J.G.S.	B
51–52		Canon at the Octave		1080/15	J.S.B.	J.J.F.S.	B
53–54		Canon at the Tenth		1080/16	J.S.B.	J.G.S.	B
55–56		Canon at the Twelfth		1080/17	J.S.B.	J.G.S.	B
57–58			Fuga a 2. Clav:	1080/18, 1	J.C.F.B.	J.H.S.	F
59–60			Fuga a 2. Clav:	1080/18, 2	J.C.F.B.	J.H.S.	F
61–65			Fuga a 3 Soggetti	1080/19	J.C.F.B.	J.H.S.	F
66–67			Choral. Wenn wir in hoechsten Noetben	668a	J.C.F.B.	J.H.S.	F

a. J.S.B. = Johann Sebastian Bach; J.H.S. = Johann Heinrich Schübler; J.C.F.B. = Johann Christoph Friedrich Bach

b. J.G.S. = Johann Georg Schübler; J.H.S. = Johann Heinrich Schübler; J.J.F.S. = Johann Jacob Friedrich Schübler

to these two principal engravers, a third artisan worked on both projects: it appears that Johann Georg's and Johann Heinrich's older half-brother, Johann Jacob Friedrich, was also involved, albeit minimally, in the engraving.[9] In Table 1, taking Koprowski's Chart 1 as my point of departure, I have indicated the distribution of the engraving of the plates among these three engravers.

Koprowski's notational styles B and D correspond almost exactly to the two principal engravers of the collection, Johann Georg and Johann Heinrich Schübler.[10] That each engraver has his own distinct notational style, even though both are transferring music notated by the same scribe to copper plate by a reverse-transfer method, can be explained by the fact that both had music training: Johann Heinrich studied with his older brother, Johann Georg, who in turn had studied with J.S. Bach in Leipzig.[11]

One of Koprowski's determinants for the identification of notational style—whether the stems of half notes descend from the left- or right-hand side of the note head—has nothing to do with the scribe of the manuscript. A strong chronological determinant for dating Bach's late hand to the last years of his life is his notation of descending half-note stems neither from the left- nor from the right-hand side of the note head but rather from its center.[12] It was the engraver then, who, according to his own notational practice, chose to have the descending stems of half notes descend either from the left- or right-hand side of the note head according to his own custom. However, both engravers were far from consistent in this respect, as the numerous exceptions in Koprowski's Chart 1 indicate. This particular parameter, then, cannot be relied on as a convincingly clear diagnostic indication for a particular notational style.

My research on the engraving of the Schübler brothers indicates that their formation of clefs reflects neither the form of the clefs in the *Vorlage* nor their own notational practice. Rather, it seems that they were interested in reproducing the appearance of the clefs in typeset music, in this case, those of the Breitkopf font.[13] Although the scope of this study does not allow me to go into greater detail on this fascinating subject, it is important because it indicates that this parameter reflects neither the engraver's nor the scribe's notational style.

The "C" of the common time and alla breve time signatures does appear to be a clear indicator of scribal notational style, however. Styles A through E, for which J.S. Bach is the scribe, represent variants of a basic scribal model, variants that can be found in autograph sources in Bach's hand. By contrast, Style F, for which Bach is not the scribe, represents a totally different notational approach to the symbol; here the style, unlike Bach's, presents a much less cursive form contained within the confines of the staff.

Finally, the notational style of rests clearly has nothing to do with the scribe and everything to do with the engraver's notational practice. For instance, the form of half rest given by Koprowski as representative of notational styles A, C, and E is certainly not characteristic of Bach's hand. Further, as I have indicated elsewhere, one of the clearest identifiers distinguishing the engraving of Johann Heinrich from that of Johann Georg Schübler is their notation of eighth-note rests.[14] It seems clear then, that the notation of rests is very much a function of the particular form favored by the engraver—and again, as in the case of half rests, the notational style may vary. Even though Koprowski's isolation of notational styles tends to conflate engraving and scribal styles, it is important. In pointing to variants, it alerts us to changes of scribe (as with the distinctive notational style of F). By indicating such changes as the notation of the half rests (notational styles A, C, and E), it points to different layers in the engraving.

In an earlier essay on ordering problems in the Art of Fugue, I argued, based on internal source evidence, that the *Canon per Augmentationem in Contrario motu*, BWV 1080/14, was intended by Bach to have followed the other three canons as the last in the series of four instead of the first,[15] an ordering for the canons now widely accepted by Bach scholars.[16] This ordering makes sense of the page numbers "*26*," "*27*," and "*28*" in J.S. Bach's hand in the upper left-hand corners on the three pages of the surviving *Abklatschvorlage* of the augmentation canon (*P 200*, Beilage 1) if one numbers from the last page in reverse order through the four canons in their correct sequence, BWV 1080/14, 17, 16, 15 (pp. 28–26, 25–24, 23–22, 21–20); the gap of six pages results from the restoration of the augmentation canon to its correct position and the removal of the redundant early version of Contrapunctus 10, BWV 1080/10a (pp. 19–17, 16–14); the two mirror canons, BWV 1080/13, 2 and 1 and BWV 1080/12, 2 and 1 (pp. 13–10, 9–6); and the second triple fugue, BWV 1080/11 (pp. 5–1). These autograph page numbers appear to be a vestige of a secondary pagination scheme for what must have been a second installment in the engraving of the plates.[17] The first, with the pagination 1–31, includes Contrapunctus 1 through Contrapunctus 10. The second (shown in Table 2), with the pagination 1–28, includes Contrapunctus 11 through Contrapunctus 13, a gap of six pages, and the four canons.[18]

It is reasonable to conclude that those plates showing notational styles B and D must have been engraved in fairly close chronological proximity to one another. Because this group of engravings crosses the boundary between the first and second installments in the original edition, those plates in notational styles A, C, and E/E^1 were in all likelihood engraved during an earlier phase of work on installment one. That is, Contrapuncti 1, 2, 5, 9, and 10 were engraved before Contrapuncti 3, 4, 6, 7, and 8.[19] The latter group constitutes a middle phase in the engraving project before the final, late phase of work was carried out after Bach's death. In Table 1 I have broken down the contents of the original print according to these early, middle, and late phases of the engraving.

Table 2. Bach's Intentions Regarding the
Disposition of Installment Two of the Art of the Fugue
According to "einen anderen Grund Plan"

Pages[a]	Title	BWV
1–5	Contrapunctus 11	1080/11
6–7	Contrapunctus 12 (recta)	1080/12, 1
8–9	Contrapunctus 12 (inversa)	1080/12, 2
10–11	Contrapunctus 13 (recta)	1080/13, 1
12–13	Contrapunctus 13 (inversa)	1080/13, 2
14–16	[Contrapunctus 14] (recta)	—
17–19	[Contrapunctus 14] (inversa)	—
20–21	Canon at the Octave	1080/15
22–23	Canon at the Tenth	1080/16
24–25	Canon at the Twelfth	1080/17
26–28	Canon by Augmentation	1080/14

a. in the engraver's copy (*Abklatschvorlage*)

The Art of Fugue project may well have started slowly, for the initial early phase seems to have been spread over a relatively long time period. This would account for Koprowski having been able to distinguish among no fewer than five distinct notational styles in this segment, even though only two different engravers were involved in the engraving and the scribe of the *Abklatschvorlage* throughout was J.S. Bach. Thus, notational style A can be seen as an early phase of notational style B (Johann Georg Schübler); likewise, notational styles C and E/E^1 are early variants of notational style D (Johann Heinrich Schübler).

In the middle phase the variants present in the first installment disappear, leaving only the two basic notational styles, B and D. This phase, in contrast to the early phase, seems to represent a short period of rather intense activity. The notational style F of the late phase, even though in each case the engraver is Johann Heinrich Schübler, differentiates itself clearly from notational style D, not only because it stems from *Vorlagen* not in the hand of J.S. Bach but also—albeit to a lesser extent—because it represents the very latest notational style of the engraver of the plates.

The breakdown of the plates in installment one into early- and middle-phase engravings provides an explanation for the engraving of three particular plates in that installment that have long puzzled Bach scholars. Since the engraving of Contrapuncti 4, 5, and 8 concluded at the end of the second system of their last pages (pages 12, 15, and 25), the lower third of all three pages was originally empty. If the works in installment one had been engraved in sequence, the first systems of Contrapuncti

5, 6, and 9 would certainly have been engraved as the third system on pages 12, 15, and 25.[20] Instead, one of the engravers (Johann Heinrich Schübler?) filled the empty spaces on each of the first two of these three pages with an extravagant *Blumenstrauss*. The third was filled with a similarly flamboyant floral cartouche containing the monogram of Johann Heinrich Schübler.[21]

It is significant that Contrapunctus 5, exhibiting all the features of notational style C, is surrounded on either side by an expanse of engraving in the late notational styles of Johann Heinrich and Johann Georg Schübler, B and D. This suggests that the three plates of Contrapunctus 5 were engraved during the early phase of work on the project by Johann Heinrich without reference to their context—which, in any case, was not yet known because, in all likelihood, Contrapunctus 4 had not yet been composed, and both it and Contrapunctus 6 had yet to be engraved. Thus, when he engraved these plates early on, the engraver simply started at the top of the first plate and left the lower third of the final plate empty when he had completed the engraving.

Similarly, Contrapunctus 9 and Contrapunctus 10 were engraved during the early phase by Johann Heinrich Schübler, the same engraver who began the engraving of the former at the top of the plate. When he later came to engrave Contrapunctus 8 as the first piece in a sequence of three, he had no engraving with which to continue, since Contrapunctus 9 and Contrapunctus 10, the final two works in installment one, were already finished. As a consequence, he did not engrave the staves for the first system of Contrapunctus 9 in the lower third of the last plate of Contrapunctus 8, as he certainly would have done if this group had been engraved in sequence, but instead signed it with an imposing monogram. He did so for the simple reason that this page marked the end of work on installment one.

The engraving of the collection in two installments, and Johann Heinrich Schübler's signing of the last plate to be engraved in the first installment, may be an indication that Bach originally considered bringing out the Art of Fugue in two volumes rather than one. This might have been in reaction to his earlier experience with *Clavierübung* III, published independently as a single, large volume of 78 pages, which apparently did not sell well because of its high purchase price of three taler.[22] Whether he ultimately decided against this plan himself or simply had no chance to make a decision before his final illness, upon his death his survivors decided to publish both installments together in a single volume.

"Und einen anderen Grund Plan": Bach's Intentions
Regarding the Contents and Layout of the Art of Fugue

One of the most persistent myths surrounding the Art of Fugue is that the collection was to be crowned with a quadruple fugue, the "incorrectly" titled *Fuga a 3 Soggetti* that survives in autograph form. Never mind that C. P. E. Bach, in his advertisement for the second edition, includes the work among the "last pieces," along with the version for two keyboards of Contrapunctus 13 and the chorale "Wenn wir in höchsten Nöten sein" after his discussion of the "manifold fugues . . . composed upon *one and the same principal theme*."[23] Never mind that the watermark of the paper and Bach's hand in the autograph score of the *Fuga a 3 Soggetti* date the manuscript to the very end of the composer's life and thus separate this source in time from the composition of the other works in the collection. Never mind that the principal subject of the Art of Fugue is uncomfortably close in its formulation to the first subject and its supposed combination with the three subjects of this fugue is far from convincing, contrapuntally.[24] Never mind that concluding the collection with a canonic appendix rather than a fugue would be much more in keeping with Bach's *modus operandi* in the late speculative works. Despite the fact that there is not a shred of evidence that this work belongs in the collection, and much that argues against this assumption, Bach scholars are unwilling to give it up, and so the myth endures. At one time I subscribed to it myself, and in my earlier essay on ordering problems I suggested that this work would have filled the hole of six pages preceding the concluding canonic complex.[25]

It is the autograph score of the *Fuga a 3 Soggetti* (P 200, Beilage 3) that argues convincingly for origins and aims totally independent of those of the pieces known to belong to the Art of Fugue proper. Its status as a source is not only that of fair autograph, but, with its *verso* faces blank, also that of engraver's *Vorlage* prepared by Bach for engraving by means of the *Abklatschvorlage* process.[26] However, unlike the surviving *Abklatschvorlage* of the augmentation canon (P 200, Beilage 1), it could never have been destined for publication as part of the Art of Fugue, because it is in keyboard score rather than open score with one voice per staff like all of the Contrapuncti.

This is not a trivial distinction. Rather, it is of critical importance. On the one hand, the partitura scoring supports the learned and theoretical designation of the works proper to the Art of Fugue as "*contrapunctus*," whereas on the other hand the keyboard scoring of the alien *Fuga a 3 Soggetti* supports the more common and practical designation, "*fuga*." Those who prepared the supplemental materials for printing after Bach's death realized this discrepancy in scoring, and it was sufficiently important to them that they went to the considerable effort of preparing a second engraver's *Vorlage* in open score when they could just as well have sent off the *Abklatschvorlage* already prepared by Bach to the engravers. It is significant, however, that they retained as the title *fuga* and not *contrapunctus*.

The *Fuga a 3 Soggetti* is just what the title suggests—a *fuga* (not a *contrapunctus*) with three subjects (not four). Given that Bach was in the process of preparing an *Abklatschvorlage* of the work for engraving,[27] I suggest that this work was originally destined for the circulating packet of Christoph Lorenz Mizler's Corresponding Society of Musical Sciences as Bach's contribution for the year 1750.[28] Because Bach was wrapping up work on his Art of Fugue at this time, he likely arranged with the Schübler shop to have it engraved at the same moment. Although a recently composed work, *vis-à-vis* the collection as a whole, the *Fuga a 3 Soggetti* has precisely the same status as the other three works engraved during the late phase of the second installment: *Contrap: a 4* (BWV 1080/10a), *Fuga a 2. Clav.* (BWV 1080/18, 1 and 2), and *Wenn wir in hoeschsten Noethen sein* (BWV 668; see Table 2). The last piece has no place in the Art of Fugue and was never intended by Bach to be included in the collection.

With these factors taken into account, the celebrated statement in Bach's obituary concerning the Art of Fugue can now be viewed in a new light: "His last illness prevented him from completing his project of bringing the next-to-last fugue to completion and working out the last one, which was to contain four themes and to have been afterward inverted note for note in all four voices."[29]

A detail in the engraving that seems to have escaped notice thus far indicates precisely where Bach, presumably through illness, was no longer able to supply engravers' copy, and it provides a clue allowing us to identify the "next-to-last fugue." It is not any radical change in the visual appearance of the musical text, but rather the ruling of barlines that distinguishes pages 41 and 42 from all others in the original print (Plate 1). These pages are the only ones in which each system contains nine measures with the barlines evenly spaced so that they are vertically aligned.[30] Clearly, the barlines in the *Vorlage* were pre-ruled in this one instance.[31] The fact that the ruling of these two pages is at odds with that of all other pages for which Bach prepared the *Vorlage* suggests that someone other than the composer was the scribe of the *Vorlage* for these two plates.

If, as I have argued, the *Fuga a 3 Soggetti* was never to have been included in the collection and the four canons were to have been the concluding group in the disposition scheme, then Contrapunctus 13 would have been the "next-to-last fugue" which Bach indeed was unable to "bring to completion" because of his final illness. However, because he had already prepared the *Vorlage* for the *recta* version of Contrapunctus 13 (*Contrapunctus inversus a 3*), it was not a complicated matter for another scribe to prepare the *Vorlage* for the *inversa* version (*Contrapunctus a 3*) with minimal (or even no) guidance from the composer. Who this scribe was must remain an open question, but given the "style" of the engraving, I suggest the engraver himself, Johann Heinrich Schübler, as the most likely candidate. The evidence indicates that Bach was in control of the project and preparing *Abklatschvorlagen* for the Schübler shop for all of the works for the collection he had composed to that point. He was unable either to prepare the *Abklatschvorlage* for Contrapunctus 13, 2 or to supply the titles for either Contrapunctus 13, 1 or Contrapunctus 13, 2 before his final illness overcame him.

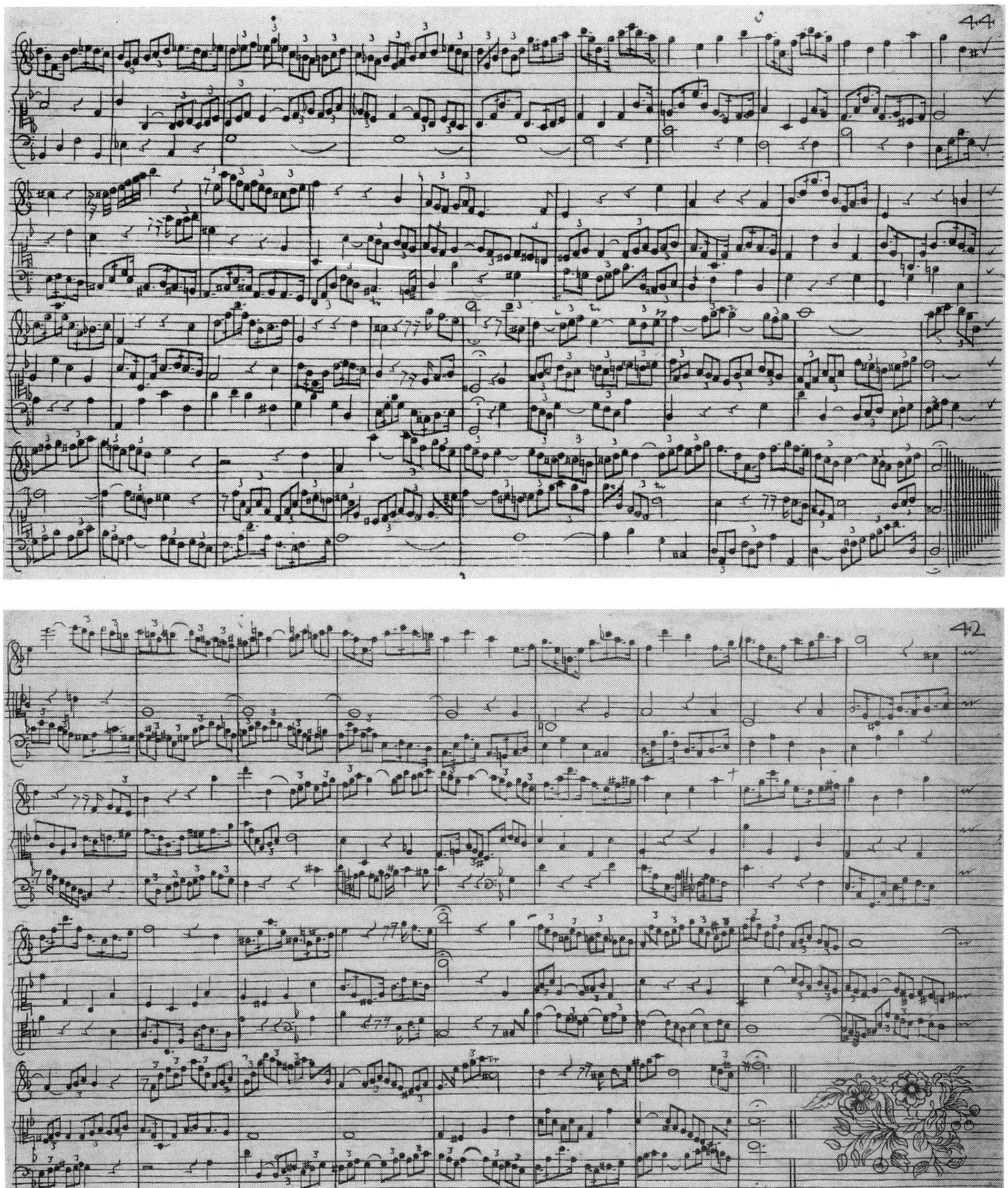

Plate 1. Top: Concluding page of *Contrapunctus inversus a 3*, BWV 1080/13, 1, p. 44 of the original print. Bottom: Concluding page of *Contrapunctus a 3*, BWV 1080/13, 2, p. 42 of the original print. Reproduced with the permission of the Riemenschneider Bach Institute, Berea, Ohio.

What, then, was "the last one," which Bach was prevented from "working out"? According to the obituary, this final work, [Contrapunctus 14, 1 and 14, 2], "was to contain four themes and to have been afterward inverted note for note in all four voices," suggesting that it was not a quadruple fugue at all but rather a "*Contrapunctus inversus a 4*," which would have completed a complex of three mirror fugues (Contrapuncti 12–14) and served as the fourth of five groups of pieces in the collection:

Contrapuncti 1–4 (simple fugues, 4)
Contrapuncti 5–7 (counter fugues, 3)
Contrapuncti 8–11 (compound fugues, 4)
Contrapuncti 12–14 (mirror fugues, 3)
Canones [1–4] (canons, 4)

This disposition may be "the other basic plan" (einen anderen Grund Plan) mentioned by Bach's pupil Johann Friedrich Agricola in a handwritten remark in Bach's autograph manuscript of the unfinished *Fuga a 3 Soggetti*.[32] If so, the definitive disposition of the collection, as Bach conceived it, consisted of a bilaterally symmetrical scheme totally in keeping with the large-scale structural principles that dominate his late works.[33]

One may surmise that Bach had at least planned in advance that the final contrapunctus was to occupy pages 45 to 50 of the original print—three pages each for the *recta* and *inversa* versions. It was this tour de force of contrapuntally and melodically invertible counterpoint—counterpoint that could be "inverted note for note in all four voices"—that would have crowned the series of fourteen *contrapuncti* that constitute the main body of the Art of Fugue.

Notes

1. The findings of this seminar were published as Christoph Wolff et al., "Bach's 'Art of Fugue': An Examination of the Sources," *Current Musicology* 19 (1975), 47–77.

2. See Chart 1 in Richard Koprowski, "Bach 'Fingerprints' in the Engraving of the Original Edition" in Wolff, "Bach's 'Art of Fugue'," 65.

3. *Abklatschvorlage* refers to a method of engraving using a mechanical transfer process. The *Stichvorlage* in this case is prepared by transcribing the musical text on one side of a sheet of paper while the other side is left blank. Each sheet is dipped in oil to render it transparent, reversed, and the face with musical text, coated with white powder, is applied face down to the varnished copper plate on which the staves have been incised. The engraver goes over the music with a blunt tool to transfer the powder adhering to the oily surface of the *Stichvorlage* to the tacky surface of the plate, after which the mirror image of the musical text is engraved on the prepared plate by means of the usual etching process.

4. See Koprowski, "Bach 'Fingerprints,'" 64.

5. Wolfgang Wiemer, *Die wiederhergestellte Ordnung in Johann Sebastian Bachs Kunst der Fuge* (Wiesbaden: Breitkopf & Härtel, 1977), 11: "erweckt den Eindruck, als seien zwei verschiedene Stecher am Werk gewesen . . . Trotz dieser Unterschiede erweist sich die Annahme, zwei Stecher hätten sich in die Arbeit geteilt, als unbegründet."

6. Wiemer, *Die wiederhergestelle Ordnung*, 20–21.

7. Wolfgang Wiemer, "Johann Heinrich Schübler, der Stecher der Kunst der Fuge," BJ 65 (1979), 77.

8. See Gregory G. Butler, "The Printing History of J.S. Bach's *Musical Offering*: New Interpretations," *Journal of Musicology* 19 (2002), 310.

9. I tentatively identified Johann Jacob Friedrich as the engraver of a number of plates in printing unit C, the performance parts for the Trio Sonata of the Musical Offering, in "The Printing History," 310–11.

10. The only exception is the notational style of Contrapunctus 2, given by Koprowski as B. I have subjected the engraving of the three pages of Contrapunctus 2 to an intensive examination and, on comparing it with the engraving of page 31, find that the form of both of the main indicators, the half rests and the C clefs, correspond not with notational style B, but rather most closely with notational style E[1]. Accordingly, I have relabeled the notational style of Contrapunctus 2 in the "Style" column of Table 1.

11. Johann Heinrich's biographical sketch of 1801–1802 states that "in his tenth year he was led by his brothers to music" (in seinem 10.ten Jahre wurde er schon von seinen Brüdern zur Music . . . angeführet) and more specifically that "after his schooling ended, he was instructed in . . . music by his second brother [Johann Georg] who had studied music in Leipzig with the famed Bach" (nach geendigten Schuljahren wurde er . . . von seinem zweyten Bruder, welcher die Music in Leipzig bey dem berühmten Bach gelernet, in der Music . . .). See Wiemer, "Johann Heinrich Schübler," 79.

12. See Yoshitake Kobayashi, "Zur Chronologie der Spätwerke Johann Sebastian Bachs—Kompositions- und Aufführungstätigkeit von 1736 bis 1750," BJ 74 (1988), 21, Plate 5d.

13. See, for example, the close resemblance of their clefs to the form of those in Johann Mattheson's *Der vollkommene Capellmeister* (1739), which, although issued by Wolfgang Deer in Hamburg, was printed by Breitkopf in Leipzig.

14. See Butler, "The Printing History," 310 and 312, Figure 1.

15. Gregory G. Butler, "Ordering Problems in J.S. Bach's *Art of Fugue* Resolved," *Musical Quarterly* 69 (1983), 58–59.

16. For example, Pieter Dirksen, in his influential monograph on the Art of Fugue, has accepted my reordering of the augmentation canon as the last in the series of four canons as a point of departure for his detailed study of the various symmetrical schemes at work in the collection. See Pieter Dirksen, *Studien zur Kunst der Fuge von Joh. Seb. Bach. (Veröffentlichungen zur Musikforschung* 12) (Wilhelmshaven: Florian Noetzel Verlag, 1994).

17. The two installments are clearly differentiated in the original print by the engraving of their page numbers. Those for installment one (pages 1–31) have no terminal dot, a feature that begins

with page 32 and is present in two-thirds of the page numbers in the second installment. The two installments must have been paginated separately.

18. Wiemer also breaks down the engraving into three phases, but his divisions are based solely on the scribe of the *Abklatschvorlage*: 1. J.S. Bach (BWV 1080/1; 3; 11; 12,1; 13,1; 15; 16; 17; 18), 2. copyists A–D (BWV 1080/2; 5; 6; 7; 8; 9; 10; 12,2; 13,2), 3. *Abklatschvorlagen* prepared after Bach's death by copyist E (BWV 1080 14; 19; 20; 21). Thus, only his phase number 3 and my late phase coincide. See Wiemer, *Die wiederhergestellte Ordnung*, 48 and 50.

19. The rather particular notation of the page numbers for Contrapuncti 1 and 2 (pp. 1–5), with a diagonal tilda over the number, indicates that these page numbers were engraved before those for Contrapuncti 3 through 10 (pp. 6–31) and that there was a lapse in time between the engraving of the page numbers on these and the rest of the plates in installment one. This evidence not only supports my contention that Contrapuncti 1 and 2 were part of the early phase of engraving in installment one but also suggests that they were the first two to be engraved.

20. This would have meant one less page to print and thus represented a not inconsiderable saving in printing and paper costs for Bach, as the independent publisher of the edition.

21. For the identification of this monogram, see Wiemer, *Die wiederhergestellte Ordnung*, 44–45.

22. As late as 1774 Carl Philipp Emanuel was still trying to unload remaining copies of *Clavierübung* III. See BDOK III, 277.

23. NBR, 257 (emphasis mine).

24. The hypothetical contrapuntal combination of the three subjects of the *Fuga a 3 Soggetti* with the principal subject of the Art of Fugue was first demonstrated by Gustav Nottebohm in *Musik-Welt* 20 (1881), 234. Christoph Wolff has pointed out that most of the possible combinations of the four subjects are not playable on the keyboard. See Wolff, "Bach's Last Fugue: Unfinished?" in *Bach: Essays on His Life and Music* (Cambridge, Mass.: Harvard University Press, 1991), 423, n. 5. In addition, the syncopation of the principal subject that is necessary for it to work in contrapuntal combination with the other three subjects seems forced and unnatural.

25. See Butler, "Ordering Problems," 56–58.

26. Christoph Wolff has suggested these were sheets that were prepared originally for the *Abklatschvorlagen* of the canons but that subsequently proved unnecessary. Instead of simply discarding them and wasting good paper, Bach reused them. See Christoph Wolff, "Bach's Last Fugue: Unfinished?," 260–61. Klaus Hofmann wonders why Bach, if he was being so frugal, as Wolff suggests, did not also make use of the empty verso faces of these sheets. See NBA VIII/2 (*Die Kunst der Fuge*), ed. Klaus Hofmann, KB, 83, n. 15.

27. Despite the fact that the work appears to trail off after the entrance of the B-A-C-H subject, both the status of this source as fair copy and also physical evidence in the source itself led Wolff to the conclusion that the work had been completed by Bach. See Wolff, "Bach's Last Fugue," 72.

28. Klaus Hofmann has suggested that Bach may have intended "to publish the fugue in keyboard notation as an 'offprint'" (*Sonderdruck*), but he does not raise the possibility that Bach never intended to include the work in the Art of Fugue. See Hofmann, KB, VIII/2, 83, n. 15.

29. NBR, 304.

30. Because Contrapunctus 13 begins with a quarter-note upbeat, the barlines of the first system on page 41 are slightly out of alignment with the other three systems on the page.

31. This is most striking in the case of m. 59, which contains only a half-note chord, quarter rest, and quarter-note chord, and in the *inversus* version, where J.S. Bach is the scribe of the *Abklatschvorlage*, takes up comparatively little space. In the *recta* version, where J.S. Bach clearly was not the scribe of the *Abklatschvorlage*, it is allotted the same space as every other measure, with the result that the wide spacing of its contents is out of all proportion to that in the other measures.

32. The full comment—"und einen anderen Grund Plan"—appears on the empty verso side of the last page (page 5) of *P 200*, Beilage 3. See NBA VIII/2, KB, 60. The remark has never been satisfactorily explained. See Christoph Wolff, "Principles of Design and Order in Bach's Original Editions," in Wolff, *Bach: Essays on His Life and Music*, 356–57.

33. Pieter Dirksen discusses this structure at some length and even applies it to a substructure within the larger disposition scheme. See Dirksen, *Studien zur Kunst der Fuge*, 94–101.

Notes on J.S. Bach and
Basso Continuo Realization

Ton Koopman

The only extant references, either directly or indirectly, to basso continuo or basso continuo performance in surviving Bach documents from the composer's lifetime are the following:

1. Christoph Ernst Sicul, reporting in an entry of October 17, 1727, in his Leipzig Chronicle, that Cantata 198, *Laß dich Fürstin, laß dich einen Strahl* ("Trauerode"), was accompanied "with *Clave di cembalo* [harpsichord], which Mr. Bach himself played."[1]

2. Georg Heinrich Ludwig Schwanenberger, after hearing Bach play the organ, remarking in a letter to Johann Daniel Bähre in Braunschweig dated November 12, 1727: "I must completely change my whole style of playing . . . and in thorough bass, too."[2]

3. *Leipziger Post-Zeitung* announcing in the issue of April 18, 1729, that exemplars of Johann David Heinichen's recently published *General-Bass in der Composition* (Dresden, 1728) are "to be found at the following locations in Germany under commission, namely . . . in Leipzig from Mr. Capellmeister Bach."[3]

4. Applying for the position of organist at the Freiberg Cathedral, Sigmund Freudenberg attests, in a letter of April 11, 1731, that during his studies with Bach he learned "how to please with a valid *Generalbass* in the modern style."[4]

5. Friedrich Schulze concerning Bach's contribution to the *Schemelli-Gesangbuch*, in the preface dated April 24, 1736, states that "the melodies . . . have been in part quite newly composed and in part improved in the thorough bass by the most noble Mr. Johann Sebastian Bach . . ."[5]

6. Lorenz Christoph Mizler writing in his *Musikalische Bibliothek* (Leipzig, 1738):

   Whoever wishes truly to observe what delicacy in thorough bass and very good accompanying mean need only take the trouble to hear our Capellmeister Bach here, who accompanies every thorough bass to a solo so that one thinks it is a piece of concerted music and as if the melody he plays in the right hand were written beforehand. I can give a living testimony of this since I have heard it myself.[6]

7. The title to a manuscript copy of a thorough-bass manual, C. A. Thieme's *Vorschriften und Grundsätze zum vierstimmigen Spielen der Generalbaß* (dated 1738), which is purported to have been prepared by Bach for his *"Scholaren in der Music"* and contains a reference to "four-voiced playing of the *Generalbass* or accompaniment."[7]

Documents originating after Bach's death that shed light on the composer's realization of figured bass are equally few in number, but they are somewhat more informative:

1. A figured bass treatise of 1756 by Johann Friedrich Daube that includes the following assessment of Bach's figured bass realization:

> The excellent Bach possessed this third species [intricate or compound counterpoint] in the highest degree. When he played [continuo], the soloist had to shine. By his exceedingly adroit accompaniment he gave the upper part life when it had none. He knew how to imitate it so cleverly, with either the right hand or the left, and how to introduce an unexpected counter-theme against it, so that the listener would have sworn that everything had been conscientiously written out. At the same time, the normal accompaniment was curtailed very little. In general, his accompanying was always like a *concertante* part—that is, it was most conscientiously worked out and added as a companion to the upper voice so that at the appropriate time the upper voice would shine. This right was even given at times to the bass, without slighting the upper voice. Suffice it to say that anyone who missed hearing him missed a great deal.[8]

2. Bach's pupil, Johann Friedrich Agricola, commenting on Bach's method of teaching thorough-bass playing: "[Bach], according to well established rules, had his pupils set down on paper the notes inserted in playing the thorough-bass, in four fair voices."[9]

3. C.P.E. Bach, writing toward the end of 1774 in a communication concerning his father:

> Thanks to his greatness in harmony, he accompanied trios on more than one occasion on the spur of the moment and, being in a good humor and knowing that the composer would not take it amiss, and on the basis of a sparsely figured continuo part just set before him, converted them into complete quartets, astounding the composer of the trios.[10]

4. Johann Nikolaus Forkel, writing in a letter of January 13, 1775, to C.P.E. Bach:

> His pupils had to begin their studies by learning pure 4-part thorough bass . . . The realization of thorough basses and preluding on chorales are without doubt the best method of studying composition as far as harmony is concerned.[11]

5. Johann Philipp Kirnberger, writing in his *Grundsätze des Generalbasses* of 1781 about Bach's four-part realization of thorough bass:

an example from a Trio by Johann Sebastian Bach, which, despite the fact that it is only a trio, must be accompanied in four parts, and this may serve to refute the common opinion that trios, sonatas for a *concertante* part and bass, as well as cantatas accompanied only by a harpsichord, must not be accompanied in four parts.[12]

6. Ernst Ludwig Gerber, son of Bach student Heinrich Nikolaus Gerber, describing his father's thorough-bass playing in the entry for his father in *Historisch-Biographisches Lexicon der Tonkünstler* (1790):

> and I must admit that I have never heard anything better than the style in which my father executed these basses according to Bach's fashion, particularly in the singing of the voices.[13]

7. Bach student Johann Christian Kittel, remarking in his organ method *Der angehende praktische Organist* (1808) on Bach's intervention in the accompaniments of students:

> One of his most capable pupils always had to accompany on the harpsichord. It will easily be guessed that no one dared to put forward a meagre thorough-bass accompaniment. Nevertheless, one always had to be prepared to have Bach's hands and fingers intervene among the hands and fingers of the player and, without getting in the way of the latter, furnish the accompaniment with masses of harmonies . . .[14]

In addition to these documents, there are short entries on continuo realization in the *Clavierbüchlein für Anna Magdalena Bach*: the "Einige höchstnöthige Regeln von General Basso" of Johann Christoph Friedrich Bach and "Einige Reguln vom General Bass" in the hand of Anna Magdalena herself.[15] Although these provide only the most basic instruction, the "Regeln der Generalbasses von dem Herrn Musico Heering," commenced in 1771 by the sixteen-year-old Otto Carol Friedrich von Voß (1755–1823), is of much greater interest for our understanding of J.S. Bach's basso continuo realization. Voß appears to have studied with Johann Friedrich Hering, a Berlin musician in C.P.E. Bach's circle. Voß's manuscript includes basso continuo realizations of an incomplete, but nevertheless impressive, part of the St. John Passion, of the Second Orchestral Suite, and of the Trio Sonata from the Musical Offering.[16] Two details from Voß's manual seem to have important implications for Bach's basso continuo realization. First, in contrast to the practice common today of doubling the upper parts in the opening entries of the imitative B section of overture movements in the orchestral suites (which, alas, leads to problems in intonation), in Voß's realization the upper part is never doubled by the basso continuo. Second, at times Voß notates a chord in the right hand when there is a rest in the bass voice.

Jörg-Andreas Bötticher, who has described the Voß document in considerable detail,[17] claims that the realizations "cannot be dismissed merely as didactic backdrops and simply as harmony exercises but must be taken seriously as proof of a historical practice."[18] I argue instead that the realizations do, in fact, represent teaching material and nothing else,[19] and consequently provide us with little information on how Bach himself realized figured basses.

Although the information is sparse, it seems undeniable, given the supporting documentation, that in his day J.S. Bach was a "phenom" in the art of figured bass realization. He taught his students by giving them both figured and unfigured basses. He never assigned treble parts, however.[20] Apparently, in continuo lessons, Bach never revealed a given model in its entirety.[21] He demanded that basso continuo parts be realized in four voices,[22] and through this process his pupils learned to compose four-part harmony.

Given that Niedt's treatise, *Musicalische Handleitung* (1700), is the source for Thieme's *Vorschriften und Grundsätze* (cited earlier among the documents from Bach's lifetime), it is possible that Bach owned a copy of Niedt's popular manual and that he used it in teaching figured bass to his students. Whatever the case, as perhaps the most important contemporary source for our understanding of figured bass in the early eighteenth century, the *Musicalische Handleitung* should be taken seriously in any assessment of Bach's figured bass practice.

Niedt's general statement concerning the realization of a figured bass is rather unorthodox. He says:

> When the singer or [obbligato] instrumentalist sounds [the interval above the bass indicated by] the numbers that are over the thorough bass, it is not necessary for the organist to play them as well. Rather, he can play merely simple thirds such as will be fitting, or he can do something more artful with it, if he should wish.[23]

Because doubling a chord tone sung by the soloist or played by the orchestra often results in problems with intonation,[24] this is eminently practical advice for the organist. In fact, it may be necessary in many instances not to realize certain figures for just this reason.[25] However, Niedt states elsewhere that in recitatives, with their long figured-bass notes, the continuo player must pay attention to the singer, for it may sometimes be necessary to double the notes of a singer who is out of tune or out of step.[26]

Johann David Heinichen's figured bass treatises *Neu erfundene und gründliche Anweisung* (1711) and *General-Baß in der Composition* (1728) are mentioned time and time again in connection with Bach's basso continuo realization. Heinichen intended both works for "*Music-liebenden*" or, as he specifies more precisely in his preface to the 1728 treatise, for "practised and unpractised, learned and unlearned, accompanists as well as composers" (geübte als ungeübte, Gelehrte und Ungelehrte, so wohl Accompagnisten als Componisten). However, we should in no way infer from the fact that Bach acted as a sales agent for the *General-Baß in der Composition* that the volume was his ideal choice as a basso continuo manual. The fact that Heinichen's examples tend to be very difficult and his realizations uninspired argues against any such assumption.

From the Hamburg theorist Johann Mattheson we have a revised edition of Niedt's *Handleitung* (1717), as well as three basso continuo methods: *Exemplarische Organisten Probe* (1719), *Grosse-Generalbass-Schule* (1731), and *Kleine-Generalbass-Schule* (1735). In his approach to basso continuo realization, Mattheson may be considerably closer to Bach than Heinichen was.

For instance, Mattheson provides trial pieces (Probestücke), often in unusual keys, and from these exercises one really learns how to realize a figured bass. But, because Mattheson finds realizing figures a dull activity, he provides in each case a second, freer realization in the manner of an "etude." He views this as an amusement or diversion in exercising the right hand ("als Belüstiging"). Mattheson wants his students to understand that continuo playing should not be noisy or a hindrance to the soloist, but rather interesting enough to keep the audience awake and an aid to the soloist in staying in tune.[27]

Let us turn now to an examination of certain of Bach's works in light of what we know of his approach to basso continuo realization. Given that Bach apparently favors four-voice basso continuo realization, it is curious to find so many different textures in the written-out continuo passages in his works.[28] In the Concerto in F Major for Harpsichord, BWV 1057 (an arrangement of the Fourth Brandenburg Concerto), full-voiced chords appear frequently in the *Cembalo concertato* part, but the chords display great variety in the number of voices. In the first movement, the *Cembalo concertato* part never plays in unison with Flauto 1, but does so with the Violino 1, which would seem to point to an alternate quartet version for obbligato harpsichord and two recorders. In the second movement, the harpsichord doubles the recorders only when the strings do so, and in the third movement the beginning resembles a keyboard transcription of the string parts, while the recorders are doubled, sometimes an octave lower (mm. 63–78, 203–218, 229–244). To judge from this evidence, the *Urform* of this arrangement may have been a concerto *senza ripieno*, like the early version of the Second Brandenburg Concerto, BWV 1047a, and the Concerto in C Major for Two Harpsichords, BWV 1061a.

On the basis of the evidence available, it seems that Bach varied the texture of his basso continuo realizations depending on the musical context. He probably would have offered the same advice as his Berlin contemporary Johann Joachim Quantz:

> For no less than a composer can set to every melody a three-, four-, or five-part accompaniment of voices . . . no less does each melody permit of an unvarying, full-

voiced accompaniment on the keyboard, because an accompanist must be guided more by the circumstance itself than by general rules of thoroughbass realization.[29]

Whenever Bach's performance of basso continuo parts is discussed, the first and third movements of the E-Major Violin Sonata, BWV 1016, and the third movement of the F-Minor Violin Sonata, BWV 1018, are routinely put forward as examples of his approach. But the B-Minor Flute Sonata, BWV 1030, could just as well serve as a model. In the Baroque era, there were extraordinary musicians like Bach who could improvise such basso continuo realizations to create what is essentially an obbligato part in the right hand. Unfortunately, this practice is beyond the capability of most continuo players today.

The sonatas for violin and transverse flute with obbligato cembalo raise certain questions. Why in these pieces are there stretches in the cembalo part where Bach neglects to write out the obbligato voice? A good example occurs at the beginning of the third movement of the B-Minor Flute Sonata. Similar examples can be found abundantly, in the first and third movements of the A-Major Flute Sonata, BWV 1032; the second movement of the B-Minor Violin Sonata, BWV 1014; the first and third movements of the A-Major Violin Sonata, BWV 1015; the second and fourth movements of the E-Major Violin Sonata, BWV 1016; the fourth movement of the C-Minor Violin Sonata, BWV 1017; the first, second, and fourth movements of the F-Minor Violin Sonata, BWV 1018; and the first and second movements of the G-Major Violin Sonata, BWV 1019.

Conversely, why does Bach sometimes write out what seem to be straightforward chordal realizations, such as, for example, those in the second movement of the B-Minor Flute Sonata? Playing the part as written lends a stiff quality to the music if it is played with no dynamic feeling.

In performing Bach's continuo parts, the average continuo player generally arrives at the limit of his capabilities. Realizing the figured bass in advance in this complex, densely figured music is already a difficult task—reading it at sight is possible for only a very few players. This may have been Kirnberger's motivation for writing out the continuo part of the Trio Sonata in the Musical Offering.[30] Apart from Bach's sons Carl Philipp Emanuel and Wilhelm Friedemann, there were decidedly few musicians able to realize such complicated masterworks faultlessly, even after extensive practicing. Peter Williams has cautioned budding continuo players not to perform the written-out parts made by Bach's students and fellow musicians.[31] Williams may be right to do so, for the parts served as lessons in counterpoint and have limited value as "sounding" continuo realizations. Bach himself, of course, knew no such hindrances —nothing was too complicated for him. As the Inventions and Sinfonias, the Well-Tempered Clavier, and other instructional collections demonstrate, even his didactic pieces are musically convincing. Bach makes the same heavy technical and musical demands on all performers—singers, instrumentalists, and continuo players alike—who attempt to play his exceedingly difficult music.

In my opinion, there is a big difference between written-out obbligato continuo parts (such as the parts for obbligato organ in various Bach cantatas) and unfigured, unprepared, improvised basso continuo parts. A genius may attempt to improvise without any preparation, as Bach did in realizing such figured bass parts. Although there were in Bach's time a good number of extraordinary players who could realize continuo with great skill, one should think twice before considering oneself in this distinguished coterie. In point of fact, it is far simpler to improvise in the manner of a Matteson, a Graupner, or a Heinichen than of a Bach.

Notes

1. BDOK II, 232: "mit *Clave di Cembalo*, welches Herr Bach selbst spielete . . ." English translation from NBR, 136.

2. BDOK II, 239: "ich mus meine Spielart gantz anders ändern . . . wie auch im *Gerneral Bass*." English translation from NBR, 325.

3. BDOK II, 260: "an folgenden Orten Deutschlandes wird in *Commission* zu finden seyn . . . in Leipzig bey dem Herrn Capell-Meister Bach . . ." English translation from NBR, 139.

4. BDOK II, no. 288: "wie auch mit einen legalen *General-Basse, in modo moderno*, zu vergnügen." This and all other translations not taken from the NBR are by Gregory G. Butler.

5. BDOK, no. 379: "theils neu componiret, theils auch von Ihm im General-Baß verbessert . . ." English translation from NBR, 170.

6. BDOK II, no. 419: "Wer das delicate im General-Baß und was sehr wohl accompagniren heist, recht vernehmen will, darf sich nur bemühen unsern Herrn Capellmeister Bach alhier zu hören, welcher einen ieden General-Baß zu einem Solo so accompagnirt, daß man denket, es sey ein Con-cert, und wäre nie Melodey so er mit der rechten Hand machet, schon verhero also gesetzet worden. Ich kan einen lebendigen Zeugen abgeben, weil ich es selbsten gehöret." English translation from NBR, 328.

7. BDOK, no. 433: "vierstimmigen spielen des *General-Bass* oder *Accompagnement*." It is clear that Bach did not correct Thieme's mistakes in this "dictation," and it may not necessarily have been Bach himself who made the selection of rules from Niedt's *Musikalische Handleitung oder gründlicher Unterricht*. Following Bach's method, everything has been worked out in four parts, but the realizations do not show a great deal of creativity, suggesting that it represents ad hoc instructional material.

8. BDOK III, no. 680: "Der vortreffliche Bach besaß diese dritte Art im höchsten Grad. Durch ihn mußte die Oberstimme brilliren. Er gab ihr durch sein grundgeschictes Accompagniren das Leben, wenn sie keines hatte. Er wußte sie, entweder mit der rechten oder lincken Hand so geschickt nach-zuahmen, oder ihr unversehens ein Gegenthema anzubringen, daß der Zuhörer schwören solte, es wäre mit allem Fleiß so gesetzt worden. Dabey wurde das ordentliche Accompagnement sehr wenig verkürzt. Ueberhaupt sein Accompagniren war allezeit wie eine mit dem größten Fleiße ausgearbei-tete, und der Oberstimme an die Seite gesetzte concertirende Stimme, wo zu rechter Zeit die

Oberstimme brilliren mußte. Dieses Recht wurde sodann auch dem Basse ohne Nachtheil der Oberstimme überlassen. Genug! wer ihn nicht gehöret, hat sehr vieles nicht gehöret." English translation
from NBR, 362. It is likely that Daube's report is a second-hand account based on information from
Carl Eugen von Würtemberg, a pupil of Carl Philipp Emanuel Bach. See Hans-Joachim Schulze's
comments in BDOK III, no. 680, commentary. In his review of Daube's treatise, Johann Friedrich
Wilhelm Sonnenkalb, a student at the St. Thomas School in Leipzig from 1746 to 1754, remarks on
this passage: "ist alles die Wahrheit. Ich für meine Person habe denselben in Leipzig sehr oft und
vielmals spielen hören, und ich kann mich mit Grunde der Wahrheit rühmen . . . Wo hat denn aber
der Herr Daube denselben gehöret? Wer weiß, ob er ihn gar gehöret hat . . . Ich zweifle daran."
("everything is the truth. I, for my person, have often and on many occasions heard the same [Bach]
play in Leipzig, and I can pride myself with reason on this truth . . . But where did Herr Daube hear
the same playing? Who knows whether he really heard it? . . . I doubt it."). BDOK, no. 703.

9. BDOK III, no. 796: "welcher nach wohl erklärten Regeln, seine Schüler, die bey dem General-
baßspielen anzubringenden Töne, in vier reinen Stimmen zu Papiere bringen ließ."

10. BDOK III, no. 801: "Vermöge seiner Größe in der Harmonie, hat er mehr als einmahl Trios accompagnirt, und, weil er aufgeräumt war, wuste, daß der Compnist dieser Trioses nicht übel nehmen
würde, aus dem Stegereif u. aus einer elend beziferten ihm vorgelegten Baßstimme ein vollkom-
menes *Quatuor* daraus gemacht . . ." English translation from NBR, 397.

11. BDOK III, no. 803: "Den Anfang musten seine Schüler mit der Erlernung des reinen 4stimmi-
gen Generalbaßes Machen . . . Das Aussetzen des Generalbaßes u. die Anführung zu den Chorälen
ist ohne Streit die beste Methode zur Erlernung der Composition, *qvoad Harmoniam.*" English
translation from NBR, 279.

12. BDOK III, no. 855: "ein Exempel von Johann Sebastian Bach aus einem Trio . . . welches,
ohngeachtet es nur ein Trio ist, dennoch vierstimmig accompagnirt werden muß, und kann dieses
zur Widerlegung der gemeinen Meinung dienen, als müßten Trios, Sonaten, für eine concertirende
Stimme und dem Baß; imgleichen Cantaten, die nur von einem Flügel begleitet werden, nicht vierstimmig accompagniret werden." English translation from *The Bach Reader* (rev. ed.), ed. Hans T.
David and Arthur Mendel (New York: W.W. Norton, 1966), 388 (facsimile reproduction of Kirnberger's realization) and 450.

13. BDOK III, no. 950: "und ich muß gestehen, daß ich in der Art, wie mein Vater diese Bässe nach
Bachs Manier ausführete, und besonders in dem Gesange der Stimmen untereinander, nie etwas
vortreflichers gehöret habe." English translation from NBR, 322.

14. Johann Christian Kittel, *Der angehende praktische Organist* (Erfurt, 1801–1808), vol. 3, 33: "Wenn
Seb. Bach eine Kirchenmusik aufführte, so mußte allemal einer von seinen fähigsten Schülern auf
dem Flügel accompagniren. Man kann wohl vermuthen, daß man sich da mit einer magern Gener-
albaßbegleitung ohnehin nicht vor wagen durfte. Demohnerachtet mußte man sich immer darauf
gefaßt halten, daß sich oft plötzlich Bachs Hände und Finger unter die Hände und Finger des Spie-
lers mischten und, ohne diesen weiter zu geniren, das Accompagnement mit massen von Harmonien
ausstaffirten." English translation from NBR, 323.

15. For a transcription of the texts of these rules, see NBA V/4 (*Die Klavierbüchlein für Anna Magdalena Bach 1722 und 1725*), ed. Georg von Dadelsen, 131.

16. See Jörg-Andreas Bötticher, "Generalbaßpraxis in der Bach-Nachfolge. Eine wenig bekannte
Berliner Handschrift mit Generalbaß-Aussetzungen," BJ 79 (1993), 103–25, and "Regeln des Gene-

ralbasses: Eine Berliner Handschrift des späten 18. Jahrhunderts," *Basler Jahrbuch für historische Musikpraxis* 18 (1994), 87–114.

17. See n. 16.

18. Bötticher, "Regeln des Generalbasses," 107: "nicht nur didaktische Hintergründe hat und als bloße Harmonieübung abgetan werden kann, sondern als Beleg für eine historische Praxis sehr ernst genommen werden muß."

19. For instance, whole passages in the Voß parts are omitted, only to be added on subsequent pages. Not only because large sections are missing, but also because of the chaotic notation, these parts could never have been used in a performance of the work. To judge from the extent of the realizations, Voß was a diligent pupil, going so far as to transcribe the basso continuo parts of forty-eight sonatas of Arcangelo Corelli alone. This seems to me, though, to be the work of a very young student writing down basso continuo exercises for his teacher, J. F. Hering. Even Bötticher is forced to admit that 95 percent of Voß's continuo realization is "rein akkordisch" and mostly in the same dull style throughout. One hopes that basso continuo playing in the "Adelshäuser" of Berlin was more creative than this!

20. In the *Exemplarische Organisten Probe* of 1719, Bach's Hamburg colleague Johann Mattheson states: "nichts kann wol hölzener klingen als einen schlechten General-Bass *solo* zu spielen" (p. 8; emphasis mine). Thus, J.S. Bach was not the only one teaching thorough bass from the bare basso continuo part alone.

21. See the example of Heinrich Nicolaus Gerber from Tomaso Albinoni's *Trattenimenti armonici per camera*, opus 6 (Amsterdam: Roger, 1712), for which Gerber realized a basso continuo part to the A-Minor Sonata "durch corrigiert von Seb. Bach." Not every mistake was corrected, however; that would have been obvious if Gerber had seen the entire score. Gerber's realization was first published by Philipp Spitta in *Johann Sebastian Bach* (Leipzig: Breifkopf & Härtel, 1873–1880), vol. 2, 293.

22. This is discussed by Peter Benary in *Die deutsche Kompositionslehre des 18. Jahrhundert* (Leipzig: Breitkopf & Härtel, 1961), 62. However, I believe that the tendency to realize figured basses in four parts common today is interpreting eighteenth-century methods too literally. This was the method taught to beginners, perhaps with a bit more information added for advanced students.

23. Friedrich Erhard Niedt, *Musicalische Handleitung* (Hamburg: auf kosten des autoris, 1700), vol. 1, ch. IV, line 8: "Wenn der Sänger oder Instrumentalist die Zahlen welche über dem General-Bass gesetzt sind singet oder spielt so ist es eben nicht nöthig daß der Organist selbige dazu nimmt sondern kann nur die blossen Tertien darnach sichs schicken wil dazu schlagen; Oder wil er etwas Künstlichers dazu machen stehts in einer eignen Beliebung."

24. Besides avoidance of doubling the melody in the realization of the basso continuo, Johann Joachim Quantz suggests an alternative solution, that of doubling the note but at the lower octave. He goes on to aver that it is better to avoid doubling altogether, as it "offends the hearing" (das Gehör zu beleidigen) and because when the thorough-bass player avoids doubling, "the solo player thereby gains his rightful freedom" (der Solospieler bekömmt dadurch seine gehörige Freiheit). See Quantz, *Versuch einer Anweisung der Flöte traversiere zu spielen* (Berlin: Johann Friedrich Boß, 1752), 233–34.

25. A case in point is that when *tasto solo* is indicated, even though basses are heavily figured, the chords indicated are not to be played. Johann David Heinichen makes the same point. See Heinichen,

Der General-Bass in der Composition (Dresden: Bey dem Autorâe zu finden, 1728), 515. Andreas Werck-meister adds an important expressive dimension when he states that an affect created by means of a dissonance in one of the other voices can be ruined if it is doubled in the realization of the basso continuo. See Andreas Werckmeister, *Harmonologica Musica* (Frankfurt and Leipzig, 1702), 64–65.

26. Niedt, *Musicalische Handleitung*, vol. 2, 16.

27. Johann Mattheson, *Exemplarische Organisten Probe* (Hamburg: auf kosten des autoris, 1719), 24: "gleich wie alle dieser Arbeit nicht dahin gehet daß man einen General-Baß mit welchem etwa eine Sing-Stimme oder ein Violino solo accompagniret wird fein bunt-verbrämen und verhudeln soll sondern daß er zu rechter Zeit lerne dem Zuhörer eine Auffmercksamkeit zu erwecken damit nicht alles in der Figural-Musique laute als das Magnificat Octavi Toni."

28. A survey of various treatises indicates that other composers and musicians of the time were rather flexible in specifying the number of voices in a figured bass realisation. For example, Georg Muffat (*Regulae concentuum partiturae*, manuscript, 1699), although he prefers three-part over four-part accompaniment, provides examples with a variety of textures. J. B. Samber, in his *Manuductio ad Organum* (Salzburg: J.B. Mayrs seel. wittib., 1704), 119, states that whether one realises a basso con-tinuo part in two, three, or four voices depends on the piece one is playing, regulating the number of voices according to the number of voices in the piece one is accompanying ("aufgelegte Musi-calische Stück wenig oder viel Stimmen habe? Darnach sole sich ein Organist reguliren"). Werck-meister, in his *Harmonologia Musica* (Frankfurt and Leipzig: T.P. Calvissi, 1702), 82, states categori-cally that a figured bass should be realised exclusively in four voices ("einen General-Baß solle nicht anders als mit vier Stimmen tractiren") but then immediately qualifies this statement by adding that three voices will also work ("Nein er kan auch gar zierlich mit dreyer gespielt werden").

29. Quantz, *Versuch einer Anweisung der Flöte traversiere zu spielen*, 224: "Denn so wenig ein Com-ponist zu allen Melodien ein drey-vier-oder fünffstimmiges Accompagnement der Stimmen setzen kann noch muß . . . eben so wenig leidet auch eine jede Melodie ein beständigen vollstimmigen Ac-compagnement auf dem Clavier weswegen ein Accompagnist sich mehr nach der Sache selbst, als nach den allegemeinen Regeln des Generalbasses, richten muß."

30. The realization appears in the manuscript *St 421*, which stems from Kirnberger's circle. See NBA VIII/1 (*Kanons, Musikalisches Opfer*), KB, 81.

31. Peter Williams, "Johann Sebastian Bach and the Basso Continuo," *Basler Jahrbuch für historische Musikpraxis* 18 (1994), 79.

Music for "Cavaliers et Dames"

Bach and the Repertoire of His Collegium Musicum

George B. Stauffer

As it is well known, Bach led the University Collegium Musicum ensemble in Leipzig from 1729 to 1737, and then once again from 1739 to at least 1741. During his tenure, the group performed once per week for two hours throughout the year: in summer on Wednesdays, from 4:00 p.m. to 6:00 p.m., in Gottfried Zimmermann's Coffee Garden in the Grimmischer Steinweg outside the east gate of the city; and in winter on Fridays, from 8:00 p.m. to 10:00 p.m., in Zimmermann's Coffee House in the Catharinenstrasse in the center of town. During the three annual trade fairs—New Year's, Easter (Jubilate), and St. Michael's—the group performed twice a week, on Tuesdays and Fridays, from 8:00 p.m. to 10:00 p.m., during the three weeks of each fair.[1]

As a consequence, Bach was responsible for approximately 61 two-hour Collegium sessions per year for at least 10 years, which works out to more than 1,200 hours of music. Moreover, he also led the Collegium in special performances, apart from the Zimmermann engagements, of celebratory music for the Elector of Saxony and other patrons. He also appeared as guest director of the ensemble now and then, both before and after his official tenure and during the period 1737 to 1739, when he handed off his duties to his assistant, Carl Gotthelf Gerlach.[2] This accounted for even more hours of Collegium music-making. By comparison, as Cantor of the St. Thomas School and music director of the city, Bach was responsible for approximately sixty cantata performances per year in the St. Thomas and St. Nicholas Churches, each lasting a half-hour or so. Given his 27 years of service in Leipzig, this accounts for just over 800 hours of music.

That Bach spent more time directing the Collegium than conducting cantatas was a fact that Philipp Spitta chose to play down in his nineteenth-century Bach biography. Spitta devoted only three pages of his monumental study to Bach's directorship of "Telemann's Musical Society" and focused instead on Bach's work as Cantor of the St. Thomas School.[3] It was Christoph Wolff, in his Bach biography *Johann Sebastian Bach: The Learned Musician*, who finally gave full due to the Collegium directorship and its central role in Bach's musical development during the Leipzig years. Drawing on the critical post-World War II studies of Werner Neumann[4] and Andreas Glöckner[5] and his own work on Bach's Leipzig chamber music,[6] Wolff outlined the history of the student ensemble founded by Telemann around 1701, traced Bach's involvement with the group, and set forth in several tables the instrumental and vocal works that Bach wrote or revised for Collegium performances.[7]

In Wolff's portrait of the composer, the Collegium directorship emerges as a major chapter in Bach's life—one that occupied a great deal of his energies from 1729 to about 1741 and shaped the music of his last two decades. We continue to learn new details about the Collegium—that members of the audience paid an admission fee of up to three groschen (approximately $9.00) to hear the ensemble perform, for instance.[8] What remains quite unclear, however, is the repertory of non-J.S. Bach works that filled out the Collegium programs. Newspaper reports and eyewitness accounts of the ensemble do not cite specific pieces that were performed. Moreover, printed programs listing the works to be played apparently were not distributed at the concerts, probably because the Collegium sessions seem to have been ad hoc "readings," with the evening's music not fully planned in advance.[9]

In the case of Bach's compositions, one can infer from the dating of manuscripts that certain pieces were intended for Collegium use. Also, for approximately a dozen celebratory vocal works (Cantatas 213, 214, 215, and others), printed text sheets were distributed—or more likely sold—to the audience. These not only identify the piece performed on a given occasion but also tell us something about the size of Bach's audience (upward of 200 for concerts in Zimmermann's Coffee House or Coffee Garden, as many as 600 to 700 for special market-square events).[10] As a result, we have a fairly good idea which compositions of Bach were earmarked for Collegium performance.

One is on much shakier ground regarding the Collegium's performance of works written by other composers. In many cases the manuscripts of the pieces have not survived or, if they have, it is difficult to establish their links with Bach's ensemble. The Collegium was a university seminar in which the members read through music. It is likely that university students and other participants brought performance materials to the concerts for consideration by the whole group. In such cases, Bach's hand would not appear in the parts or scores, since they were not written under his supervision. Nor would there be a direct link with Bach's personal library. Although the scribes attending St. Thomas's School who copied the parts of Bach's church cantatas have been heavily scrutinized and largely identified, most of the scribes of the Collegium materials—presumably university students—remain anonymous. It is possible that the Collegium repertory is reflected in the secular works listed in the sales catalogs of the Breitkopf firm, which appears to have acquired the manuscript estate of

Bach's assistant Gerlach after his death in 1761,[11] and in the estate catalog of Carl Philipp Emanuel Bach, who inherited much of his father's music collection.[12] Still, it has yet to be determined precisely which music from the Gerber and Emanuel Bach estates is related to Collegium performances and which is not—if, indeed, it can ever be discerned.

Thus, establishing the repertory of the Collegium beyond Bach's compositions remains a work in progress. In his Bach biography, Wolff laments this gap in our knowledge and mentions the small number of non-J.S. Bach pieces that can be securely linked to Collegium performances: music by Johann Bernhard Bach, Locatelli, Handel, Porpora, Alessandro Scarlatti, and Telemann.[13] To flesh out a bit further the skeletal picture of the Collegium repertory and performances, I would like to review the list of established works and propose a few new pieces to add to it.

For Bach, the opportunity to study and perform secular vocal and instrumental music of his contemporaries must have been a central factor in his decision to assume the directorship of the Collegium Musicum. As he expressed it in his petition of 1730 to the Leipzig Town Council, seeking better resources for church performances, "the state of music is quite different from what it was, since our artistry has increased very much, and the *gusto* has changed astonishingly, and accordingly the former style of music no longer seems to please our ears."[14] The progressive forces leading to this change are most clearly evident in secular works of Bach's Italian and Italian-oriented contemporaries, whose cutting-edge orchestral overtures, sinfonias, concertos, chamber sonatas, cantatas, and operas ushered in the new *galant* style. Features of *galant* writing include an emphasis on singable melodies rather than complicated counterpoint; transparent homophonic textures; symmetrical phrases; light scoring with strings as the core of the ensemble; straightforward forms; and, in vocal music, the use of Italian language.[15] These qualities appealed to the tastes of the coffee-drinking, tobacco-smoking audiences of "Cavaliers et Dames" (as announcements of the time put it) that attended the Collegium concerts, and they appear to be the common denominator in the non-J.S. Bach works that were performed by the university ensemble.

Instrumental Music

OVERTURES (ORCHESTRAL SUITES)

Johann Bernhard Bach: Five Ouvertures

It was Spitta who first pointed to Bach's copies of orchestral suites or "Ouvertüren" by his Eisenach colleague, Johann Bernhard Bach.[16] Four works are extant: the Orchestral Suites in D Major, G Major, and G Minor, in partly autograph parts (*St 318,*

St 319, and *St 320*, respectively), and an Orchestral Suite in E Minor preserved in a secondary score (*P 291*) copied by "S. Hering," a scribe from Carl Philipp Emanuel Bach's circle. A fifth orchestral suite, in G minor, is known to have existed from an entry in Emanuel Bach's estate catalogue.[17]

The obituary of 1754, written principally by Emanuel Bach and Johann Friedrich Agricola, mentions that Johann Bernhard Bach wrote "many fine overtures in the manner of Telemann." Indeed, the extant works show many Telemann-like qualities, including an emphasis on *galant* dances (passepied, gavotte en rondeau, rigaudon, marche), dances with whimsical names (*La Joye, Caprice, Les plaisirs*), and the use of ripieno-concertino forces in the overture movements. In the Overture to the Suite in G Minor, the use of solo violin in the episodes may have spurred Bach to use solo flute in a similar way in the Overture to the Orchestral Suite in B Minor, BWV 1067.[18] This trait, too, is found in Telemann's suites, such as those of the *Musique de Table* set of 1733. In the original materials of the G-Minor Suite, the intricate *Violino Concertino* part with very few articulation marks (indeed, fewer than the violin 1 part) and the continuo part with copious figures throughout suggest that for this work, at least, Bach led the Collegium from the concertmaster position, playing the solo violin part himself. This underscores Emanuel Bach's remark that until the approach of old age his father "played the violin cleanly and penetratingly and thus kept the orchestra in better order than he could have done with the harpsichord."[19]

The original performance materials for the Overtures in D Major, G Major, and G Minor point to a performance date of ca. 1730[20]—that is, just after Bach assumed the directorship of the Collegium. The presence of duplicate violin 1 and violin 2 parts in the D-Major and G-Minor Suites and three continuo parts in the D-Major and G-Major Suites suggests the use of large forces.

Agostino Steffani: Overture "La Tempête" from Il zelo di Leonato

The Overture from Steffani's *Il zelo di Leonata* appears as an "extra movement" in Johann Bernhard Bach's G-Major Orchestral Suite, written into the performance parts, *St 319*, after the concluding gigue. The Steffani overture appears to be hastily written, and in the violin 1, viola, bassoon, and figured continuo parts, Bach stepped in for the copyists to add the music, which is in the same key—G major—as the Bernhard Bach suite. This suggests a last-minute insertion, written under time pressure.

Titled *La Tempête*, the Steffani overture is a short, engaging work cast in the composer's progressive, turn-of-the-century Italian style (*Il zelo di Leonata*, a revision of *La superbia d'Alessandro*, premiered in Hanover in 1691).[21] The B section, marked *"très vite,"* is very animated and suggestive of a storm. It may be that Bach viewed this appealing programmatic piece as an encore, played in response to applause after Bernhard Bach's attractive orchestral suite.

Johann Friedrich Fasch: Ten Overtures

Hugo Riemann first referred to the manuscripts of ten orchestral suites by Fasch in the library of the St. Thomas School, partly in Bach's hand.[22] Of these manuscripts, only that of the Suite in B♭ Major for Two Oboes, Bassoon, Strings, and Continuo survived World War II, in the form of a set of performance parts (Leipzig, Thomasschule, on loan to the Stadtarchiv). Andreas Glöckner has shown that the parts to the B♭-Major Suite were written not by Bach but by Gerlach, most probably during the period 1747 to 1749.[23] This suggests that the suites were performed by the Collegium after Bach's departure, or by the Grand Concert Ensemble (*Grosse Concert-Gesellschaft*), a rival group established by Leipzig aristocrats and merchants in 1743 that Gerlach soon joined.

SINFONIAS

Franz Benda: Sinfonia in B♭ Major

Among the composers Bach "esteemed highly in his last years" and knew personally, according to his son Carl Philipp Emanuel,[24] was Franz Benda. A musician at the court of Frederick the Great in Berlin and a colleague of Emanuel there, Benda was the writer of progressive works, including preclassical sinfonias. He appears to have met Bach and his sons for the first time in March 1734, while passing through Leipzig,[25] and was later an eyewitness to Bach's visit with Frederick the Great in Potsdam in May 1747.[26]

In the Becker Collection of the Leipzig Music Library (Leipzig, Musikbibliothek), one finds a set of manuscript parts, *III.11.14*, for a Benda Sinfonia in B♭ Major for Two Violins, Viola, and Basso Continuo that can be linked to Bach's Collegium years. The parts, written on paper with a watermark found in Bach manuscripts from the 1730s,[27] were copied out and owned by "Kirchhoff," presumably Johann Friedrich Kirchhoff, *Stadtpfeifer* in Leipzig from 1737 to 1769, who probably played in Bach's Collegium before eventually joining the Grand Concert Ensemble, where his name appears as first oboist ("Hautbois 1. Concert.") in a roster dating from 1746 to 1748.[28] Given the date of the manuscript, it is possible that the piece was performed by Bach's Collegium in the late 1730s, under either Bach's direction or Gerlach's.[29]

The work follows the conventional three-movement sinfonia format—*allegro, andante, presto*—and has light, Italianate, preclassical textures (Example 1) similar to those espoused later by Johann Christian Bach, especially, in his sinfonias.

CONCERTOS

Pietro Locatelli: Concerto Grosso in F Minor, op. 1, no. 8

Arnold Schering appears to have been the first to note a performance of this work by Bach,[30] which is verified by an extant set of instrumental parts (Leipzig, Bach-Archiv,

Example 1. Franz Benda: Sinfonia in B♭ Major, movement 2, mm. 1–7.

Go.S. 4). Recent datings identify three performances by Bach: the first circa 1734, the second circa 1739, and the third circa 1748 (when a new *Violoncello Concertino* part was written out).[31] Bach made numerous corrections in the original set of parts and, at a much later date, wrote out the title and initial measure of the *Violoncello Concertino* part before turning over the copying to an anonymous scribe. Bach's stiff, awkward hand-writing in this source (Plate 1) closely resembles that of the divider pages of the B-Minor Mass, written in 1748–1749.[32] This suggests that Bach was involved with the Collegium in a hands-on way, from time to time at least, even during the very last years of his life. Several of the copyists of the earlier parts (those from circa 1734) were also involved in the preparation of the performance materials for the Christmas Oratorio, BWV 248, which led Hans-Joachim Schulze to suggest that the closing *Pastorale ad libitum* movement of the Locatelli may have influenced Bach's decision to write the so-called Pastoral Symphony ("Sinfonia" in the score) to Part II of the Christmas Oratorio.[33]

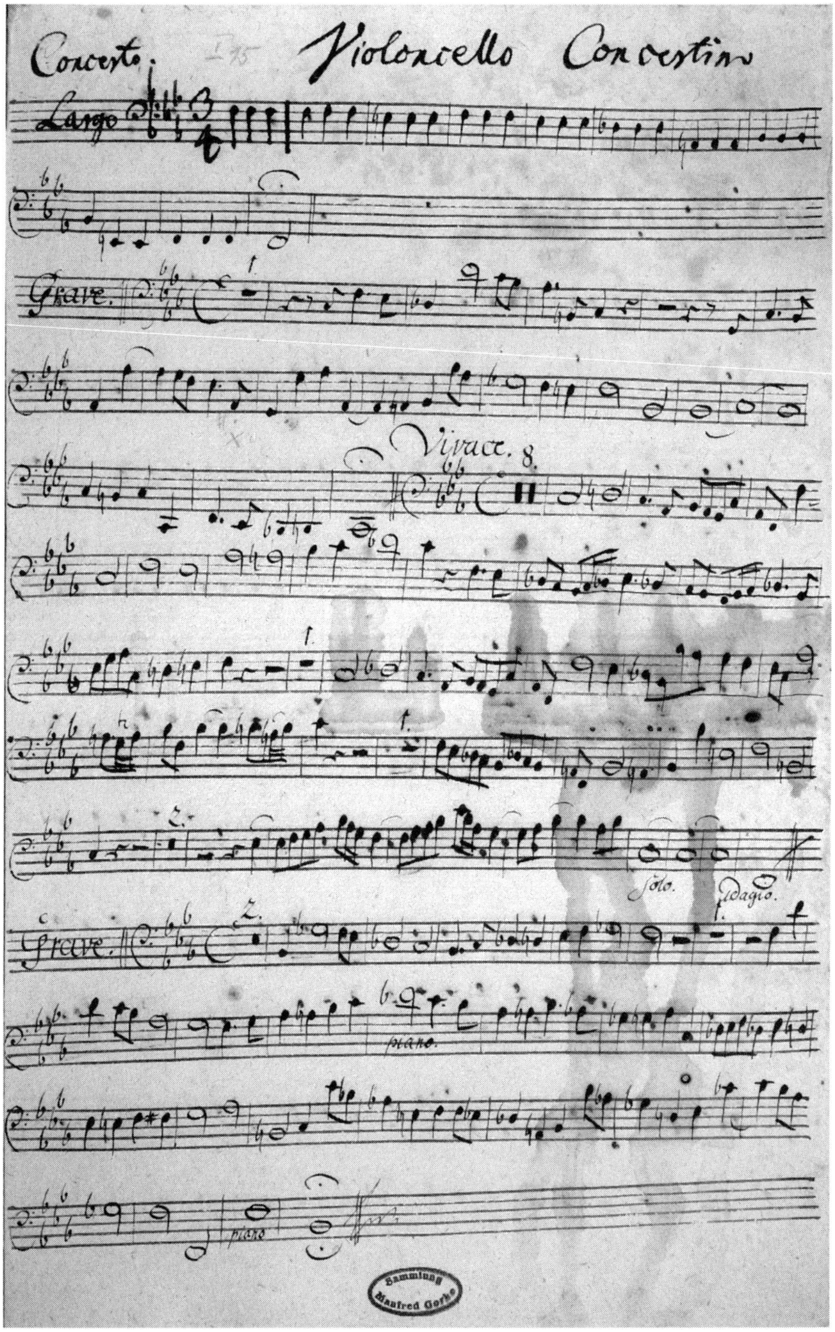

Plate 1. Pietro Locatelli: Concerto Grosso in F Minor, op. 1, no. 8. *Violoncello Concertino* part with title, initial tempo indication, clef, key and meter signatures, and first measure in the hand of J.S. Bach, ca. 1748, with remainder by an anonymous scribe. Leipzig, Bach-Archiv, *Go.S. 4*. Reproduced with permission of the Bach-Archiv.

One of the most striking features of the Locatelli concerto is the division of the string forces into grosso and concertino groups, in the manner of Corelli but with expanded forces, including a concertino of two violins, two violas, cello, and violone and a ripieno of two violins (violin 2 is missing in the extant set of parts), two violas, and basso. Locatelli's opus 1 was published in Amsterdam by Estienne Roger in 1721.

Wilhelm Friedemann Bach: Concerto for Two Harpsichords in F Major, Fk 10
A Leipzig performance of this work is indicated by a set of performance parts, *St 176*, copied out by J.S. Bach on Leipzig paper around 1742.[34] It is not surprising that Bach would have wanted to showcase his sons' compositions in performances with the Leipzig Collegium, in this instance championing a work in the form of a double harpsichord concerto, a genre he had developed in his own works performed with the ensemble in the 1730s.

In the performance of the F-Major Concerto, it is likely that father and son took the two harpsichord parts. When copying from Friedemann's autograph score, *P 325*, Sebastian remained faithful to his son's text, aside from clarifying notation and articulation and thickening chords here and there. Friedemann's concerto is cast in a progressive homophonic idiom that is markedly different from the heavily contrapuntal double-concertos of his father. Still, Sebastian's faithfulness to his son's score suggests that he respected the new style, even if he himself did not adopt it in his own concertos.

Johann Friedrich Wilhelm Sonnenkalb described Friedemann performing to great approbation with the Grand Concert Ensemble,[35] but this would not have taken place until after 1746, when Sonnenkalb first enrolled as a student at the St. Thomas School. A 1742 performance would have fallen to the Collegium.

Carl Philipp Emanuel Bach: Harpsichord Concerto in A Minor, H 403
Carl Philipp Emanuel is also represented by a harpsichord concerto, a work in A minor for which a set of performance parts (Krakow, Biblioteka Jagiellońska, *St. 495*) was copied on Leipzig paper by Emanuel and his father around 1746–1747.[36] Whether the work was performed by the Collegium under Bach's or Gerlach's direction, or by the newly formed Grand Concert Ensemble, cannot be determined with any degree of certainty. What is clear is that Bach had a hand in the preparations for the performance, and it appears that the parts remained in his possession and were inherited by Emanuel only after Sebastian's death.[37] This points to Bach's Collegium as the performing group. The work is the revised version of a concerto written in the 1730s, which raises the possibility that the piece may have been performed by the ensemble at that time, too.

Like the F-Major Concerto of Wilhelm Friedemann Bach, Emanuel's A-Minor Concerto displays qualities of the preclassical keyboard concerto, with an emphasis on *galant* gestures rather than severe counterpoint.

Johann David Heinichen: Trio Sonata in C Minor

This sonata is transmitted in a manuscript, *P 609*, written around 1731 by Christoph Nichelmann, a student at the Thomasschule from 1730 to 1733 and occasional copyist for Bach.[38] It seems safe to assume that Nichelmann copied the work from a manuscript owned by Bach[39] and that it served as repertoire for the Collegium in the early 1730s. The sonata, in four-movement format, is fully in accord with the progressive Italian style that Heinichen learned first-hand during his travels in Italy, before taking up residence at the Dresden court in 1717.

Georg Philipp Telemann: "Paris" Quartets

Bach's name appears on the list of subscribers published in the 1738 Paris edition of Telemann's Six Quartets for Transverse Flute, Violin, Bass, and Continuo: "Nom des Souscrivans des Pays Etrangers . . . Mr Bach . . . de Leipzig."[40] Bach's copy of the quartets is lost, but it is reasonable to assume that he would have ordered the music for Collegium performances in the late 1730s.

The quartets capitalize on the "sensitive" nature of the transverse flute and are written in the most fashionable French dance-suite style, employing light chamber meters (3/8, 2/4, 6/4, etc.) and affective movement titles (*Tendrement, Gaiment, Flatteusement, Gracieusement, Triste*, etc.).

Johann Gottlieb Graun: Trio Sonata in C Minor

Riemann referred to a now-lost manuscript, in Bach's hand, of a Trio Sonata in C Minor by Johann Gottlieb Graun in the possession of the Kaiserin-Augusta-Gymnasium, Berlin-Charlottenburg.[41] It carried the date "30. August 1742," the day Bach was in Kleinzschocher performing the *Cantate Burlesque, Mer hahn en neue Oberkeet* (Peasant Cantata), BWV 212, with his Collegium Musicum. The Graun sonata, cast in a progressive, sensitive Berlin *empfindsamer Stil* idiom in three movements (*Adagio, Allegro moderato*, and *Scherzo*), may well have been performed on this occasion. Graun was also included in Carl Philipp Emanuel's list of contemporary composers whom his father esteemed highly in his last years.[42]

Vocal Works

Nicola Antonio Porpora: Six Cantatas

In his examination of Gerlach's activities as organist and music director at the New Church, Andreas Glöckner identified three secular Italian cantatas by the Neapolitan composer Nicola Antonio Porpora that can be linked with Bach's Collegium: *Dal primo foco in cui penai*; *Ecco, ecco l'infausto lido*; and *Sopra un colle fiorito*.[43] They appear in two Leipzig manuscripts (Leipzig, Musikbibliothek, *III.5.24* and *III.5.25*), written around 1734 with Italian texts in the hand of Gerlach and music in the hand of Johann Ludwig Dietel, a student at St. Thomas School and the university and occasional copyist for Bach. Three other Porpora cantatas appear in the same manuscripts in Gerlach's hand alone: *D'amor la bella pace*, *La viola che languiva*, and *Tu ten vai cosi fastoso*. These, too, can be linked to performances by the Collegium. The six works are for soprano, alto, or contralto and harpsichord continuo, and Glöckner proposes that Gerlach intended them for his own use as a singer with Bach's Collegium (Gerlach sang alto and played violin and harpsichord as well).[44]

All six cantatas consist of sequences of alternating recitatives and arias, either in three movements (aria-recitative-aria) or four (recitative-aria-recitative-aria). They are cast in the advanced Neapolitan style that was sweeping through Europe at the time (Example 2). There is no indication of any accompanimental instrument other than the harpsichord, and thus the six cantatas can be viewed as a link with the "cembalization" of the continuo seen in Bach's chamber works calling for obbligato harpsichord without additional bass instrument, such as the violin, flute, and gamba sonatas and Cantata 203, *Amore traditore*.

Alessandro Scarlatti: Se Amor con un contento
Glöckner also identified as a Collegium work the Italian solo cantata *Se Amor con un contento* by Alessandro Scarlatti, which appears in Gerlach's hand in a manuscript from ca. 1734 (Leipzig, Musikbibliothek, *III.5.27*).[45] Like the Porpora cantatas, the work is written in the Neapolitan style, but for mezzo soprano and continuo (rather than harpsichord alone). Noteworthy here is the harmonically adventurous *da capo* aria "A'un povero cuore," which is cast in E♭ minor, with modulations to A♭ minor and B♭ minor in the B section.

George Frideric Handel: Dietro l'orme fuggaci *("Armida abbandonata"), HWV 105*
Handel's cantata *Dietro l'orme fuggaci* ("Armida abbandonata"), written in Rome in 1707, is passed down in a set of original performance parts (Darmstadt, Hessische Landesbibliothek, *Mus. ms. 986*) from ca. 1731. The parts were copied out by Bach, his son Carl Philipp Emanuel, and an anonymous scribe,[46] presumably for Collegium use. The parts are accompanied by an older manuscript score that may stem from Melchior Hofmann,[47] one of Bach's predecessors as Collegium director in Leipzig (Hofmann inherited the ensemble from Telemann in 1705 and led it until his death in 1715).

The seven-movement sequence of recitatives and arias is scored for soprano (missing from the Darmstadt parts), two violins, and continuo. Bach's parts are informative not only about the repertory of the Collegium, but also about the nature of its performances. Revealing in this regard are Bach's changes in the aria "Venti, fermate."

Example 2. Nicola Antonio Porpora: "Chieggo al lido" from *Ecco, ecco l'infausto lido*, mm. 1–24.

Handel notated the movement using two meters: the soprano and violins are in 2/4, and the continuo, with its extensive triplet figures, is in 6/8. In performance, the dotted figures of the upper parts were presumably absorbed into the triplet patterns of the continuo. When writing out the parts, Bach altered the meter of the continuo from 6/8 to 2/4, bringing it into metrical accord with the upper voices (Example 3).[48]

In Bach's new version of "Venti, fermate," the issue of rhythmic assimilation remains: Dotted figures must still be adjusted to fit into triplet patterns when they occur. Now, however, the overall spirit of the movement is uniform: The continuo joins the upper parts in playing in 2/4, a meter in which triplets, especially, are performed lightly and playfully—"just with the tip of the bow," according to Bach's student Johann Philipp Kirnberger.[49] This produces a metrical, rhythmic, and expressive

Example 3. a) Handel: "Venti, fermate" from *Dietro l'orme fuggaci* ("Armida abbando-nata"), HWV 105, mm. 1–8, as notated by the composer. b) Handel: "Venti, fermate" from *Dietro l'orme fuggaci* ("Armida abbandonata"), HWV 105, mm. 1–8, as notated by Bach. c) Bach: Brandenburg Concerto No. 5 in D Major, BWV 1050, movement 3, mm. 1–8.

similarity with the last movement of Brandenburg Concerto No. 5 in D Major, BWV 1050, which Bach notated in 2/4 meter rather than 6/8 despite its dominating triplet figures, presumably because the triplets would have been too "heavy" in 6/8 (see Example 3).

Bach also changed the rhythm in the continuo and violin 1 parts in a number of places, to clarify for the performer that the short notes should be "sharpened." Up to the return of the ritornello in m. 26, Bach notated isolated upbeat notes as eighth notes, in accordance with Handel's notation. From there onward, he "sharpened" them by turning them into sixteenth notes. Meanwhile, Carl Philipp Emanuel, who was writing out violin 2, continued to use the eighth notes of Handel's score (Example 4). One assumes that in performance, the player (or players) of violin 2 would have made rhythmic adjustments upon hearing the shorter notes of violin 1 and the continuo.

Finally, in the violin 2 part the music for the last movement, "In tanti affanni miei," does not appear at all. Violin 1 and violin 2 play in unison in this aria, and it seems

Example 4. Handel: "Venti, fermate," mm. 51–60 as they appear in Bach's performance parts (Darmstadt, Hessische Landesbibliothek, *Mus. ms. 986*).

likely that the player (or players) of violin 2 read off the violin 1 part for the duration of the movement.[50] This suggests intimate performance forces, in this instance, and considerable time pressure in preparing the parts.

Handel: Cantata and Three Arias

In Leipzig manuscripts from the Collegium period one also finds another cantata, *Dica il falso, dica il vero* (Leipzig, Musikbibliothek, *III.5.13*), for soprano, solo violin, strings, and harpsichord, along with three arias: "Amico il fato" (*III.15.45*), "E si dolce il mio contento" (*III.15.44*), and "Passagier ch'in selva oscura" (*III.15.43*) for soprano, two violins, and continuo ("E si dolce" also includes a viola part).[51] Although all four works are attributed to Handel, the cantata and last aria are not found among his known pieces and may be the work of another composer. The four works are listed in the Breitkopf catalog of 1768 (p. 31, where they are credited to "Hendel") and thus may represent music from Gerlach's estate performed by Bach's Collegium. This can be no more than speculation, however, as the two scribes of the manuscripts (one for the cantata, one for the arias) remain anonymous and cannot be securely linked to Bach or Gerber.

OPERA EXCERPTS

Handel: Two Arias from Alcina

Also handed down in Gerlach's hand are two arias from Handel's *Alcina*: Ruggiero's "Mi lusinga il dolce affetto" from Act II and Alcina's "Di, cor mio, quanto t'amai" from Act I, scored for soprano, strings, and continuo. The surviving materials (Leipzig, Musikbibliothek, *III.15.42*) (Plate 2), which appear to date from the same time as the manuscripts of the Porpora arias—that is, ca. 1734—include an abbreviated score for soprano and harpsichord (Plate 3) and additional parts for violin 1, violin 2, viola, basso (also labeled "Cembalo" and containing more continuo figures than the abbreviated score). This arrangement allows for two performance options: soprano and harpsichord alone, or soprano with string ensemble, much in the fashion of the aria "Schlummert ein, ihr matten Augen" from Cantata BWV 82, *Ich habe genug*, which is scored for alto, strings, and continuo in the cantata version but also appears as a continuo aria in the Notebook for Anna Magdalena of 1725.

Whereas *Dietro l'orme fuggaci* is one of Handel's early works, *Alcina* is a mature composition that premiered in London on April 16, 1735. If the two arias from *Alcina* were performed by Bach's Collegium in the mid-1730s with Gerlach as singer or ensemble leader, as now seems likely, they would have represented the very latest in fashionable opera music from the London stage.

Summary

The present discussion of the non-J.S. Bach works that were performed by the Collegium is summarized in Table 1, which lists the works of contemporary composers that can be connected with Bach's ensemble. Although the pieces represent only a tiny fraction of what must have been a vast repertory, they verify that the group focused on music written in an advanced, popular style. Among the instrumental works, the Benda sinfonia, Telemann quartets, Graun trio, and harpsichord concertos by Wilhelm Friedemann and Carl Philipp Emanuel Bach were especially progressive.

Of the vocal works, it is striking that all are in Italian and in the Neapolitan vein. The Leipzig opera house, opened by Nicolaus Adam Strungk in 1693 and later directed by Bach's Collegium-Director predecessors Georg Philipp Telemann and Melchior Hoffmann, provided fifteen performances during each of the annual trade fairs. The house closed in 1720, however, and was razed in 1729. From then until the construction of the Comödienhaus in 1766, opera was provided by itinerant Italian

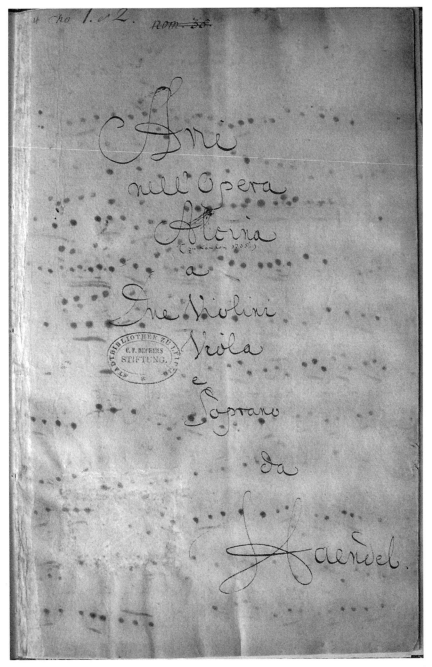

Plate 2. George Frideric Handel: Two arias from *Alcina*. Title page to a set of performance parts in the hand of Carl Gotthelf Gerlach, ca. 1734. Leipzig, Musikbibliothek, *III.15.42*. Reproduced with permission of the Musikbibliothek Leipzig.

Plate 3. George Frideric Handel: "Mi lusinga il dolce affetto" from Act II of
Alcina. Abbreviated score for soprano and harpsichord in the hand of Carl
Gotthelf Gerlach, ca. 1734. Leipzig, Musikbibliothek, *III.15.42*. Reproduced
with permission of the Musikbibliothek Leipzig.

Table 1. The Repertory of Bach's Collegium: Works by Contemporary Composers

Composer	Work	Date(s) of Performance
Instrumental Music		
Overtures (Orchestral Suites)		
Johann Bernhard Bach	Orchestral Suite in E Minor	ca. 1730
	Orchestral Suite in D Major	ca. 1730
	Orchestral Suite in G Major	ca. 1730
	Orchestral Suite in G Minor	ca. 1730
	Orchestral Suite in G Minor	ca. 1730
Agostino Steffani	Overture "La Tempête" from *Il zelo di Leonata* (1691)	ca. 1730
Sinfonias		
Franz Benda	Sinfonia in B♭ Major	ca. 1737
Concertos		
Pietro Locatelli	Concerto Grosso in F Minor, op. 1, no. 8 (1721)	ca. 1734, ca. 1739, ca. 1748
Wilhelm Friedemann Bach	Concerto for Two Harpsichords in F Major, Fk 10	ca. 1742
Carl Philipp Emanuel Bach	Concerto for Harpsichord in A Minor, H 403	ca. 1746
Chamber Sonatas		
Johann David Heinichen	Trio Sonata in C Minor	ca. 1731
Georg Philipp Telemann	"Paris" Quartets (1738)	ca. 1738
Johann Gottlieb Graun	Trio Sonata in C Minor	ca. 1742

(continued)

151

Table 1. (continued)

Composer	Work	Date(s) of Performance
Vocal Works		
Italian Chamber Cantatas		
George Frideric Handel	Cantata: *Dietro l'orme fuggaci* ("*Armida Abbandonata*"; 1707), HWV 105	ca. 1731
Nicola Antonio Porpora	Cantata: *Dal primo foco in cui penai*	ca. 1734
	Cantata: *Sopra un colle fiorito*	ca. 1734
	Cantata: *Ecco, ecco l'infausto lido*	ca. 1734
	Cantata: *D'amor la bella pace*	ca. 1734
	Cantata: *Tu ten vai così fastoso*	ca. 1734
	Cantata: *La viola che languiva*	ca. 1734
Alessandro Scarlatti	Cantata: *Se Amor con un contento*	ca. 1734
Opera Excerpts		
George Frideric Handel	*Alcina* (1735): "Mi lusinga il dolce affetto" and "Di, cor mio, quanto t'amai"	ca. 1735

troupes that performed on temporary stages during the fair times. Although the Leipzig chronicler Johann Salomon Riemer reported seeing the intermezzo *Amor fa l'uomo cieco* with Italian castratos and prima donnas during the 1744 Easter Fair,[52] such productions were few and far between.

The Collegium performances of Italian cantatas and opera arias by Porpora, Scarlatti, Handel, and others helped to fill the gap. They underscore the strong interest in Italian-texted works and present a broader context for Bach's two secular compositions in that style, Cantata 203, *Amore traditore*, and Cantata 209, *Non sa che sia dolore*. The "Cavaliers et Dames" who attended the Collegium concerts wanted to hear new, fashionable music. Bach and his ensemble appear to have provided it.

Notes

1. On the three-week duration of the fairs, see George B. Stauffer, "Leipzig: A Cosmopolitan Trade Centre," in *Music and Society: The Late Baroque Era*, ed. George J. Buelow (Englewood Cliffs, N.J.: Prentice-Hall, 1993), 256–57.

2. See Andreas Glöckner, "Bachs Leipziger Collegium Musicum und seine Vorgeschichte," in *Die Welt der Bach Kantaten*, vol. 2 (*Johann Sebastian Bachs weltliche Kantaten*), ed. Christoph Wolff (Kassel: Bärenreiter/Stuttgart: J.B. Metzler, 1997), 111 and 116.

3. Philipp Spitta, *Johann Sebastian Bach* (Leipzig: Breitkopf & Härtel, 1873–1880); English translation: Clara Bell and J.A. Fuller-Maitland, trs. (London: Novello, 1889; reprint New York: Dover, 1951), vol. 3, 17–19.

4. Werner Neumann, "Das Bachische Collegium Musicum," BJ 47 (1960), 5–27, and the KBs to NBA I/36 (*Festmusiken für das Kurfürstlich-Sächsische Haus I*), NBA I/37 (*Festmusiken für das Kurfürstlich-Sächsische Haus II*), NBA I/38 (*Festmusiken zu Leipziger Universitätsfeiern*), NBA I/39 (*Festmusiken für Leipziger Rats-und Schulfeiern/Huldigungsmusiken für Adlige und Bürger*), and NBA I/40 (*Hockzeits-kantaten — Weltliche Kantaten Verschiedener Bestimmung*).

5. Andreas Glöckner, "Neuerkenntnisse zu J.S. Bachs Aufführungskalender zwischen 1729 und 1735," BJ 67 (1981), 66–75; "Die Musikpflege an der Leipziger Neukirche zur Zeit Johann Sebastian Bachs," published as *Beiträge zur Bachforschung* 8 (1990); and "Bachs Leipziger Collegium Musicum," 105–17.

6. Christoph Wolff, "Bach's Leipzig Chamber Music," *Early Music* 13 (1985), 165–75, reprinted in Wolff, *Bach: Essays on His Life and Music* (Cambridge, Mass.: Harvard University Press, 1991), 223–38.

7. Christoph Wolff, *Johann Sebastian Bach: The Learned Musician* (New York: W.W. Norton, 2000), 351–65.

8. As revealed in the testimony of Bach's student Johann Friedrich Schweinitz, cited by Hans-Joachim Schulze in "Johann Friedrich Schweinitz, 'A Disciple of the Famous Herr Bach in Leipzig,'" chapter 7 in this book, 82. The estimated dollar value of the groschen is taken from NBR, 527.

9. Johann Adam Hiller's description of Johann Christoph Götze and Johann Georg Pisendel reading through Torelli concertos in the Collegium in 1709 gives a clear sense of the impromptu nature of the sessions. It is quoted in Glöckner, "Bachs Leipziger Collegium Musicum," 108–9.

10. Hellmuth von Hase, "Breitkopfsche Textdrücke zu Leipziger Musikaufführungen zu Bachs Zeiten," BJ 10 (1913), 69–127.

11. See especially Andreas Glöckner, "Fasch-Ouvertüren aus Johann Sebastian Bachs Notenbibliothek?," BJ 76 (1990), 66–69. The Breitkopf catalogs and supplements with music incipits have been issued in a modern reprint: *The Breitkopf Thematic Catalogue: The Six Parts and Sixteen Supplements 1762–1787*, ed. Barry S. Brook (New York: Dover, 1966).

12. *Verzeichniß des musikalischen Nachlasses des verstorbenen Capellmeisters Carl Philipp Emanuel Bach* (Hamburg, 1790). The catalog has been transcribed in BJ 35 (1938), 36 (1939), and 37 (1940–1948), and issued in a modern facsimile, *The Catalog of Carl Philipp Emanuel Bach's Estate*, ed. Rachel W. Wade (New York: Garland, 1981).

13. Wolff, *Johann Sebastian Bach*, 355.

14. NBR, 149.

15. The features of the *galant* style in Bach's time are nicely summarized by Robert L. Marshall in "Bach the Progressive: Observations on His Later Works," in Marshall, *The Music of Johann Sebastian Bach: The Sources, the Style, the Significance* (New York: Schirmer Books, 1989), 23–58, especially 32–34.

16. Spitta, *Johann Sebastian Bach*, vol. 1, 25–26.

17. Carl Philipp Emanuel Bach, *Verzeichniß*, 83.

18. See Hermann Max's comments in the modern edition of the work (Stuttgart: Carus-Verlag, 1988), preface; and, most recently, Joshua Rifkin, "The 'B-Minor Flute Suite' Deconstructed: New Light on Bach's Ouverture BWV 1067," in *Bach Perspectives 6: J.S. Bach's Concerted Ensemble Music, The Overture*, ed. Gregory G. Butler (Urbana and Chicago: University of Illinois Press, 2007), 1–98.

19. NBR, 397.

20. Glöckner, "Neuerkenntnisse," 61.

21. A keyboard arrangement of the overture from Steffani's *La Briseïde* (Hanover, 1696) appears in the Möller Manuscript (Berlin, Staatsbibliothek zu Berlin, *Mus.ms. 40644*) from ca. 1705, suggesting that Bach was familiar with Steffani's music at an early age.

22. Hugo Riemann, "Die französische Ouverture (Orchestersuite) in der ersten Hälfte des 18. Jahrhunderts," *Musikalisches Wochenblatt* 30 (1898–1899), nos. 1–9, 113–15 and 129.

23. Glöckner, "Fasch-Ouvertüren," 65–69. According to Glöckner, the manuscripts to the Fasch suites were purchased from Gerlach's estate by Breitkopf, who subsequently listed the works in their catalogs.

24. NBR, 400.

25. BDOK III, 731.

26. NBR, 412.

27. "Heraldische Lilie, auf Steg," no. 74 in NBA IX/1 (*Katalog der Wasserzeichen in Bachs Originalhandschriften*). It is found in Bach compositions and documents from 1729, 1734, and 1737. On the Benda manuscript and watermark, see also Douglas A. Lee, *Franz Benda (1709–1786): A Thematic Catalogue of His Works* (New York: Pendragon Press, 1984), 5–6 and 207 (Watermark 104). Lee dates the work "before 1766" on the basis of its appearance in the Breitkopf catalog of that year (see n. 29).

28. The roster appears as part of a diagram of the ensemble found in Johann Salomon Riemer's manuscript chronicle of Leipzig life (Leipzig, Stadtarchiv).

29. The work later appears in the Breitkopf catalog of 1766 (p. 3), and hence it may be connected with Gerlach's estate.

30. Arnold Schering, *Musikgeschichte Leipzigs* (Leipzig: B.G. Teubner, 1941), vol. 3, 134.

31. Hans-Joachim Schulze, in *Katalog der Sammlung Manfred Gorke* (Leipzig: Musikbibliothek der Stadt Leipzig, 1977), 15, proposes dates of 1734–1735 and circa 1748; Yoshitake Kobayashi, in "Zur Chronologie der Spätwerke Johann Sebastian Bachs," BJ 74 (1988), 42, puts forward an additional date of 1738–1739.

32. See *Johann Sebastian Bach. Messe in h-moll BWV 232. Faksimile der autographen Partitur* (Kassel: Bärenreiter Verlag, 1965; reprint 1984).

33. Hans-Joachim Schulze, "Ein apokryphes Händel-Concerto in J.S. Bach's Handschrift," BJ 66 (1980), 30.

34. Kobayashi, "Zur Chronologie," 51.

35. BDOK III, no. 703.

36. Hans Joachim Marx, "Wiederaufgefundene Autographe von Carl Philipp Emanuel Bach und Johann Sebastian Bach," *Musikforschung* 41 (1988), 150–56.

37. Marx, "Wiederaufgefundene Autographe," 155.

38. Hans-Joachim Schulze, "Der Schreiber 'Anonymus 400': ein Schüler Johann Sebastian Bachs," BJ 58 (1972), 104–17.

39. Kirsten Beißwenger places the work in Bach's personal music library, in *Johann Sebastian Bachs Notenbibliothek* (Kassel: Bärenreiter, 1992), 359–60.

40. BDOK II, no. 425.

41. *Johann Gottlieb Graun: Sonata a tre*, ed. Hugo Riemann (Collegium Musicum series) (Leipzig: Breitkopf & Härtel, 1906), no. 26.

42. NBR, 400.

43. Glöckner, "Neuerkenntnisse," 57–69.

44. As Glöckner notes in "Neuerkenntnisse," 60, Gerlach received payment as an alto during Bach's visit to Weißenfels on February 23, 1729. See BDOK II, 187–88.

45. Glöckner, "Neuerkenntnisse," 68.

46. The parts were first described by Oswald Bill in "Die Liebesklage der Armida. Händels Kantate HWV 105 im Spiegel Bachscher Aufführungspraxis," in *Ausstellung aus Anlaß der Händel-Festspiele des Badischen Staatstheater Karlsruhe 1985* (Karlsruhe: Badische Landisbibliothek und Badisches Staatstheater, 1985), 25–40. The dating given here is that proposed by Glöckner in "Neuerkenntnisse," 50.

47. Andreas Glöckner, cited by Hans Joachim Marx in *Hallische Händel-Ausgabe*, V/3 (*Kantaten mit Instrumenten II*) (Kassel: Bärenreiter, 1995), XXIII.

48. Both the Handel-Gesamtausgabe (*The Works of George Frederic Handel*, ed. Friedrich Chrysander [Leipzig: German Handel Society, 1888], vol. 52A, 158–59) and the *Hallische Händel-Ausgabe* (XXIII,

47–48) print "Venti, fermate" as an odd compilation, using Bach's meter (2/4) with Handel's note values (appropriate for 6/8) for the continuo part.

49. Johann Philipp Kirnberger, *Die Kunst des reinen Satzes in der Musik* (Berlin and Königsberg, 1776), vol. 2, part 1, 118–20.

50. This possibility was first proposed by Bill, in "Die Liebesklage der Armida," 34.

51. The manuscripts are tied to the Collegium era by their watermarks, which appear in Bach manuscripts from the 1730s and 1740s: *III.5.13* = NBA IX/1, no. 74; *III.15.45* = NBA IX/1, no. 111; *III.15.44* = NBA IX/1, no. 46; *III.15.43* = NBA IX/1, no. 110.

52. Stauffer, "Leipzig: A Cosmopolitan Trade Centre," 284.

A Print of *Clavierübung* I from J.S. Bach's Personal Library

Andrew Talle

Over the course of his long career in Leipzig, Johann Sebastian Bach saw seven editions of his works into print (Table 1). Each of these publications generated several hundred exemplars,[1] most of which were sold to colleagues, friends, students, and the general public (often at the three annual Leipzig trade fairs) or given away as special gifts. Each time Bach issued a publication, however, he seems to have kept a certain number of prints for himself, at least one of which served as his personal copy, or *Handexemplar*, of the work. Into these prints he often entered, by hand, corrections and small changes to the musical text. In many cases scholars have been able to identify these personal copies from among the surviving original prints preserved in libraries and private collections today. In 1951 Walter Emery identified Bach's personal copy of *Clavierübung* II,[2] and in the late 1970s Christoph Wolff was able to identify the *Handexemplare* of *Clavierübung* III and the Schübler Chorales.[3] Most spectacularly, Wolff identified Bach's personal copy of *Clavierübung* IV (Goldberg Variations), which included fourteen canons on the opening bass notes of the work's aria.[4] Only two of the canons had been known previously.

By contrast, the identity of the *Handexemplar* of Bach's first keyboard publication, *Clavierübung* I, has never been entirely secure. The existence of a personal copy of this print was documented as early as 1774, when Carl Philipp Emanuel Bach mentioned it to the historian (and later author of the first Bach biography) Johann Nicolaus Forkel in a letter from August 9 of that year:

> From my deceased father's published music there are no more prints available; also the plates are no longer extant. What I have of these, namely the first and third parts [of the *Clavierübung* series], I can offer you bound so that you might copy them, or I can even sell them to you. These two prints together formerly cost six *Reichstaler*; if you don't wish to make copies I can sell them to you, cleanly bound and very well preserved, for eight *Reichstaler*. I have the deceased man's manuscript, which serves my purposes, and you would have the print, which he himself formerly possessed. You need not feel at all awkward about this.[5]

Table 1. Original Prints Issued During J.S. Bach's Leipzig Years

Date	Publication	Contents	BWV
1726–1731	*Clavierübung* I	Six Partitas for keyboard	825–830
1735	*Clavierübung* II	Italian Concerto, French Ouverture	971, 831
1739	*Clavierübung* III	Various works for organ	552, 669–689, 802–805
1741	*Clavierübung* IV	Goldberg Variations	988
1747	The Musical Offering	Variations and canons on a theme by Frederick the Great	1079
1748	Canonic variations on *Vom Himmel hoch*	Canonic variations for organ	769
ca. 1748	Schübler Chorales	Six chorales for organ	645–650

The sale to Forkel of both exemplars, along with Bach's personal copy of the Schübler Chorales, was finalized two weeks later, as revealed in Emanuel's letter to Forkel of August 26:

> Herewith you receive the two books; thank you very much for the correct payment. Bound in at the back of the first book [*Clavierübung* III] you will also find the 6 printed chorales. The manuscript markings in this print are from the hand of the late composer himself.[6]

When Forkel died in 1818, Bach's personal copy of *Clavierübung* I was still in his possession. His estate catalogue of 1819 contains an entry that reads: "Clavierübung best. in Präludien, Allemanden etc. [1]731. in 4. O[pus]. I." Later in the catalogue the print is described as "des Verfassers eigenes Exemplar" (the composer's own exemplar).[7]

In the 1978 critical report accompanying his edition of *Clavierübung* I for the *Neue Bach Ausgabe*, Richard Douglas Jones was able to locate twenty-four surviving exemplars of the original print. He noted that among the copies there are five that contain a substantial number of handwritten corrections and revisions dating from the eighteenth century.[8] These exemplars are listed here in Table 2, together with their numbering from Jones's critical report, their present locations, and their call numbers.

Jones observed that the corrections in these exemplars overlap in complex ways. Copies G23 and G25 contain the same detailed emendations, some of which concern minute refinements—for example, the same mordent changed into a turn,[9] an upward stem added to the same quarter note that already had a downward stem,[10] and grace notes added in the same places.[11] Similarly, the writer or writers who corrected G23 and G24 decided to correct the same mordent to a turn[12] and erase another mordent

Table 2. Exemplars of the Original Print of *Clavierübung* I
with Substantial Corrections

Print (NBA listing)	Location	Call Number
G23	London, British Library	*Hirsch III, 37*
G24	Berlin, Staatsbibliothek zu Berlin	*DMS 224 676 (1) Rara*
G25	Washington, Library of Congress	*LM3. 3B2 CASE*
G26	Urbana, Illinois, University of Illinois Library	*xq. 786. 41/B 12 cu*
G28	Vienna, Österreichische Nationalbibliothek	Hoboken Collection, *J. S. Bach 56*

to move it back one note.[13] G25, G26, and G28 have in common a substantial re-working of the second half of the *Gigue* from Partita 3.[14] Despite striking similarities of the five prints, in terms of the corrections they contain, each has a large number of unique readings, suggesting that no set of revisions was copied entirely from one surviving print to another.

Given that the texts in Bach's personal copies normally contain handwritten changes, the five prints identified by Jones seem a logical place to begin the search for Bach's *Handexemplar* of *Clavierübung* I. In 1952 Emery proposed that G23, the copy owned by the British Library, might be the print that C.P.E. Bach sold to Forkel in 1774.[15] He based his argument on three points:

1. G23 has many more emendations and additions than any other surviving print, including the other four in the highly corrected group.
2. The changes resemble in appearance and character those in Bach's known *Handexemplar* of *Clavierübung* II.
3. The handwriting could be that of J.S. Bach—at least in some cases.

Jones accepted Emery's argument and put it on a more solid footing by systematically detailing the changes to the printed text.[16] Despite objections from Christoph Wolff that Jones's identification of G23 as Bach's personal copy of *Clavierübung* I was "hypothetical" and led him to neglect important manuscript variants in the other four heavily corrected exemplars when editing the *Neue Bach-Ausgabe*,[17] Jones's conclusion has gained widespread acceptance. Ernest May listed G23 as Bach's *Handexemplar* in his survey of the connections between Breitkopf and J.S. Bach published in 1996,[18] and the publishing firm of J.M. Fuzeau issued a facsimile edition of G23 with a preface written by Philippe Lescat in which he, too, asserts without qualification that the annotations in the print are those of J.S. Bach.[19] Jones himself responded to Wolff's criticism by devoting a great deal of attention to the handwritten variants in G24, G25, G26, and G28 in his 1988 doctoral dissertation[20] and in a nineteen-page supplement (1997) to his critical report of 1978 for the *Neue Bach-Ausgabe*. In all these writings, Jones has held fast to his belief that G23 is Bach's *Handexemplar* and that handwritten additions to the other corrected prints can be accepted only "in so far as these readings accord with those of G23."[21]

There are, however, reasons to doubt that G23 is the print referred to by C.P.E. Bach as his father's personal copy. The earliest known owner of G23 was Johann Gottfried Schicht (1753–1823), Cantor of the St. Thomas School from 1810–1823. As noted earlier, Bach's personal print belonged to Forkel until 1819. It is conceivable that Schicht acquired the print sometime between 1819 and his own death four years later. Given the binding of G23, however, this scenario is unlikely. In the letter to Forkel quoted earlier, C.P.E. Bach described his father's *Handexemplar* as "sauber gebunden"—that is, "finely," or professionally, bound. Indeed, the luxurious binding seems to have led Emanuel to ask Forkel for an additional *Reichstaler*.[22] An idea of the type of high-quality binding one would expect to find in Bach's personal copy of *Clavierübung* I can be gained from an examination of the *Handexemplar* of *Clavierübung* III (now Leipzig, Stadtbibliothek, *PM 1403*) that Emanuel sold to Forkel for the same price around the same time. It is professionally bound in solid, multiple-ply pasteboard with a leather spine and corners.[23] G23, by contrast, is not properly bound at all, but rather wrapped in a crude, single-ply, blue cardboard cover that bears Schicht's signature, indicating that it dates from before his death in 1823. It seems very unlikely that this shoddily bound copy of *Clavierübung* I is the exemplar that C.P.E. Bach described to Forkel as "sauber gebunden" and for which he demanded an extra *Reichstaler*.[24] It seems equally unlikely that either Forkel, during the forty-five years he owned the print, or Schicht, during the four years he theoretically might have owned it, would have replaced the solid eighteenth-century binding described by C.P.E. Bach with a slipshod cardboard wrapper.

Further arguing against G23 as the exemplar C.P.E. Bach sold to Forkel is a keyboard manuscript now catalogued as *P 212* in the Berlin Staatsbibliothek and labeled H1 by Jones in his critical report. H1 has a title page in Forkel's hand that reads: "Sammlung einiger auserlesenen Claviercompositionen aus den grösten Werken von *Johann Sebastian, Wilhelm Friedemann* und *Carl Phil. Emanuel* Bach gezogen" (Collection of selected keyboard compositions drawn from the greatest works of Johann Sebastian, Wilhelm Friedemann and Carl Philipp Emanuel Bach).[25] The music by J.S. Bach in this manuscript is drawn from numerous collections, including individual movements from the Well-Tempered Clavier, the English Suites, the French Suites, and *Clavierübung* I.[26] H1 was prepared by Forkel together with an anonymous scribe, apparently an assistant. Given that it does not appear in Forkel's estate catalogue, it seems likely that the manuscript was prepared on behalf of a third party. Forkel's extensive library of works by the Bach family was almost certainly the source from which the movements in this manuscript were chosen and copied. If Forkel indeed owned G23, one would expect to find its handwritten corrections reflected in the music copied by Forkel and his associate into H1. This is not the case, however.[27] On the same grounds, it seems unlikely that G24 and G25 were owned by Forkel.[28]

Interestingly, another manuscript once owned by Forkel does in fact transmit a large number of revisions documented in one of the corrected exemplars. This manuscript, containing a complete copy of *Clavierübung* I and labeled H68 by Jones, was formerly in the possession of Carl Bär in Rapperswil, Switzerland, and is now owned by an anonymous private collector.[29] It represents a complete copy of *Clavierübung* I. As in the case of H1, the bulk of the musical text was written by an anonymous scribe working on behalf of Forkel, but the title page and the meticulous corrections of copying errors were carried out by Forkel himself.[30] Like H1, H68 does not appear in Forkel's estate catalogue, suggesting that it, too, was copied from a source in his library on behalf of a third party, who acquired the manuscript upon its completion.[31] H68 includes each and every one of the many manuscript corrections found in G28 and displays no other deviations from the printed text. Judging from the estate catalogue, Forkel owned only one copy of *Clavierübung* I. The leather binding of G28 is certainly "sauber," though its origin remains unknown.[32] Thus, it seems safe to conclude that G28, whose text is reflected in H68, was in fact owned by J.S. Bach before 1750, by C.P.E. Bach before 1774, and by Forkel from 1774 to 1818.[33]

The provenance of G28 after Forkel's death is not entirely clear. Anthony van Hoboken (1887–1983) donated it to the Österreichisches Nationalbibliothek in 1974. An *ex libris* sticker on the inside cover of the print reads "Ex Bibliotheca J. W. Six," suggesting that it once belonged to the Dutch collector Jan Willem Six van Vromade (1874–1936). Six's extensive library was auctioned in Amsterdam in three lots between 1925 and 1930, and the 1925 auction catalogue contains an entry for *Clavierübung* I.[34] It may have been around this time that van Hoboken acquired the print. Although it is possible that Six himself purchased the print before 1925, it is perhaps more likely that he inherited it from one of his ancestors. The Six family, famous for its patronage of the arts, traces its lineage back to Jan Six (1616–1700), who was portrayed by Rembrandt in 1654. The family's early interest in music is well documented.[35] Is it possible that a member of the Six family acquired the exemplar of *Clavierübung* I from Forkel's estate around 1819? To date there is no evidence concerning the matter.

The handwritten revisions to the musical text of G28 were comprehensively documented for the first time by Jones in his 1988 doctoral dissertation.[36] Emendations are found in six movements of the suites, though only those in the following three movements can be considered musically substantive:

Plate 1. *Capriccio* from Partita 2 in C Minor, BWV 826, first half, in copy of the original print of 1731 now located in Vienna, Österreichische Nationalbibliothek, Hoboken Collection, *J. S. Bach 56*.

PARTITA 2: *ALLEMANDE*: Turns have been added to the soprano voice in mm. 2 and 26 (the analogous passage in the second half of the binary form). They both appear on eighth notes at the ends of phrases consisting primarily of faster notes, and they lend vitality to the phrase elision that takes place in each case.

PARTITA 2: *CAPRICCIO*: Mordents have been added to the second note of the theme wherever it occurs in the first half (mm. 1, 5, 19, 28, 37, 40, and 42; see Plate 1). They serve to accent the off-beat nature of the figure. Curiously, the mordents do not appear in the second half, possibly because the theme never appears again in its original guise (ascending fourth) but only inverted (descending fifth, as in m. 49) or melodically altered (ascending fifth or seventh, as in mm. 89 and 93). In addition to the mordents, turns have been added to the final eighth notes of the soprano voice in mm. 32 and 34. Like the turns in the *Allemande*, those in the *Capriccio* add energy and flair to cadential passages.

PARTITA 3: *GIGUE*: As noted earlier, G28 has in common with G25 and G26 a substantial reworking of the second half of this movement (Plate 2). Of the three slightly different revisions of the *Gigue*—G25, G26, and G28—one suspects that G28 was written last, as G25 and G26 were part of the second print run and G28 was part of the third.[37] Each of the three revised versions of the *Gigue* is unique; none was

Plate 2. *Gigue* from Partita 3 in A Minor, BWV 827, second half, in copy of the original print of 1731 now located in Vienna, Österreichische Nationalbibliothek, Hoboken Collection, *J. S. Bach 56*.

directly copied from another. Yet all share a common goal: to arrive at a more exact inversion of the fugal theme.

Although the revisions to the *Allemande* and *Capriccio* of the second partita seem uncontroversial, the changes to the *Gigue* of Partita 3 raise perplexing issues. Jones has drawn attention to what he considers unsatisfactory musical aspects of the reworking of the *Gigue* in all three revised versions. Indeed, inverting the theme more exactly leads to counterpoint problems during the course of the second half of the binary form, and none of the three versions is able to solve them all.[38]

A further strike against G28 as Bach's personal copy comes from the fact that the handwritten changes were not made by the composer himself. The handwriting does not match that of J.S. Bach, nor does it match that of any of his four sons whose handwriting is well documented: Wilhelm Friedemann, Carl Philipp Emanuel, Johann Christoph Friedrich, or Johann Christian Bach. Certain graphological characteristics suggest that the scribe was relatively young and that the print was altered before 1750,[39] but beyond this virtually nothing can be said about the identity of the scribe. Might this be the work of Johann Gottfried Bernhard Bach, who died in 1739 at age 24?

G28 thus places us in an interesting interpretive predicament. This print seems clearly to be the one C.P.E. Bach described as "the print which he [J.S. Bach] himself formerly possessed," and yet the handwritten additions arouse suspicion rather than confidence because of their questionable musical merit and lack of scribal connection to Bach. Even if Bach sanctioned the manuscript changes in G28, I see no reason to believe that he saw them as constituting a more successful version of the piece. In fact, in 1748 Bach presented his thirteen-year-old son Johann Christian (1735–1782) with an individual print of Partita 3 in which the *Gigue* remains unaltered.[40] This suggests that even at the end of his life Bach did not feel that the altered versions of the *Gigue* were superior to his original conception. Thus, despite the favorable pedigree of G28, for which I have argued in this chapter, its contrapuntal problems, its scribe's unknown identity, and its failure to have served as a model for J.C. Bach's print all conspire to prevent us from accepting it as the composer's *Fassung letzter Hand*.

In my view, however, G28 represents something more interesting than a final, fixed version of the piece. Since one of the three sources for the alternate reading of the *Gigue* can now be connected directly with J.S. Bach, it seems all the more appropriate to follow Wolff's suggestion that we see these readings as viable supplements to the printed musical text.[41] To be sure, the exact circumstances under which these prints were revised remain a matter of speculation. The most plausible scenario, perhaps, is that sometime after 1731 the inconsistent inversion of the second half of the *Gigue* of Partita 3 came to interest or perhaps even irritate Bach. In the course of giving lessons, he brought this passage to the attention of his students, offering guidance as to how the theme might be more exactly inverted. The three surviving solutions in G25, G26, and G28 differ because Bach's suggestions changed from one lesson to the next—a process one can observe in student manuscript copies of the Well-Tempered Clavier, the Inventions and Sinfonias, and other keyboard works used for didactic purposes. Perhaps after some initial instruction the composer left each student to resolve the counterpoint problems for himself.[42]

Whether or not the exact scenario suggested here is true, it seems clear that the revisions in G25, G26, and G28 were set in motion by a single mind, though they were copied down by separate hands. Recognizing now the connection of G28, the Österreichische Nationalbibliothek exemplar of *Clavierübung* I, to the composer's personal library of prints (Table 3), it is difficult to imagine a scenario in which this mind belonged to someone other than J.S. Bach himself. The identification of G28 as the print that C.P.E. Bach singled out as his father's personal copy of *Clavierübung* I lends welcome support for the idea that the composer was involved in inspiring the altered versions of the *Gigue* from Partita 3 that were first highlighted by Christoph Wolff in 1979. The print itself can serve not as Bach's definitive version of the piece, but rather as a testament to the flexibility of printed texts in the eighteenth century.

Table 3. Original Prints of Bach's Music Once Contained in the Composer's Personal Library

Publication	*Personal Copy*
Clavierübung I	Vienna, Österreichische Nationalbibliothek, Hoboken Collection, *J. S. Bach 56*
Clavierübung II	London, British Library, *K.8.g.7*
Clavierübung III	Leipzig, Stadtbibliothek, *PM 1403*
Clavierübung IV	Paris, Bibliothèque Nationale, *Ms. 17669*
Musical Offering	unidentified
Canonic variations on *Vom Himmel hoch*	Berlin, Staatsbibliothek, *P271*
Schübler Chorales	Princeton, New Jersey, Princeton University Library, Scheide Collection

Notes

1. The printing runs were normally of modest size, since the copper plates used in the engraving process were of limited durability. In the case of the Musical Offering, Bach ordered 200 title pages and forewords from the Breitkopf printing firm to accompany the engraved music. See BDOK II, no. 556.

2. See Walter Emery, "An Introduction to the Textual History of Bach's *Clavierübung*, Part II," *Musical Times* 92 (1952), 205–9 and 260–62. Bach's *Handexemplar* of *Clavierübung* II is deposited in the British Library, London, under the call number *K.8.g.7.*

3. See Christoph Wolff, "Bachs Handexemplar der Schübler-Choräle," BJ 63 (1977), 120–29. Bach's *Handexemplar* of *Clavierübung* III is deposited in the Stadtbibliothek, Leipzig, under the call number *PM 1403*, and his personal copy of the Schübler Chorales is located in the Scheide Library, Princeton University, without call number.

4. See Christoph Wolff, "Bach's Handexemplar of the Goldberg Variations: A New Source," *Journal of the American Musicological Society* 29 (1976), 224–41. Bach's *Handexemplar* of *Clavierübung* IV is now deposited in the Bibliothèque Nationale, Paris, under the call number *Ms. 17669.*

5. BDOK III, no. 792: "Von meines seeligen Vaters Kupfersachen sind keine Exemplare mehr zu haben; auch die Platten sind nicht mehr da. Was ich davon habe, nehmlich den ersten u. 3tten Theil, will ich Ihnen gebunden zur beliebigen Abschrift, oder gar käuflich überlaßen. Die Materie von beyden kostete ehemahls 6 rthl., wenn Sie sie nicht abschreiben wollen, so will ich beyde Theile Ihnen, sauber gebunden, u. sehr gut conservirt, für 8 rthl. überlaßen. Ich habe des seeligen Mannes manuscript u. damit will ich mich behelfen, u. sie haben das Exemplar, was er ehedem selbst für sich hatte. Doch müßen Sie Sich gar nicht genieren." The English translations in this chapter are my own.

6. BDOK III, no. 793: "Hierbey erhalten Sie die 2 Bücher, für deren richtige Bezahlung ich Ihnen bestens danke. Bey dem einen finden Sie die 6 gestochenen Choräle hinten mit gebunden. Die dabey geschriebene Anmerckungen sind von der Hand des seeligen Autors."

7. Johann Nicolaus Forkel, *Verzeichniß der von dem verstorbenen Doctor und Musikdirector Forkel in Göttingen nachgelassenen Bücher und Musikalien* (Göttingen: F. E. Huth, 1819), 136 (entry no. 60) and 200.

8. See NBA V/1 (*Erster Teil der Klavierübung*), ed. Richard Jones, KB (1978), 28–32; Richard Jones, *The History and Text of Bach's Clavierübung I* (PhD diss., Oxford University, 1988), 30–36.

9. Partita 2: Courante, m. 8. NBA V/1, KB, 58.

10. Partita 2: Courante, m. 6. NBA V/1, KB, 58.

11. Partita 3: Fantasia, m. 101 and 102. NBA V/1, KB, 59.

12. Partita 3: Corrente, m. 55. NBA V/1, KB, 60.

13. Partita 3: Corrente, m. 54. NBA V/1, KB, 60.

14. Christoph Wolff, in "Textkritische Bemerkungen zum Originaldruck der Bachschen Partiten," BJ 63 (1979), 72–74, first drew attention to the revisions of this movement in G25, G26, and G28. Jones responded to Wolff by printing the entire second half of the *Gigue*, as it appears in G25, in his 1988 dissertation and in the 1997 supplement to the KB of NBA V/1. See Jones, *The History and Text of Bach's Clavierübung I*, 262–63, and NBA V/1, KB, Supplement, 16–17.

15. Walter Emery, "Bach's Keyboard Partitas: A Set of Composer's Corrections?" *Musical Times* 93 (1952), 495–97.

16. NBA V/1, KB, 28–32.

17. Wolff, "Textkritische Bemerkungen zum Originaldruck der Bachschen Partiten," 64–74, especially 66–67.

18. Ernest May, "Connections between Breitkopf and J.S. Bach," in *Bach Perspectives 2: J.S. Bach, the Breitkopfs, and Eighteenth-Century Music Trade*, ed. George B. Stauffer (Lincoln: University of Nebraska Press, 1996), 13.

19. Philippe Lescat, *Johann-Sebastian Bach: Clavier Übung 1ère Partie (Partitas) 1731, Chorals Schübler 1746* (Courlay: J.M. Fuzeau, 1991), preface, 10. Unfortunately, this facsimile edition is so poorly executed that the manuscript changes are impossible to distinguish from the printed text.

20. See n. 8.

21. Jones, *The History and Text of Bach's Clavierübung I*, 33. See also his remarks in NBA V/1, KB, Supplement, 3–5.

22. Apparently, the binding of *Clavierübung* I cost one *Reichstaler*, and the binding of *Clavierübung* III (together with the Schübler Chorales) cost a second *Reichstaler*.

23. Wolff, "Bach's Handexemplar der Schübler-Choräle," 124–25. Bach's personal copy of the Schübler Chorales was originally bound with his personal copy of *Clavierübung* III, apparently by C.P.E. Bach.

24. Emanuel had by this point sent Forkel numerous musical works and other materials relating to his father, and there is no evidence that he was ever dishonest or misleading in his transactions.

25. A second title page, also in the hand of Forkel, reads: "Auswahl einigen vorzüglichen Clavier-Compositionen von Joh. Sebastian, Wilhelm Friedemann und Carl Phil. Emanuel Bach."

26. The works excerpted from *Clavierübung* I are the *Præludium, Allemande, Corrente,* and *Giga* from Partita 1, the *Ouverture, Sarabande, Menuet,* and *Gigue* from Partita 4, and the *Præambulum, Allemande,* and *Gigue* from Partita 5. For a full description of the contents, see NBA V/6.2 (*Das wohltemperierte Klavier, Teil II. Fünf Praeludien und Fughetten*), ed. Alfred Dürr, KB, 90–91.

27. In G23, at m. 61 of the *Gigue* from Partita 5, there is a correction of the fifth note in the tenor voice from a dotted eighth to a dotted quarter note; H1 has the unaltered dotted eighth.

28. In G24, mm. 7, 9, and 13 all have mordents added above the first notes in the measure. In G25, at m. 25 of the *Gigue* from Partita 1, the descending stems of the first three notes in the treble staff are changed to ascending stems. None of these corrections are reflected in H1. Unfortunately, none of the movements that have corrections in G26 or G28 appear in H1, and for this reason their association with Forkel can be neither confirmed nor denied.

29. I would like to thank Dr. Uwe Wolf and Dr. Christine Blanken, Bach-Archiv, Leipzig, for making available to me a photocopy of this manuscript.

30. This anonymous primary scribe of H68 is not, however, identical with any of the anonymous copyists of H1. It was Alfred Dürr who first recognized Forkel's involvement in the preparation of H68. See NBA V/6.1 (*Das Wohltmperierte Klavier, Teil I*), ed. Alfred Dürr, KB, 30–31.

31. A complete manuscript of the Well-Tempered Clavier I, prepared by the same scribe (again with Forkel's assistance), was copied around the same time on paper with the same watermark, presumably on behalf of the same recipient. These two manuscripts were both in the possession of former Gewandhaus Kapellmeister Franz Konwitschny before ca.1960, at which time they were acquired by Kurt Wagner. The whereabouts of both manuscripts is currently unknown. See NBA V/6.1, KB, 30–31.

32. The paper of the flyleaves in G28 presents a watermark (anchor above an "R") that to this point has not been successfully attached to a particular time or place. I would like to thank Dr. Jen-yen Chen for initially examining this watermark on my behalf and Andrea Lothe of the Deutsches Buch- und Schriftmuseum der Deutschen Bücherei Leipzig, Papierhistorische Sammlungen, for looking into its history.

33. One possible objection to the argument that G28 was owned by Forkel is that Forkel's edition of the six partitas for Hoffmeister & Kühnel (1801–1802) reflects none of the manuscript changes to G28. Forkel himself, however, seems to have had very little to do with the production of this edition, a situation that irritated him to the point that he remarked in a letter of March 5, 1802, to the publishing house: "[S]enden Sie mir Ihre Abschriften zu, ehe Sie sie stechen lassen. Denn ich gebe Ihnen mein Wort, daß Sie außerdem stets in Gefahr sind, unrichtige Sachen zu liefern, wie sogar schon in dem ersten Theil der Clavierübung hin u. wieder geschehen ist, den Sie doch von einem gestochenen Exempl. haben abstechen lassen." See George B. Stauffer, ed., *The Forkel-Hoffmeister & Kühnel Correspondence: A Document of the Early 19th Century Bach Revival* (New York: C. F. Peters, 1990), 30.

34. Jan Willem Six van Vromade, *Catalogue de la Bibliothèque de M.-J. W. Six de Vromade* (Den Haag: Van Stockum's Antiquariaat, 1925), vol. 1, 89. Entry 484 in this catalogue reads as follows: "Bach. Johann Sebastiaan, Clavir Ubung bestehend in Praeludien, Allemanden, Couranten, Sarabanden, Giguen, Menuetten und andern Galanterien, denen Liebhabern zur Gemüths Ergoetzung verfertiget. Opus 1. In Verlegung des Autoris. 1731. Titre et musique gravé. in-4. oblong. reliure originale en veau marbré à ornements estampés à froid. Première édition d'un des chefs-d'oeuvre de Bach: les 6 partita's pour le piano-forte. Sa première publication. Il l'a lui-même mise en distribution. La gravure en a été faite sur l'autographe même du compositeur. Bel exemplaire."

35. In 1763 the Six family purchased a clavichord made by the well-known Hamburg builder Johann Adolph Hass. The instrument is now in the Russell Collection of Historical Keyboards in Edinburgh.

Four years later, in 1767, the nine-year-old Mozart visited the Six household while passing through the Low Countries. In 1819 J. W. Six's grandfather, Hendrik Six van Vromade (1790–1847), commissioned for his fiancé, Lucretia Johanna van Winter (1785–1845), a wedding present of a barrel organ that could play works by Haydn, Cimerosa, and an otherwise undocumented set of variations by Mozart, said to have been written especially for the family. See Arthur Ord-Hume, *The Barrel Organ: The Story of the Mechanical Organ and its Repair* (New York: A. S. Barnes, 1978), 185. I would like to thank Tom Brockmeier of the Gemeentearchif, Amsterdam, as well as Eric Solsten and Kathryn Anderson of the Library of Congress, Washington, for their help in researching the musical background of the Six family.

36. See n. 8.

37. NBA V/1, KB, 17–32.

38. NBA V/1 KB, 32; and Jones, *The History and Text of Bach's Clavierübung I*, 35–36.

39. This is suggested above all by the upright (rather than reclining) notational style of the ornaments in the *Allemande* and *Capriccio* of Partita 2, an orthography confined for the most part to the first half of the century. I would like to thank Peter Wollny of the Bach-Archiv, Leipzig, for this insight.

40. The print, designated C2 by Jones, exhibits two ownership markings, both of which read "p.p. J.C.B. 1748."

41. Wolff, "Textkritische Bemerkungen zum Originaldruck," 71.

42. Jones suggested a scenario along these lines in *The History and Text of Bach's Clavierübung I*, 36.

After Bach

Carl Reinecke's Performance of Mozart's *Larghetto* and the Nineteenth-Century Practice of Quantitative Accentuation

Robert Hill

A performance-practice convention among classically trained musicians holds that metric accentuation in tonal and post-tonal Western music is qualitative rather than quantitative in nature. Accentuation of strong beats is clarified primarily by stress accents—dynamic inflection and articulation—although where applicable it can be aided by additional expressive devices such as arpeggiation or ornamentation. Stylistic exceptions to this principle that take the form of lengthening accented beats, such as French Baroque *inégalité* or the "shuffle" inequality of jazz performance, are deemed to apply foremost to rapid or flowing note values at the bottom of the metric hierarchy.[1] Metrical units occurring in pairs are intended to be equal or symmetrical in length, regulated by a clear, relatively rapid pulse.[2] Although our bias toward qualitative accentuation over quantitative accentuation is now deeply ingrained in our habits of performing and listening, it is a performance-practice convention that, historically speaking, has probably been firmly in place only for the past eighty to one hundred years or so. Thus, this convention may not represent a universal constant of what musicians today understand as "good" musicianship.

I use the term *quantitative accentuation* to denote the asymmetry between the lengths of complementary metric units—the two quarter-note beats within a half-bar, for example, or the two half-note beats within a whole bar. In the realm of tempo inflection, asymmetric expression occupies a middle position between rhythmic inequality at the low end of the metric hierarchy (sixteenth and eighth notes) and tempo modification at higher levels of the phrase structure. Differences between accented and unaccented metric units can be very marked, but most often they are rather subtle. Because of its subtlety, quantitative accentuation is easily masked by other performance gestures, making it challenging to isolate as a performance-practice criterion. In this chapter I present a method for analyzing quantitative accentuation in expressive piano-roll recordings from the early twentieth century and then consider the implications of my findings.

Wax cylinders, shellac disks, and paper piano rolls from the earliest period of acoustic recording constitute a vast corpus of acoustic documents. These sources, drawn from the late-nineteenth century through World War I, strongly suggest that the best musicians of the late nineteenth century held to a standard of musicianship that embraced, among other things, a more flexible approach to tempo than modern audiences are accustomed to or than modern musicians may feel comfortable with. A new open-mindedness in recent scholarly studies suggests that today, a hundred years later, we are more receptive to the customs of late-Romantic performance practice[3] than was usually the case during the twentieth century.[4]

In view of the misgivings that have surrounded late-Romantic performance practice in the past, it is tantalizing to think that among the trove of early acoustic recordings are some that might reliably shed light on even earlier stylistic practices. Recordings from the beginning of the twentieth century, made by musicians born ca. 1820–1850, provide a unique perspective on the performance conventions of the mid-nineteenth century. Musicianship is, among other things, a complex interaction of mental and physical habits usually acquired early in life through highly repetitive behavior. Ingrained performance habits are rather difficult for musicians to change in later life (as my own performing experience, as well as instructional work with elderly students, attest), and I believe that it is quite the exception for a mature musician to break aesthetically with his or her training and adopt a new style. If we wish to assemble a body of recordings that most probably reflect practices current in the mid-nineteenth century, we should look for the oldest possible musicians in the earliest generation of recordings, and then select from this group those musicians with reputations as conservatives who shunned late-Romantic musical influences. In the present study I focus on one such recording, a piano roll made by the oldest keyboard player—and quite possibly the oldest musician—to leave an acoustic record: the German conductor, composer, and pianist Carl Reinecke (1824–1910). The recording in question is a Welte piano roll of Reinecke's own transcription of the middle movement, *Larghetto*, from Mozart's Piano Concerto in D-Major ("Coronation"), K 537.[5]

Now known mainly for his compositions, Reinecke was an influential musician and teacher in his day. Conductor of the Gewandhaus Orchestra in Leipzig from 1860 to 1895 and Professor of Piano and Composition at the Leipzig Conservatory, he was an acquaintance of Robert Schumann and the teacher of Hugo Riemann, the well-known lexicographer. Reinecke's conservative musical tastes contributed to his eventual dismissal as Gewandhaus conductor. His high-profile position in late-nineteenth-century German music circles, his disdain for innovation, and his championing of

Mozart's works all underscore the significance of the recordings he made in 1905, his eightieth year, for the newly developed Welte reproducing piano system.

In view of the relative importance of tempo inflection in late-nineteenth-century performance, it is not surprising that contemporary inventors of music-reproduction devices strove to develop technological means of reproducing those performance features valued by consumers. Introduced commercially in 1904, Welte was the first piano-roll system capable of reproducing the dynamic inflections and tempo nuances of the pianist. Although the reproduction of touch and dynamics was soon improved upon by Welte and by competing makers, the early Welte system records timing details with sufficient accuracy to be useful for analysis.[6]

Early enthusiasm for the reproduction quality of expressive piano rolls notwithstanding, one normally senses the machine as an unwelcome intermediary in piano-roll recordings. This is not the case in Reinecke's vivid recording. Dispelling any sense of the mechanical, Reinecke's performance presents us with a view of Mozart's music that balances a gestural vigor—at times verging on the ecstatic—with a sense of demure respect.

In an article on Reinecke's tempo-modification practice, as well as in his dissertation on the analysis of piano-roll recordings, Hermann Gottschewski uses the term "tempo-arch" (*Tempobogen*) to describe a phrase in which the tempo accelerates toward the middle of the phrase and then relaxes toward the end.[7] Using a simple but effective software tool that he devised to represent changing tempo relationships graphically, Gottschewski examined Reinecke's treatment of tempo over entire phrases and sections based on measurements of half and whole measures. In my analysis, I have included the lengths of quarter-note beats in order to look more closely at Reinecke's manner of representing strong and weak metric accents. Doubling the level of magnification increases the significance of the margin of error in the paper-punching process, which Gottschewski identifies as being on the average "up to one millimetre."[8] Because my goal was to ascertain patterns in Reinecke's habits of quantitative accentuation, I believe that the problem of potential inaccuracy in the position of punchings does not significantly affect my findings. Nonetheless, I have allowed for the margin of error by treating measurements that differed by one millimeter or less as if they were equal.

Working with an at-scale photocopy of the exemplar of Reinecke's performance in the piano-roll collection of the Augustinermuseum in Freiburg/Breisgau, Germany, I measured the distance in millimeters on the paper roll from the beginning of one quarter-note beat to the beginning of the next for the entire movement (102 measures, in Reinecke's transcription). Mozart's *Larghetto* facilitates the measurement procedure, for it has a straightforward, relatively homogeneous rhythmic structure with

Example 1. Mozart: *Larghetto* from Piano Concerto in D Major ("Corona-tion"), K 537, mm. 1–8.

frequent internal motivic repetition and a clear leading voice that acts as a frame of reference for determining where beats begin. The latter quality is especially impor-tant when one analyzes late-nineteenth-century piano performance, since at the time it was usual for the player to attack with the left hand in advance of the right.

The main theme (Example 1) is made up of two four-bar units that are alike ex-cept in the shape of the cadences in m. 4 (half cadence) and m. 8 (full cadence). In Reinecke's transcription, the theme recurs a total of four times. Table 1 presents in

Table 1. The Theme from Mozart's *Larghetto* in Its Initial Form: Whole Bars, Half Bars, Quarter Bars

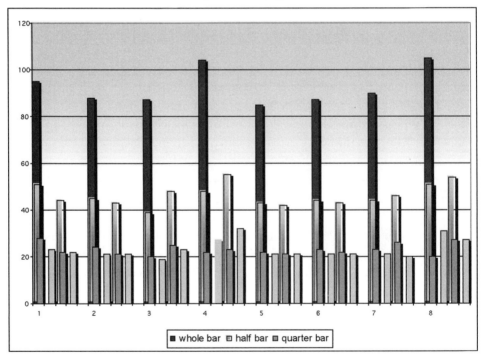

graph form the tempo inflections in the first eight measures of Reinecke's recording—the higher the column, the longer the length of the unit. The top level of columns compares the relative lengths of whole bars, the middle level compares half bars, and the shortest columns compare quarter bars. To interpret the graph, it is most helpful to compare pairs of measurements: mm. 1 + 2 or 3 + 4, for example.

The Y axis shows the length in millimeters, the X axis the values for each measure in the eight-measure theme. Whole measures range in length from 85 to 105 millimeters, half measures from 39 to 55 millimeters, and quarter measures from 19 to 31 millimeters. (The median measure length for all four statements of the theme is 92.4 millimeters.) Taking advantage of the fact that the eight-measure theme returns three more times in Reinecke's transcription, I averaged the values for all four statements to correct for possible idiosyncrasies in the performance of any given statement. To improve the resolution of the resulting graph at the quarter-beat level, I have not averaged whole-measure lengths. The averaged version (Table 2) confirms the characteristic length differences seen in the individual phrases (Table 1).

These graphs indicate that Reinecke tends to lengthen stronger metric units and to foreshorten weaker units in the first two measures of each phrase. The third measure in both phrases tends to be quite stable. In the fourth measure the tempo slows after the slight acceleration into the third measure. In the eight-measure theme, the quantitative disposition found at the half-note level tends to be mirrored in the

Table 2. The Theme from Mozart's *Larghetto*—Average of the Four Versions: Half Bars and Quarter Bars

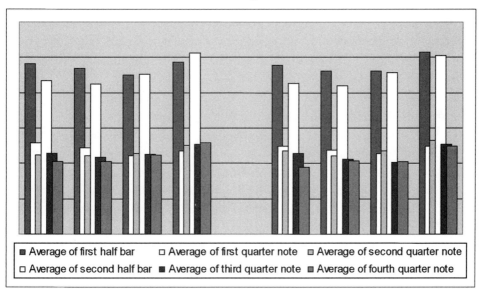

Table 3. Mozart's *Larghetto:* Preponderance of Long–Short, Short–Long, and Equal Relationships in Fifteen Four-Measure Phrases

Whole-Measure Pairs (30)			Half-Measure Pairs (60)			Quarter-Measure Pairs (120)		
Long–Short	Short–Long	Equal	Long–Short	Short–Long	Equal	Long–Short	Short–Long	Equal
8 (26.7%)	15 (50%)	7 (23.3%)	30 (50%)	19 (31.7%)	11 (18.3%)	46 (38.3%)	33 (27.5%)	41 (34.2%)

relationships at the underlying quarter-note level as well—if the half bars are long–short, the quarter bars within them tend also to be long–short, creating nested long–short pairs. Looking at the movement as a whole, however, the picture is less clear-cut. Although such parallelism in disposition between the half-measure and quarter-measure levels is common, it is certainly not imperative: I can identify no rule predicting the relationship between the quantitative disposition of the quarter bars and that of the half bars of which they are a part.

Rather than present an unwieldy graph representing the entire performance,[9] I have decided, for study purposes here, to compare the proportions of long–short, short–long, and equal relationships between members of pairs. In order to compare whole measures with one another, I have restricted my selection to those phrases that are exactly four measures long. Of the total of 102 such measures, 60 are composed of 15 four-measure phrases, yielding 30 pairs of full measures, 60 pairs of half measures, and 120 pairs of quarter measures, for a total of 210 pairs. Of these, 84 (40%) are long–short, 67 (32%) are short–long, and 59 (28%) are equal. Table 3 breaks down these pairs by metric unit.

In the sixty measures examined, Reinecke emphasizes long–short structures more than short–long, and he equalizes the length of two members of a complementary pair a bit more than one-quarter of the time. He tends to lengthen strong metric units and to shorten weak ones at the beginnings of phrases, reversing the proportions when slowing down at the ends of phrases.

When comparing the graph with the listening experience, there is a perceptual difference between the lengths as measured and the apparent durations. This seems to be due to the influence of the arpeggiated accompaniment beginning before the beat, thereby perceptually lengthening certain beats for the listener. Because the pre-beat gesture seems to rise up to the melody note, I am calling this effect *portamento*. Table 4 compares the whole- and half-measure lengths of the opening eight-measure

Table 4. The Theme from Mozart's *Larghetto*, with and without Portamento:
Whole Bars and Half Bars

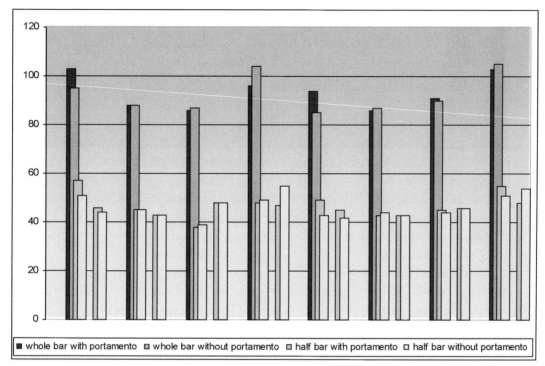

whole bar with portamento   whole bar without portamento   half bar with portamento   half bar without portamento

theme, with and without portamento.[10] Here we can see that the portamenti appear to lengthen the strong beat that begins a four-measure phrase.

To summarize: In Reinecke's performance of Mozart's *Larghetto*, quantitative differences in length between the complementary units of a metric pair occur about 72% of the time in the 210 pairs analyzed at the quarter-, half-, and whole-measure levels. Reinecke's use of quantitative accentuation is analytical in character, in the sense that the degree of asymmetry is a function of the local musical context. The differences in length between the strong and weak members of a metric unit range from subtle to extreme. Reinecke's tendency to underscore the standard strong–weak accent patterns of the metric hierarchy with long–short quantitative accentuation is balanced by frequent use of a mirror shape, short–long, often in order to create a larger, complementary unit: long–short—short–long.

Most importantly, the principle of asymmetry within metric pairs acts concurrently at several levels of the metric hierarchy: quarter-measure level, half-measure level, and whole-measure level. The levels of asymmetry are coordinated and often nested with each other. At the same time, they remain highly unpredictable.[11] Equal or near-equal pairs occur about 28% of the time, and they certainly do not represent a "norm." Reinecke often exaggerates the quantitative accentuation of the accompaniment to underscore the quantitative accentuation of the melody.

I propose that Reinecke's expressive use of quantitative differences reflects a performance-practice tradition current in European art music in the mid-nineteenth century, a time when Reinecke, then in his mid-twenties, would have been a fully trained musician.[12] Testing this assertion will involve analysis of recordings by other musicians who had finished their training by circa 1850–1870, to see how their handling of metric-unit relationships compares with Reinecke's.

The dichotomy between Reinecke's practice of quantitative accentuation and the modern convention of symmetry in metric expression raises a question. If metric asymmetry emerges as a style characteristic of performance practice in the mid-nineteenth century, on what authority can the modern concept of metric symmetry claim to be a stylistic constant? The usual arguments for the status quo hold that the tempo-modification practices of the late-Romantic period represent an extreme departure from the practice of the Baroque and Classic periods, in which performance norms represent the stylistic constant to which we purportedly returned with Neoclassicism. Although the written record from the second half of the nineteenth century does reflect increasing awareness and conscious application of tempo modification in large-scale phrase structures, there is no lack of documentation for tempo flexibility of various kinds going as far back as the Renaissance period. Could it be that, for the last century, the perception of tempo flexibility as a stylistic value has been categorically biased by the simplistic assumption that earlier practices—from which late-Romantic performance practice allegedly departed—were essentially identical with our own practice of metric symmetry?

It is challenging to dispute the conventional view of the history of tempo nuancing. Our reconstructions of past musical practices inescapably mirror our own values and conditioning. We lack an adequate and accepted vocabulary for discussing the expressive use of musical time. Ambiguities in the written record on tempo flexibility can all too easily be interpreted as supporting the dominant paradigm. More than simply looking beyond our own shadow to correct for our engendered anti-Romantic bias, we have to look beyond the shadow cast by the late Romantic period as well, if we wish to try to recover anything of earlier traditions.

Until now, the reconstruction of earlier performance traditions from vestiges captured by early acoustic recording technology has scarcely been touched upon by performance-practice specialists, much less openly discussed or applied. Nevertheless, projecting backward in time to reconstruct missing cultural artifacts based on surviving traces is accepted scientific practice. Doing the intellectual work will be only the first, and indeed, the easier part of the challenge. As scholars and musicians

become more familiar with the fine points of late-Romantic style and attempt to revive this style or to extrapolate even earlier styles, it will become ever more apparent
that the modern convention of quantitative symmetry in expression of meter has
corseted us. Musicians will have to master a new mode of metric expression and inte-
grate it into their bodily reflexes if they are to begin to express tempo, meter, and
rhythm according to the principles that thrived before the First World War.[13]

Notes

1. Among specialists in historical performance practice, agogic accentuation in the form of a slight
lengthening of stressed notes is admitted (on the first of four sixteenth notes, for example), but since
it is held to be a subjective expression of individual taste, it plays only a marginal role in performance-
practice theory.

2. One of the principles of metric organization in music is that metric events are organized in layers.
In binary meter, two metric units make a pair consisting of one "strong," or accented, member and
one "weak" member. For example, two quarter notes equal one half note. The metric unit resulting
from the total of two lower units makes, together with its complement, a pair, as, for example, two
half notes equalling a whole note. According to the modern convention, the two units within a pair
are normally equal in length, or are intended to be so by the player. The weight or emphasis of a
unit is expressed by the duration that a note sounds within the beat, by a stress accent on the stronger member of the pair; by articulation (releasing the note preceding the accented note early so as
to emphasize the *ictus* of the accented note, complemented by slurring or tending to slur the accented note to the unaccented complement that follows); or by a combination of these means. In
modern practice the two units of a pair are intended to be equal to each other in length, so I am calling them "symmetrical."

3. For example, Clive Brown, *Classical and Romantic Performing Practice 1750–1900* (Oxford, UK:
Oxford University Press, 2004); Robert Philip, *Early Recordings and Musical Style: Changing Tastes in
Instrumental Performance, 1900–1950* (Cambridge, UK: Cambridge University Press, 1992).

4. On the stigmatization of late-Romantic performance practice, see Robert Hill, "'Overcoming
Romanticism': On the Modernization of Twentieth-century Performance Practice," in *Music and
Performance during the Weimar Republic* (Cambridge Studies in Performance Practice 3), ed. Bryan
Gilliam (Cambridge, UK: Cambridge University Press, 1994), 37–58.

5. The performance has been issued on the compact disk *The Closest Approach to 19th-Century Piano
Interpretation* (Archiphon 106, 1992).

6. The resolution of the Welte rolls as a function of the roll speed was higher than with competing
technologies. On the problems inherent in the piano-roll recording technology, including roll speed
during the course of playback and inaccuracy in the punching of commercially sold copies made
from the master roll, see Hermann Gottschewski, "Theorie und Analyse der musikalischen Zeitge-
staltung. Neue Wege der Interpretationsforschung, gezeigt an Welte-Mignon-Aufnahmen aus dem
Jahre 1905" (PhD diss., Freiburg im Breisgau, 1993).

7. Gottschewski, "Theorie und Analyse"; and "Tempoarchitektur—Ansätze zu einer speziellen Tempotheorie oder: Was macht das Klassische in Carl Reineckes Mozartspiel aus?" *Musiktheorie* 8 (1993),
99–117.

8. Gottschewski, "Theorie und Analyse," 42.

9. A graph of the exposition section is found in Gottschewski, "Tempoarchitektur—Ansätze zu einer speziellen Tempotheorie," 108.

10. For a contemporary definition of the term *portamento*, as well as the related term *cercar la nota*, see Hugo Riemann, *Musik-Lexikon*, 5th ed. (Leipzig: Hesse Verlag, 1900). To measure portamento, I determined where the accompanimental chordal notes began in advance of the main melody note and added that amount of time to the value of the length of the whole or half measure. This method requires that the portamento value for a given unit be subtracted from the previous length, as bringing in the accompaniment before the beat effectively shortens the length of the previous beat. The fact that portamento values often cancel each other out in the analysis, yet remain acoustically perceivable as lengthening of the beat, is a limitation of the measurement and representation method.

11. The resulting asymmetrical hierarchical structures bear certain resemblances to the phonological "prosodic tree structure" described and diagrammed in Fred Lerdahl and Ray Jackendoff, *A Generative Theory of Tonal Music* (Cambridge, Mass.: MIT Press, 1983), 315.

12. Reinecke's Mozart performance should be compared with his few other piano-roll recordings, which include Schumann's "Warum" and Beethoven's "Ecossaises." Reinecke recorded the same Mozart *Larghetto* transcription again for the Hupfeld piano-roll system, although there the roll speed is lower, making for lower resolution and hence less detailed information about low-level tempo nuances. See Gottschewski, "Tempoarchitektur—Ansätze zu einer speziellen Tempotheorie," 114.

13. For a modern example of quantitative accentuation applied to eighteenth-century piano music, see my upcoming CD recording (Naxos, 2007) of keyboard works by Wilhelm Friedemann Bach, in particular the slow movements, performed on a replica of a fortepiano by Bartolomeo Cristofori.

"Grand Miscellaneous Acts"

Observations on Oratorio Performance in London after Haydn

Mark Risinger

In the early weeks of Lent, 1814, the Theatre Royal in Covent Garden, London, presented a concert featuring Part I of *The Creation*, "composed by Dr. Haydn."[1] It was followed by "Two Grand Miscellaneous Acts" consisting of arias and choruses by various composers. Although the choice of the word "Acts" for Parts II and III of the program on the title page of the libretto suggests a dramatic performance, nothing about the sequence of numbers constitutes a thematically consistent—much less dramatically unified—musical experience. A number of the selections in Parts II and III of the program were drawn from the works of Handel, both in their original versions and in their later guises as "pasticcio oratorios" arranged by other hands. A significant portion of the remaining music, however, seems to have been chosen for the evening's soloists, with only passing concern for thematic or dramatic relevance.

A libretto from this performance (Plate 1), located today in the collection of the Harvard University Library,[2] provides a glimpse of the breadth and variety that constituted an evening's entertainment for the London public in the generation after Haydn. In addition, the text suggests that by this time, the driving organizational principle behind oratorio performances in London was no longer the veneration of the composer as musical icon, as it had been in the past, but rather the cult of the individual performer.

The concert that took place at the Theatre Royal during Lent, 1814, reflects a trend that had been developing over several decades in the late eighteenth century. During the half-century following Handel's death, performances of his works proliferated both in England and on the Continent, particularly in the aftermath of the Handel Commemoration of 1784. Within a relatively short period, however, performances of complete oratorios became more the exception than the rule, and by the end of the century they had all but vanished. Music historian Simon McVeigh, while acknowledging the persistent popularity of *Messiah* and *Judas Maccabaeus*, nevertheless

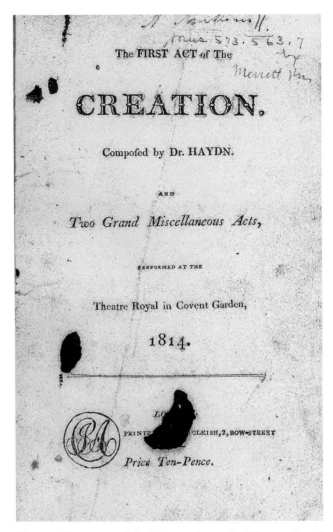

Plate 1. First page of the libretto from the Theatre Royal concert of Lent, 1814. Harvard University, Eda Kuhn Loeb Library of the Harvard College Library, Merritt Room, *Mus 573.563.7*. Reproduced by permission.

traces the beginnings of the decline of complete oratorio performances to the middle of the century and provides a concise summary of their demise at the end of it:

> But in general the tide was against Handel's biblical oratorios, even if *Samson* and other Old Testament dramas were never completely forgotten. Instead, the lighter secular works (*Alexander's Feast*, *L'Allegro*, *Acis and Galatea*) were clearly favored . . . A

more ominous development was the practice of making selections from the orato-rios. Admittedly Handel had initiated the concept with his *Occasional Oratorio* (1746), but this had had a special purpose . . . Several new libretti were fitted out with Han-del selections in ensuing decades; even the Concert of Ancient Music unambigu-ously put on miscellaneous programmes.

    Despite all these experiments, support for public oratorios was waning by the early 1780s . . . It seems likely that the oratorio season would have died altogether had it not been for the Handel Commemoration.[3]

The "special purpose" of the *Occasional Oratorio*, the original "pasticcio oratorio," was the celebration of the English victory at the Battle of Culloden in 1746. To com-memorate this occasion, Handel used music borrowed from a number of his own works, including *Samson, Judas Maccabaeus, Athalia, Israel in Egypt,* and various instru-mental concertos. The *Occasional Oratorio* relates more closely to the pasticcio orato-rios arranged in the 1760s, 1770s, and 1780s by the younger John Christopher Smith and Samuel Arnold than it does to the "miscellaneous programmes" that became popular a bit later. The compilers of the pasticcio oratorios made an attempt to find a unifying theme when crafting a libretto, to which Handel's music was then refitted. In the miscellaneous programs, movements from Handel's works, usually in their original form and with their original texts, were extracted and presented *ad seriatim* alongside the music of other composers. Little effort was made to provide a continu-ous narrative.

The movement away from performing complete oratorios and toward extracting Handelian movements and presenting them in "anthology concerts" was not limited to the London oratorio series: it became increasingly popular on the Continent as well. In Germany, Handel's reputation initially rested on four works: *Messiah, Alexan-der's Feast, Judas Maccabaeus,* and the "Utrecht" *Te Deum. Alexander's Feast,* mentioned by McVeigh, was performed in Berlin as early as 1766, in a translation by Karl Wilhelm Ramler (the poet of *Der Tod Jesu*). In Hamburg, Michael Arne, C.P.E. Bach, and others started to conduct complete performances of *Messiah* and *Alexander's Feast* (both were sung in German) in the early 1770s.[4] C.P.E. Bach stated his intention to perform *Al-exander's Feast* as early as 1769 in a letter to Johann Philipp Kirnberger, in which he also expressed a desire to acquire scores of the "Funeral Anthem for Queen Caro-line" and an unspecified "Te Deum" (adding in clear anticipation, "I can scarcely wait for it").[5] C.P.E. subsequently appears to have conducted six or seven performances of *Messiah* between 1774 and 1786, a performance of *Judas Maccabaeus* in 1774, multiple performances of *Alexander's Feast* in 1783, and the "Funeral Anthem" in 1786.[6] By 1780 or so, we find references to a concert program that began with a Haydn sym-phony and included other instrumental concertos, but whose first part finished with the "Hallelujah" chorus and whose second part concluded with "Worthy Is the Lamb," both from *Messiah*.[7]

What ties all of these performances together, whether they consist of a complete oratorio or a selection of individual numbers, is the almost complete absence of dramatic librettos. With occasional exceptions, the oratorios that received the greatest number of performances and won the affection of the public were those with lyrical and narrative texts, rather than those with dramatic librettos based on biblical episodes. By the time Haydn made his famous journey to London in 1791—a trip that brought him into contact with Handel's music in a way that profoundly influenced his late development—the opportunity to hear a complete performance of a dramatic oratorio was virtually nonexistent. The two works that most directly influenced Haydn as he composed *The Creation* were *Israel in Egypt* and *Messiah*, both with librettos adapted from the Bible and, in the case of *Messiah*, the Book of Common Prayer. The first two parts of *The Creation* are closely adapted, translated, and retranslated from Milton's *Paradise Lost*, with occasional insertions from Scripture as well. The librettos of *Israel in Egypt* and *Messiah*, which were arguably the most popular Handel works with both English and Continental audiences, stem from the nondramatic oratorio tradition rather than the dramatic. The use of music from the dramatic biblical oratorios was ordinarily limited to large choral movements—the hallmark of the Handelian style. And this brings us back to Lent, 1814, and the concert in Covent Garden.

A heading across the top of the first page of the libretto characterizes the offerings for the evening as "A Grand Selection." Part I was the only portion of the concert that contained a full segment of a large-scale work presented more or less intact: "The First Act of the Creation." With Part II of the concert, the "miscellaneous" nature of the offerings becomes evident (Table 1). The structure of Part II strongly resembles the architecture of a standard oratorio: an introductory overture leads to two solo numbers, which in turn lead to a chorus, then two recitative and aria pairs, then another chorus, and so forth. Rounding out this part of this "Grand Miscellaneous Act" is the chorus-trio-chorus finale of Part II of *The Creation*. This raises the question as to why it was not preferable simply to perform Part II of *The Creation* complete, rather than substituting unrelated but structurally similar numbers for the entire contents, save the finale.

A few unifying elements among the pieces help to compensate for the lack of a common composer or librettist. The first three vocal and choral movements—"Sad my soul," "Lord! remember David," and "Join voices all"—share an emphasis on praise. Furthermore, the third number in the group, the "Galliard & Cooke" chorus, takes its text from Milton (three lines from Book V of *Paradise Lost*), which makes a rather nice connection to *The Creation*. The two recitative–aria pairs that follow, by

Table 1. Theatre Royal Concert of Lent, 1814: Part II of the Program

Entry in Program	Text Incipit	Source of Music
Overture. Anacreon. *Cherubini.*	—	Cherubini: Overture from *Anacreon*
Song, *Miss Rennell.* Winter.	"Sad my soul, I sigh and weep"	Winter: *Il Ratto di Proserpina*
Air, *Mr Braham.* Redemption.	"Lord! remember David"	Arnold: *Redemption* (pasticcio)
Chorus. Galliard & Cooke.	"Join voices all ye living souls"	Cooke: "Join voices"
Recit. *Mr Tinney.* Callcott	"Friend of the brave, in perils darkest hour"	Callcott: unidentified work
Air	"When all is still on death's devoted soil"	
Recit. *Mrs. Salmon.* Judas Mac.	"O let eternal honours crown his name"	Handel: *Judas Maccabaeus*
Air:	"From mighty kings he took the spoil"	
Chorus. Dr. Boyce.	"Blessed be the name of the Lord"	Boyce: Anthem *Lord Thou Has Been Our Refuge*
Air, *Mr Kellner.* Deborah	"Tears, such as tender fathers shed"	Handel: *Deborah*
Scena, *Madame Catalani.*	"Vittima sventurata, Di crudelta da more"	Pucitta: *La vestale*
Aria.	"Voi che in amore, Felici siete"	
Chorus. Creation—*Dr. Haydn.*	"Achieved is the glorious work"	Haydn: *The Creation*
Trio,	"On thee each living soul awaits"	
Chorus.	"Achieved is the glorious work!"	

John Wall Callcott and Handel, respectively, introduce a militaristic tone with images of battle: first "stormy floods and carnage cover'd fields" and "the march-worn soldier" and then Judas's heroic acts ("Judah rejoiceth in his name, And triumphs in her heroes [sic] fame").

The pieces in Part II display a wide range of adaptation and divergence from published editions of the time, suggesting that numerous editorial hands were at work. The music of "Sad my soul," for instance, comes from an aria in Peter von Winter's opera *Il Ratto di Proserpina*, first produced in London in 1804 with a libretto by Lorenzo da Ponte. The version performed on this occasion, however, is an arrangement by Joseph Addison with English words by Thomas Moncrieffe. Of more contemporary vintage was John Wall Callcott's "Friend of the brave" and "When all is still," both settings of texts from Thomas Campbell's 1814 publication *Pleasures of Hope*. The chorus "Blessed be the name of the Lord," from William Boyce's anthem *Lord, Thou Hast Been Our Refuge*, by contrast, was composed for the Sons of the Clergy's annual performances at St. Paul's Cathedral in 1755. Within Part II it comes at approximately the same point as Haydn's chorus, "The Lord is great and great his might," and it serves a similarly affirmative role.

Up to this point, each number in the "Grand Act" shares some tie with another number—a trait that provides a degree of internal consistency, if not dramatic cohesion. However, after a brief air from Handel's *Deborah*, any cohesion evaporates with the most jolting insertion in the proceedings: an unattributed and untranslated *scena* sung by "Madame Catalani." The soloist in this work, Angelica Catalani, had made her London debut in 1806 after triumphant appearances in Venice, Milan, Florence, and Rome during the previous ten years.[8] The *scena* and aria that she performed on this occasion were drawn from Vicenzo Pucitta's *La vestale*, one of the operas conceived and composed expressly for her as the *prima donna* of the King's Theatre from 1808 to 1814. What makes this part of the concert so remarkable is the shift in focus from composer to performer: neither the musical style nor the text of Pucitta's pieces are of any relevance to the music that surrounds them. All that counts is the power of a star performer in a vehicle presumably of her own choosing.[9] Strange indeed must have been the segue from the end of "Felici siete," an *aria di lamento*, to the finale of Part II of *The Creation*, "Achieved is the glorious work."

Matters of thematic consistency do not improve in Part III of the concert (Table 2), though the overall structure is somewhat similar to that of Part II. This portion of the concert exhibits a more Handelian flavor than the second, with the inclusion of two "grand choruses" (one, from *Saul*, serving as the final number) and two airs from the pasticcio *Redemption*. Once again, however, certain solo items display the decidedly personal stamp of the performers themselves: the tenor John Braham sang "by desire" (that is—by popular demand) a song of his own composition portraying military

Table 2. Theatre Royal Concert of Lent, 1814: Part III of the Program

Entry in Program	Text Incipit	Source of Music
Hymn. *Marcello.* Harmonized with Accompaniments, and an	—	Marcello: Hymn
Introductory Voluntary for the Organ By Mr. S. Wesley	—	Wesley: Organ Voluntary
Verse, *Master Williams and Chorus.*	"There is a river, the streams whereof"	Unidentified work (Wesley anthem?)
Air, *Mrs. Salmon. Redemption*	"He was eyes unto the blind"	Arnold: *Redemption* (Handel: *Siroe*)
Song, (by desire) *Mr. Braham.* Braham	"In this cottage my father once dwelt"	Braham: "In this cottage"
Grand Chorus. Samson	"Fix'd in his everlasting seat"	Handel: *Samson*
Recit. *Mr. Kellner.* Redemption	"But, who is He? Tremendous to behold"	Arnold: *Redemption*
Air.	"Awful, pleasing being, say"	
Bravura, *Madame Catalani.* Portogallo	"Frenar vorrei le lacrime"	Fonseca Portugal: *La Morte di Semiramide*
Grand Chorus. Saul.	"Gird on the sword, thou man of might"	Handel: *Saul*

glory and loss, and Madame Catalani returned to perform another Italian *scena* from an opera of special significance to her career. "Portogallo" is a reference to the composer Marcos Antonio da Fonseca Portugal, and the aria in question stems from his *La Morte di Semiramide*, the work in which Catalani had made her London debut in 1806.[10]

The remaining numbers stem from one piece or another by Handel. Certainly the most intriguing movements in Part III are the pieces from the pasticcio *Redemption*. Samuel Arnold, the arranger of *Redemption*, explained in the preface to the libretto of 1786 his motives for assembling the work:

> The judicious selection of Music, performed at the Commemoration of Handel at Westminster-Abbey, and at the Pantheon, first gave me the idea of compiling and bringing into one performance, or regular drama, those great and favorite works of this justly-admired author; and I have only to regret, that the compass of time allotted for the performance of an Oratorio is so short, as to deprive me of adding many more of his capital compositions, that would have greatly enriched the performance.[11]

Arnold, in fact, produced what Howard E. Smither describes as "a concert of Handel's music placed within a context created by a new libretto of monumental scope."[12] The music was not derived exclusively from the oratorios, however. Whereas the aria, "Awful, pleasing being, say," is taken from Act I of *Joshua*, "He was eyes unto the blind" is a recast version of "Non vi piacque ingiusti Dei" from Handel's *opera seria Siroe*. McVeigh characterizes the success of Arnold's new libretto as an "astute move" that capitalized on the success of the Commemoration performances. After this point, "complete oratorios were declared out of fashion. The way was paved for the miscellaneous selections that dominated the [oratorio] series of the 1790s."[13] By the spring of 1814, more than two decades after the use of complete oratorios in the Commemoration performances, *Redemption*, a pasticcio arranged from "original" Handelian compositions (operas, oratorios, and anthems), had itself become a type of "original work" that could be used as a source of material for creating "Grand Miscellaneous Acts."

The program that was presented during Lent, 1814, in the Theatre Royal in Covent Garden reflects both the trend toward extracting and "anthologizing" works by master composers (most notably Handel) and the tendency to grant star performers the opportunity to excel in music that suited them, regardless of its relationship to the pieces preceding or following.[14] Fortunately for Handelians, the pasticcio craze was shorter-lived than the desire for bravura performances, and the persistent popularity of *Messiah*, presented with large choral forces and star singers, guaranteed its regular appearance, intact. Indeed, the grandiose productions in London's Crystal

Palace at mid-century, featuring immense choruses and the best soloists of the time, eventually led to the return of other oratorios in full form.

Notes

1. The only date on the title page of the surviving libretto (see Plate 1 and n. 2) is 1814, but the last page contains an advertisement for an upcoming concert on Friday, March 4. Given that oratorio performances were a feature of the Lenten season, it is likely that the concert in question took place between Ash Wednesday, which fell on February 23, and March 4, 1814.

2. Harvard University, Eda Kuhn Loeb Library of the Harvard College Library, Merritt Room, *Mus 573.563.7*. I am grateful to Virginia Danielson and Douglas Freundlich of the Harvard Music Library for their assistance in granting access to this libretto.

3. Simon McVeigh, *Concert Life in London from Mozart to Haydn* (Cambridge, UK: Cambridge University Press, 1993), 31. A more extensive survey of this period can be found in Eva Zöllner, *English Oratorio after Handel, 1760–1800* (Marburg: Tectum Verlag, 2002).

4. Magda Marx-Weber, "Hamburger Händel-Pflege im späten 18. Jahrhundert," in *Händel und Hamburg: Ausstellung anlässlich des 300. Geburtstages von Georg Friedrich Händel: Staats- und Universitätsbibliothek Hamburg Carl von Ossietzky*, ed. Hans Joachim Marx (Hamburg: Karl Dieter Wagner, 1985), 135–36.

5. *Letters of C. P. E. Bach*, ed. and trans. Stephen L. Clark (Oxford, UK: Oxford University Press, 1997), 18.

6. Josef Sittard, *Geschichte des Musik- und Concertwesens in Hamburg vom 14. Jahrhundert bis auf die Gegenwart* (Altona und Leipzig: A. C. Reher, 1890), 109–14.

7. Sittard, *Geschichte des Musik- und Concertwesens in Hamburg*, 129.

8. Elizabeth Forbes, "Catalani, Angelica," in *The New Grove Dictionary of Opera*, ed. Stanley Sadie (London: Macmillan, 1992), vol. 1, 771.

9. The insertion of the Italian *scena* into the composite oratorio was quite like the use of *arie di baule* in late-eighteenth-century operas. Such arias were carried from place to place by virtuoso singers (hence the epithet "suitcase aria") and inserted randomly into whatever opera the singers happened to be performing. Mozart wrote such pieces: "Un baccio di mano," K 541, of May 1788, for instance, was composed for the virtuoso bass Francesco Albertarelli for insertion into Pasquale Anfossi's *Le gelosie fortunate* (Albertarelli sang the title role in the first Vienna performance of *Don Giovanni*). Three months later Mozart recycled the closing melody of the aria as the second theme of the first movement of the "Jupiter" Symphony, K 551. I am indebted to George B. Stauffer for this observation.

10. An 1807 edition (London: M. Kelly) of this aria, presently found in the British Library, London, under call number *G.811.(23.)*, bears the title "Frenar vorrei le lagrime [sic], with the Embellishments & Graces, as sung by Madame Catalani."

11. Quoted in Howard E. Smither, *A History of the Oratorio* (Chapel Hill: University of North Carolina Press, 1987), vol. 3, 242.

12. Smither, *A History of the Oratorio*, vol. 3, 243.

13. McVeigh, *Concert Life in London*, 31.

14. In the Theatre-Royal libretto, the upcoming concert on March 4, 1814 (see n. 1), is described as "A Grand Selection of Sacred Music, from the compositions of the most favorite Authors." The pieces listed include further choruses from *Joshua*, *Judas Maccabaeus*, and *Israel in Egypt*, as well as airs from *Theodora*, *Samson*, and *Athalia*. Along with this music are other miscellaneous pieces by Mozart, Beethoven, and Pergolesi, in addition to a special treat: "End of Part I: Madame Catalani will sing the National Air of 'Rule Brittania.'" This performance may well have constituted a musical farewell for the diva, who left London later that year to assume directorship of the Théâtre Italien in Paris.

Back from B-A-C-H

Schumann's Symphony No. 2 in C Major

Douglass Seaton

For much of the year 1845, Robert Schumann was occupied with the composition of his Six Fugues on the Name B-A-C-H, op. 60. For some critics, this retrospective shift to a rigorous genre from the early eighteenth century seems symptomatic of a new pursuit of classicist control, one that marks the climactic point in Schumann's journey from the fantasy of the piano miniature and the poetic Lied to the mastery of larger, more self-contained works. Others interpret the B-A-C-H fugues as manifestations of a particular subtype of the character piece, for Schumann had regarded the fugues of the Well-Tempered Clavier as "character pieces of the highest sort, to some extent truly poetic creations, of which each asserts its own expression, its own lights and shadows."[1] Still others, like Georg von Dadelsen, assert that these compositions represent a downturn for Schumann, in which "[m]elody and form, originally manifestations of poetic fantasy, should now be built on 'laws and rules.' The creative work thereby attained a level of self-consciousness that it had not possessed earlier. It was brought to the edge of the 'mechanical.'"[2]

However one evaluates Schumann's fugues, the work on B-A-C-H in op. 60 exerted a significant impact on the composer's next major work, the Symphony No. 2 in C Major, op. 61. The symphony presents intriguing problems of interpretation. Widely admired in the nineteenth century for its perceived metaphysical content, it became less popular in the twentieth, mainly because its structural peculiarities resisted analysis.[3] Indeed, both its form and its content confront the listener and the music historian with unexpected challenges. Significant for the understanding of the symphony is Schumann's engagement with Bach.

Schumann's interest in Bach's music emerges in several different aspects of the symphony. The musical spelling of B-A-C-H appears in the second trio of the *Scherzo*, stated both in half-note and quarter-note values, at pitch and transposed (movement 2, mm. 230–232 and 257–262). The motive is introduced in a passage of regularly flowing eighth notes that evoke the steady rhythmic momentum of Bach's music.

Listeners since Brahms have noted a similarity between the melody of the symphony's slow movement and the opening of the first movement of the Trio Sonata

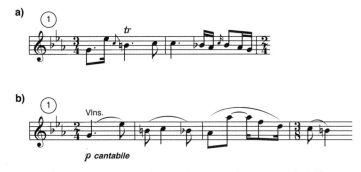

Example 1. a) Opening theme from Bach's Musical Offering, movement 1. b) Opening theme from Schumann's Symphony No. 2 in C Major, movement 3.

from the Musical Offering.[4] This theme is an example of a pathopoeia, a Baroque figure characterized here by the upward leap of a minor sixth (from g' to e♭"), followed by the highly expressive descent of a diminished fourth (e♭" to b-natural') and then the resolution upward by a semitone (b-natural' to c"; Example 1). Linda Correll Roesner, crediting Bernhard Appel,[5] points out the resemblance of this theme to the melody of the soprano aria "Seufzer, Tränen, Kummer, Not" from Bach's Cantata 21, *Ich hatte viel Bekümmernis*, which, however, does not begin with an ascending minor sixth but rather a descending major third. We might rather agree with John Daverio that the melody resembles the theme of the aria "Erbarme dich, mein Gott" from the St. Matthew Passion.[6] Whether or not Schumann intended a direct citation from a single Bach work can be questioned, but his reference to a recognizable *topos* seems unambiguously clear.

In addition, conspicuous instances of "walking bass" effects, a common feature of Baroque music, occur in both of the symphony's inner movements (movement 2, mm. 240–254; and movement 3, mm. 62–74). Christopher Reynolds identifies this device as a "topic for faith, resolve, and strength, whether in the special context of the Credo . . . or in operatic scenes that portray the same traits."[7]

Schumann's work on the C-Major Symphony occupied the last weeks of 1845 and much of 1846. He began sketching on December 12, 1845, just a few weeks after he completed the B-A-C-H fugues, and by December 28 he had practically finished a draft of the whole symphony.[8] He started the orchestration on February 12, 1846, but worked only slowly because of trouble with ringing in his ears. The score was not finished until October 19. The first performance of the symphony—not a particularly successful one—took place on November 5, 1846, in the Leipzig Gewandhaus under Mendelssohn's direction.[9] The second performance, a week and a half later, received a more enthusiastic response. The work was published in 1847. A number of leading scholars have examined the C-Major Symphony in depth, each yielding particular insights about the work.[10] In this chapter, I approach the symphony from a narratological viewpoint, looking first at its plot and narrative voice and then at its use of citations, in order to set forth a new interpretation.

It is helpful to start by noting the overall trajectory of the symphony. As Anthony Newcomb points out, the plot archetype to which it belongs is the "end-accented" or "heroic" symphony, for which Beethoven's Fifth and Ninth Symphonies serve as the most important models.[11] In such works, the course of the music suggests struggle leading to victory or suffering leading to healing or redemption. Typical is the shift from minor mode to major mode at the end. Despite its presumptive major tonality, Schumann's symphony resembles Beethoven's Fifth on the large scale, since the arrival of the final movement brings a brilliant C major to supersede the C minor that shadowed the first two movements and was the key of the third.[12]

The first movement consists of a strikingly serious slow introduction leading to a sonata form in C major. The sense of the major key seems rather attenuated because of the strong presence of E♭, heard already in the first measure (as d♯ in the violins) and structurally significant as a stopping point in the main modulation of the exposition from C major to G major: the fourteen measures of stable E♭ major (the entire dominant section lasts only twenty measures) suggest that C minor (as the relative minor of E♭ major) is nearly as important an aspect of the tonic as C major.

The second-movement *Scherzo* likewise leans heavily toward C minor. Perhaps taking a cue from the "Wedding March" of Mendelssohn's *Midsummer Night's Dream*, the movement opens not on the tonic but on an F♯ diminished seventh, here with E♭ prominently in the top voice on the first downbeat. Again the dominant is reached (m. 12) only after a strong move to E♭ major (m. 8). Throughout the *Scherzo* there is heavy emphasis on the flat-key side of the tonal spectrum (even in the first trio, which is in G major), including the music in which C major has been firmly established. As already noted, the second trio contains the B-A-C-H citation, along with the allusion to the Baroque gesture of continuous eighth-note motion.

The third movement, an *Adagio espressivo*, is explicitly in C minor, with the pathos-filled theme that recalls that of the Musical Offering and the middle section that presents the strikingly Baroque-sounding walking-bass effect. At the end of the movement, although the key signature changes to C major, the penultimate cadential harmony is a fully diminished seventh chord based on (i.e., spelled from) the leading B, with a strong A♭ in the bass line substituting for the dominant, G.

At the opening of the finale, however, the minor shading is abruptly obliterated. The movement begins with a tremendous acclamatory gesture in C major, with subordinate tonicization of G major and no hint of E♭ major to intervene in the modulatory scheme of tonic to dominant. Even in the development section the flat harmonies seem to warm rather than darken the overall effect. The whole ending centers on C major.[13]

The general trajectory in the symphony from semi-darkness to light constitutes the overall plot outline. We must also observe that the work explores strongly the experience of a single leading character, established—as usual in music of the Classic-Romantic period—by rhythmic/melodic material. Newcomb points out that in the opening measures of the introduction, Schumann already presents the thematic material that dominates the symphony, even as it grows and changes. The fanfare-like brass motive, with its dotted rhythms and leaps of fifth and fourth, contrasts with the crawling line that appears simultaneously in the strings and is marked by smooth rhythmic flow and stepwise chromatic motion. These two ideas create a sort of dual, Florestan-versus-Eusebius, character. Because of the extreme contrasts between these elements, it is almost inevitable that whatever follows will appear as a development, reflecting some aspect of the character of the opening. Beyond this, Schumann repeatedly makes sure that new ideas arise out of existing ones. The effect is not merely one of intermittent cyclic thematic resemblances, but rather step-by-step character development.[14]

Thus, although the symphony is ostensibly "absolute" music, since it displays the usual structural conventions of that mode of composition, it presents certain problems. The way the work moves forward, in terms of both harmony and character, together with the idiosyncrasies in its treatment of the conventions of sonata and symphonic forms, suggests a deliberate and coherent plot, comparable to a heroic drama or novel. Writing in 1850, Ernst Gottschald described the symphony as recounting "the *victorious* striving of the particular individuality for its most sincere fusion with spiritual universality, in which all egoistic limits, limits that divided individual spirits from each other, are annihilated, so that [those spirits] love each other as equals, for they live in the realm of liberty, equality, and fraternity."[15] This is certainly a provocative view, and we shall return to it shortly.

For many commentators the symphony's principal character is the composer. Gottschald identified the "particular individuality" as representing "the composer's personality, still caught up in an estranged isolation."[16] More recently, Michael Steinberg argues that Schumann's personality comes through most intimately in the third movement.[17] Others, too, have wanted to make Schumann the protagonist of the narrative. They have been led to do so by some comments that the composer himself made about his situation during the composition of the work. Schumann had experienced a breakdown in August 1845, and he was still recuperating in December, when he drafted the symphony. In addition, as we have already noted, during the orchestration of the work Schumann had trouble with the ringing in his ears that presaged his ultimate collapse. On April 2, 1849, a few years after completing the symphony, Schumann wrote to D. G. Otten: "I wrote the symphony in December 1845, still half sick; it seems to me that one would have to hear this in it. Only in the last movement did I begin to feel like myself again; actually I became better only after the completion of the whole work. Otherwise though, as I say, it reminds me of a dark time."[18] Thus, it is tempting to think that the plot of the symphony represents an episode in the composer's life. Newcomb, for example, writes: "Although the plot archetype of a particular work may have no connection with the life of the composer, that of op. 61 had an autobiographical dimension. The struggle in the symphony from suffering to healing and redemption seems also to have been Schumann's own."[19]

We should be extremely reluctant, however, to fall into the biographical fallacy—which should more correctly be called the "autobiographical" fallacy—in this way. To interpret any work as merely recounting an episode in its author's experience trivializes the music. It risks demoting the work of art to the paltry business of personal diary-keeping. What is more, Schumann's letter to Otten does not justify such an interpretation, for he wrote, "I became better only after finishing the whole work." He did not suggest that it represents his experience of illness and recovery. Rather, he simply noted "it recalls to me a dark time." If the plot archetype truly belongs to that of the "end-accented" or "heroic" symphony, then it represents something more significant than the course of Schumann's health.

Nevertheless, any credible interpretation must account for the undeniable occurrence of this plot archetype. As we have seen, the narrative contour of the symphony was identified by its earliest reviewers. In fact, even Schumann validated this view. Writing to Taubert on March 3, 1847, within a few months of the completion and first performances of the symphony, he noted that the work was "as a whole a dark piece—only in the last part do a couple of friendly beams break through."[20] The story in the symphony is indeed one of heroic struggle leading to victory or of suffering leading to redemption. The protagonist simply is not the ailing and recovering Robert Schumann.

Let us leave the discussion of the thematic and tonal plot of this symphony for the moment and consider the other peculiar aspect of the work: its use of citations. Besides incorporating the letters B-A-C-H and alluding to Bach's music and his style, the symphony contains several other explicit citations and allusions. The most famous references are to the slow introduction of Haydn's Symphony No. 104 in D Major (Haydn, movement 1, mm. 1–4; Schumann, movement 1, mm. 1–4; Example 2)[21] and to Beethoven's *An die ferne Geliebte* at the end, where it substitutes for the expected reprise of the finale (Beethoven, "Nimm sie hin denn" from *An die ferne Geliebte*, mm. 1–2, 9–10; Schumann, movement 4, mm. 394–397; Example 3).

Example 2. a) Haydn: Symphony No. 104 in D Major, movement 1, mm. 1–4.
b) Schumann: Symphony No. 2 in C Major, movement 1, mm. 1–4.

There are, however, some other allusions that reward fresh scrutiny. A consideration of these, as well as a rethinking of the meaning of the recognized citations, can add new perspective to this feature of the symphony. A citation that might be considered debatable occurs in the finale at mm. 445–452 (which itself is a reference back to mm. 5–8 of the slow introduction). The resemblance here is to the fugue on the text "Danket dem Herrn" in Mendelssohn's *Lobgesang* (no. 10, mm. 87–186; Example 4).

Example 3. a) Beethoven: "Nimm sie hin denn diese Lieder" from *An die ferne Geliebte*, op. 98/6, mm. 9–10. b) Schumann: Symphony No. 2 in C Major, movement 4, mm. 394–397.

Example 4. a) Mendelssohn: "Danket dem Herrn" from *Lobgesang*, op. 52/10, mm. 87–90. b) Schumann: Symphony No. 2 in C Major, movement 4, mm. 445–452.

The general contour of this theme—a leap of a fourth followed by a scalar descent, beginning with a dotted rhythm, through a whole tone, semitone, whole tone, and so forth—might be deemed sufficiently generic to undermine this possible connection, however. So, let us proceed to another possible citation. A bit later in Schumann's finale (mm. 544–551), we find a reference that should be unmistakable. It is to the choral finale of Beethoven's Ninth Symphony, at the words "Alle Menschen, alle Menschen . . . werden Brüder" (mm. 806–811; Example 5).

I would like to draw special attention to yet another allusion, and this is to Mozart, who otherwise seems conspicuously absent from the pantheon of composers in the great German tradition that Schumann invokes. This is a reference that Daverio, at least, has already noted,[22] but one that has not been drawn closely enough into interpretations of the symphony. This citation occurs in conjunction with the "walking bass" passage in Schumann's third movement, and it is a reference to Mozart's Magic Flute (Mozart, Act 2, mm. 196–207; Schumann, movement 3, mm. 62–74; Example 6a and b).

Why is all this significant? Clearly, music of the past must have been in the foreground of Schumann's creative imagination as he composed the C-Major Symphony. Naturally, this would be true for any composer undertaking symphonic writing in the decades following Beethoven. Here, though, the response to "the anxiety of influence"[23] is not to avoid the past but to acknowledge and embrace it—not only the music of Beethoven but the full German classical tradition as Schumann knew it. However, it is not necessary to regard the Symphony in C Major in the manner suggested by Mark Evan Bonds, who has proposed that Schumann's work is a misreading of an earlier piece, presumably Beethoven's Fifth.[24]

The idea that Schumann's C-Major Symphony deals consciously with the symphonic tradition is by no means a new one. Arnfried Edler notes that the choice of C major, combined with Schumann's statement to his Dutch admirer Johann Verhulst

Example 5. a) Beethoven: Symphony No. 9 in D Minor, movement 4, mm. 806–811. b) Schumann: Symphony No. 2 in C Major, movement 4, mm. 544–551.

that the work would be a "rechte Jupiter," suggests that the composer had in mind a particular relationship to Mozart.[25] Edler considers the reference to Haydn's Symphony No. 104 even more important, describing it as embodying "the symphonic tradition itself, represented by the Haydn citation."[26] Ludwig Finscher notes succinctly that in this symphony "the idea of musical work itself becomes thematicized —there is hardly another symphony before Brahms in which substantive and structural unification is wrestled with so rigorously and so strenuously as here, and hardly any in which at the same time the idea of musical work is set up with such historical depth . . ."[27] I pursue this idea now, drawing together the symphony's narrative design and its allusions.

Of great interest is what the citations suggest about the narrative voice of Schumann's work. Having identified the shape and nature of the plot of the symphony, we

Example 6a. Mozart: The Magic Flute, Act. 2, Finale, mm. 196–207.

can now see more clearly what the music itself reveals about the symphonist as story-teller. Through its use of multiple citations and allusions, the narrative voice of the work establishes a certain kind of identity. The listener is forced to understand that the narrative persona for the symphony is particularly conscious of the great composers of the German musical tradition, from Bach to the present. The motivation for the symphony, as well as its plot, must be understood within the framework of the symphonist's narrative position. The desire—indeed, compulsion—to express an heroic plot is linked to an awareness of the German musical tradition. The struggle and fulfillment represented in the work relate directly to the symphonist's experience. In other words, the symphonist persona is responding to the influence of his musical heritage by narrating the "through suffering to joy" plot[28] and by explicitly bringing

Example 6b. Schumann: Symphony No. 2 in C Major, movement 3, mm. 62–74.

the composers of the past into the text itself. I find this far more interesting than a viewpoint that reduces the C-Major Symphony to a mere autobiographical reflection of the composer's physical ailment and improving health. The allusions and citations offer a form of self-identification for the narrative voice.

Moreover, the reference to Mozart's Magic Flute points to what may have been the composer's own understanding of the meaning of the unusual plot in this symphony: the process of self-realization. This is strongly underscored in a neglected remark in Schumann's correspondence that appears in a letter to Joseph Fischhof November 23, 1846. Here Schumann writes that the music was "etwas geharnischt."[29] *Geharnischt*, which describes a knight girt up in armor, is an unexpected description of music, as the word suggests belligerence. This might lead one to believe that the narrative voice of the piece represents someone who is in a mood to take on his predecessors in the great German musical tradition and do battle with them.

One must recall, however, the connection with the most famous instance of the word *geharnischt* in the history of music—the "zwei geharnischte Männer" in the finale of Act 2 of The Magic Flute. Schumann could not have missed this tie when he wrote to Fischhof, and the allusion to the music of the armed men in the C-Major Symphony further reinforces the connection. So what is its significance?

The two armed men in The Magic Flute sing the following:

Der, welcher wandelt diese Straße	He who wanders this path
voll Beschwerden,	full of burdens,
wird rein durch Feuer, Wasser,	becomes pure by fire, water,
Luft, und Erden;	air, and earth;
wenn er des Todes Schrecken	if he can conquer
überwinden kann,	the fear of death,
schwingt er sich aus der Erde	he ascends from earth
Himmel an.	to heaven.
Erleuchtet wird er dann	Enlightened, he will then
im Stande sein,	be in a position
sich den Mysterien der Isis	to dedicate himself fully
ganz zu weih'n.	to the mysteries of Isis.

This could hardly be bettered as a formulation of the plot archetype to which the Symphony in C Major belongs. The story is not one of sickness and recovery, but rather one of trials on the way to self-realization.

The early reviewers of the C-Major Symphony had some inkling of this, it appears —something that later commentators seem to have overlooked. In reviewing the first edition of the score in 1848, Alfred Dörffel wrote that "the music is none such as is discovered by the lucky grasp of the genius. It is one attained by effort and has behind it a great world view, a great life."[30] Gottschald, responding at length to Dörffel, referred to the "most profound soul, which endures firmly and without trembling the trial by fire of the 'forms.'"[31] We can also return here to Gottschald's suggestion that the work's *Grundidee* was "the *victorious* striving of the particular individuality for its most sincere fusion with spiritual universality, in which all egoistic limits, limits that divided individual spirits from each other, are annihilated, so that those spirits love each other as equals, for they live in the realm of liberty, equality, and fraternity."[32]

The theme of universality and objectivity (especially in contradistinction to Schumann's highly personal expressions in his early work) that runs through both Dörffel's and Gottschald's comments on the symphony had already been mentioned by Franz Brendel in his review of the second performance: "If in the works of Schumann's first period the fantastic dominated, then here it is the plastic, objective stamp of the thoughts, mediated by his contrapuntal studies, a direction that characterizes the works of his second period generally."[33]

Thus, a narratological approach to the work, uniting plot and voice, brings us closer to the core of Schumann's symphony. The integration of these elements permits a compelling interpretation.

The autobiographical fallacy may be put to rest by Schumann's own description of the music: the persona is not Schumann, but a more general voice with an experience related to struggle and recovery, the symphony as a genre, and German musical culture and tradition. The citations that Schumann chose lead directly enough to the recognition of this. As Newcomb noted, the allusion to Haydn at the opening of the symphony "proclaims as effectively as a poetic preamble one quite specific program: Schumann's courageous and ambitious decision to measure for the first time his particular methods and abilities against the overwhelmingly, even terrifying prestigious tradition of the Viennese Classical symphony."[34] Reynolds points out that "in the nineteenth century [the B-A-C-H motive] gained symbolic status, a change that followed inevitably from the cultural progression that replaced the image of Bach the Leipzig cantor with one of him as the source of German musical nationalism."[35]

One final reference demands our attention. As the development section of the fourth movement of the symphony is drawing to a close, it introduces Schumann himself in a rather remarkable way. In mm. 343–349 of the finale, Schumann quotes mm. 131–135 of the last fugue of his own B-A-C-H series (Example 7). By including this self-reference with those to Bach, Haydn, Mozart, Beethoven, and Mendelssohn, Schumann adds his own name to the list of canonical composers in the German tradition. Yet it is no characteristic passage from Schumann's oeuvre that is quoted here; instead, it is specifically Schumann at the moment when he looks back to Bach. In other words, the symphony makes a claim that Schumann belongs to the tradition of German music not directly in his own right, but specifically as one who acknowledges his dependence on his forebears.

By way of closing, let us go back once more to the plot and the allusions and consider Gottschald's formulation, Mozart's Magic Flute, and Beethoven's Ninth Symphony. The ultimate accomplishment of the plot, represented by the symphony finale, is, according to Gottschald, the "attainment" of a "spiritual universality" in which the separate spirits "live in the realm of liberty, equality, and fraternity." In Mozart's opera, too, the hero, Tamino, enters the realm of the enlightened—an Elysium where, indeed, "all men become brothers." In the final analysis, the self-identification and self-realization in the Symphony in C Major amount to Schumann's claim for incorporation into the community that the narrator-symphonist understood by the 1840s

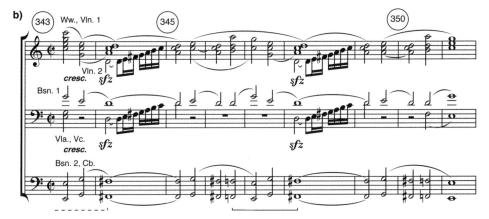

Example 7. a) Schumann: Fugue 6 from Six Fugues on the Name B-A-C-H, mm. 130–135. b) Schumann: Symphony No. 2 in C Major, movement 4, mm. 343–351.

as the canon of great German composers. This canon began, both in history and in Schumann's inspiration for the C-Major Symphony, with Bach.

Notes

1. Robert Schumann, *Gesammelte Schriften über Musik und Musiker*, 5th ed., ed. Martin Kreisig (Leipzig: Breitkopf & Härtel, 1914), vol. 1, 354: "Charakterstücke höchster Art, zum Teil wahrhaft poetische Gebilde, deren jedes seinen eigenen Ausdruck, seine besonderen Lichter und Schatten verlangt." The English translations throughout this chapter are my own.

2. Georg von Dadelsen, "Robert Schumann und die Musik Bachs," *Archiv für Musikwissenschaft* 14 (1957), 59: "Melodie und Form, ursprünglich Ergebnis der dichterischen Phantasie, sollen jetzt nach 'Gesetz und Regel' gebildet werden. Das Schaffen erreicht damit einen Grad der Bewußtheit, den es früher nicht besessen. Es wird an die Grenze des 'Mechanischen' geführt."

3. An important critique of the symphony from the point of view of its structure may be found in Carl Dahlhaus, "Studien zu romantischen Symphonien—Das 'Finalproblem' in Schumanns Zweiter

Symphonie," in *Jahrbuch des Staatlichen Instituts für Musikforschung Preussischer Kulturbesitz*, ed. Dagmar Droysen (Berlin: Staatliches Institut für Musikforschung Preussischer Kulturbesitz, 1973), 104–19.

4. See *Clara Schumann, Johannes Brahms: Briefe aus den Jahren 1853–1896*, ed. Berthold Litzmann (Leipzig: Breitkopf & Härtel, 1927), vol. 1, 158.

5. Linda Correll Roesner, "Tonal Strategy and Poetic Content in Schumann's C-Major Symphony, Op. 61," in *Probleme der symphonischen Tradition im 19. Jahrhundert, Internationales Musikwissenschaftliches Colloquium, Bonn 1989*, ed. Siegfried Kross and Marie Luise Maintz (Tutzing: Hans Schneider, 1990), 299, n. 9. See also Christopher Alan Reynolds, *Motives for Allusion: Context and Content in Nineteenth-Century Music* (Cambridge, Mass.: Harvard University Press, 2003), 41 and 195, n. 31.

6. John Daverio, *Robert Schumann: Herald of a "New Poetic Age"* (Oxford, UK: Oxford University Press, 1997), 319.

7. Reynolds, *Motives for Allusion*, 10.

8. Clara Schumann reported to Felix Mendelssohn, in a letter of December 27, 1845, that Schumann had surprised her at Christmas with the sketches for his symphony. See Nancy B. Reich, "The Correspondence between Clara Wieck Schumann and Felix and Paul Mendelssohn," in *Schumann and His World*, ed. R. Larry Todd (Princeton, N.J.: Princeton University Press, 1994), 222. Schumann also noted some of the important stages of the symphony-drafting in his journal. See Robert Schumann, *Tagebücher (Haushaltbücher: Teil I, 1837–47)*, ed. Gerd Nauhaus (Leipzig: VEB Deutscher Verlag für Musik, 1982), vol. 3, 408–10.

9. Preparations for the concert are discussed in Clara Schumann's letters to Mendelssohn. See Reich, "Correspondence," 223–25.

10. Especially notable among these studies is Anthony Newcomb, "Once More 'Between Absolute and Program Music': Schumann's Second Symphony," *19th-Century Music* 7 (1984), 233–50. This detailed examination lays out much of the central evidence, both analytical and documentary. Newcomb's bibliography is also especially useful.

11. Newcomb, "Once More 'Between Absolute and Program Music,'" 234.

12. For an extensive analysis of the harmonic progress of the symphony, see Roesner, "Tonal Strategy," 295–306, especially 296–301.

13. There is much to be said about the finale of the work, but space and time do not permit a complete analysis here. Among the most useful studies of the movement are Jon R. Finson, "The Sketches for the Fourth Movement of Schumann's Second Symphony," *Journal of the American Musicological Society* 39 (1986): 143–68; Gerd Nauhaus, "Final-Lösungen in der Symphonik Schumanns," in *Probleme der Symphonischen Tradition im 19. Jahrhundert*, ed. Siegfried Kross and Marie Luise Maintz (Tutzing: Hans Schneider, 1990), 307–20, translated by Susan Gillespie as "Schumann's Symphonic Finales," in *Schumann and His World*, ed. R. Larry Todd (Princeton, N.J.: Princeton University Press, 1994), 113–28.

14. Newcomb emphasizes this point in "Once More 'Between Absolute and Program Music,'" 242, n. 21. Roesner, in "Tonal Strategy," also demonstrates the evolution of the third-movement theme into the "substitute-reprise theme" of the finale.

15. Ernst Gottschald, "Robert Schumann's zweite Symphonie: Zugleich mit Rücksicht auf andere, insbesondere Beethoven's Symphonien. Vertraute Briefe an A. Dörffel," *Neue Zeitschrift für Musik* 32 (1850), 137–38: "das *sieggekrönte* Ringen der besonderen Individualität nach ihrer innigsten Verschmelzung mit der geistigen Allgemeinheit in der alle egoistischen Schranken, vernichtet sind, Schranken, welche die einzelnen Geister von einander trennten, die sich nun als Gleiche lieben, denn sie wohnen im Reiche der Freiheit, Gleichheit und Brüderlichkeit."

16. Gottschald, "Robert Schumann's zweite Symphonie," 138: "des Tondichters Gemüth, noch mitten in befremdeter Einsamkeit befangen."

17. Michael P. Steinberg, "Schumann's Homelessness," in *Schumann and His World*, ed. R. Larry Todd (Princeton, N.J.: Princeton University Press, 1994), 75. Steinberg, however, denies the plot framework that others find in the work.

18. Robert Schumann, *Briefe: Neue Folge*, 2d ed., ed. F. Gustav Jansen (Leipzig: Breitkopf & Härtel, 1904), 300: "Die Symphonie schrieb ich im December 1845 noch halb krank; mir ist's als müßte man ihr dies anhören. Erst im letzten Satz fing ich an mich wieder zu fühlen; wirklich wurde ich auch nach Beendigung des ganzen Werkes wieder wohler. Sonst aber, wie gesagt, erinnert sie mich an eine dunkle Zeit."

19. Newcomb, "Once More 'Between Absolute and Program Music,'" 237.

20. Quoted in Newcomb, "Once More 'Between Absolute and Program Music,'" 237, n. 12: "im ganzen ein finsteres Stück—erst im letzten Teil tun ein Paar freundlichen Strahlen hervorbrechen."

21. R. Larry Todd is suspicious of this allusion, however. See his article "On Quotation in Schumann's Music," in *Schumann and His World*, ed. R. Larry Todd (Princeton, N.J.: Princeton University Press, 1994), 80 and 109, n. 3.

22. Daverio, *Robert Schumann*, 318–19.

23. The phrase and the idea came to prominence in critical theory through the 1973 book by Harold Bloom, *The Anxiety of Influence: A Theory of Poetry*, 2d ed. (New York: Oxford University Press, 1997).

24. Mark Evan Bonds, *After Beethoven: Imperatives of Originality in the Symphony* (Cambridge, Mass.: Harvard University Press, 1996), 7.

25. Arnfried Edler, "Ton und Zyklus in der Symphonik Schumanns," in *Probleme der symphonischen Tradition im 19. Jahrhundert, Internationales Musikwissenschaftliches Colloquium, Bonn 1989*, ed. Siegfried Kross and Marie Luise Maintz (Tutzing: Hans Schneider, 1990), 194. The letter to Verhulst is cited from Schumann, *Briefe: Neue Folge*, 517, n. 314.

26. Edler, "Ton und Zyklus," 202: "die symphonische Tradition selber, repräsentiert durch das Haydn-Zitat."

27. Ludwig Finscher, "'Zwischen absoluter und Programmusik': Zur Interpretation der deutschen romantischen Symphonie," in *Über Symphonien: Beiträge zu einer musikalischen Gattung. Festschrift Walter Wiora zum 70. Geburtstag*, ed. Christoph-Hellmut Mahling (Tutzing: Hans Schneider, 1979), 112: "der Begriff der musikalischen Arbeit thematisiert wird—es gibt vor Brahms kaum eine andere Symphonie, in der substantielle und strukturelle Vereinheitlichung so rigoros und so angestrengt erzwungen sind wie hier, und kaum eine, in der der Begriff der musikalischen Arbeit zugleich so geschichtstief gefaßt wird . . ."

28. I take this expression from its appearance in Akio Mayeda, *Robert Schumanns Weg zur Symphonie* (Zurich: Atlantis/Mainz: Schott, 1992), 523. Mayeda refers to "Das Beethovensche Grundkonzept: 'Durch Leiden zur Freude'" and cites Beethoven's letter to Countess Maria von Erdödy of October 19, 1815.

29. Schumann, *Briefe: Neue Folge*, 262.

30. Alfred Dörffel, "Für Orchester: Robert Schumann, Op. 61. Zweite Symphonie für großes Orchester," *Neue Zeitschrift für Musik* 28 (1848), 99: "Die Musik ist keine solche, die ein glücklicher Geist gefunden: sie ist eine errungene und hat eine große Weltanschauung, ein großes Leben hinter sich."

31. Ernst Gottschald, "Robert Schumann's zweite Symphonie," 138: "innerste Seele, welche fest und unerschütterlich die Feuerprobe der 'Gestalten' besteht."

32. See n. 15.

33. Franz Brendel, report on Leipzig *Abonnementskonzerte, Neue Zeitschrift für Musik* 25 (1846), 181: "Wenn in den Werken der ersten Epoche bei R. Schumann das Phantastische überwog, so ist es hier, vermittelt durch seine contrapunktischen Studien, die plastische, objective Ausprägung der Gedanken, eine Richtung, welche überhaupt die Werke seiner zweiten Epoche charakterisirt."

34. Newcomb, "Once More 'Between Absolute and Program Music,'" 240.

35. Reynolds, *Motives for Allusion*, 138.

CONTRIBUTORS

GREGORY G. BUTLER is Professor of Music History at the University of British Columbia and President of the American Bach Society. His early research on the relationship between rhetoric and music led quite naturally to Bach studies, where he has become an authority on the early editions of the composer's works. He is author of *J.S. Bach's Clavier-Übung III: The Making of a Print* (Duke University Press, 1990), and editor of *Bach Perspectives* 6 and 7.

JEN-YEN CHEN is Assistant Professor in the Graduate Institute of Musicology at National Taiwan University. He has published essays in the *Journal of Musicological Research* and *Ad Parnassum*, and he has edited volumes of music for the Johann-Joseph-Fux Gesamtausgabe and A-R Editions. His research focuses on eighteenth-century Austria, and his interests include sacred music, aristocratic patronage, and performance practice.

ALEXANDER J. FISHER is Assistant Professor of Music and director of the Collegium Musicum at the University of British Columbia. His research focuses on music and issues of religious practice and identity in central Europe during the Reformation and Counter-Reformation. He is author of *Music and Religious Identity in Counter-Reformation Augsburg, 1580–1630* (Ashgate, 2004) and editor of *Virginalia Eucharistica* for A-R Editions.

MARY DALTON GREER is Artistic Director of "Cantatas in Context," a Bach cantata series, and Vice President of the American Bach Society. She has served as Christopher Hogwood Research Fellow at the Handel & Haydn Society and has taught at Yale University. She has published on Bach cantatas in *BACH: The Journal of the Riemenschneider Bach Institute* and on the reception of Bach's music in New York in the ninteteenth century in *Bach Perspectives*.

ROBERT HILL, Professor of Harpsichord, Chamber Music, and Performance Practice at the Musikhochschule in Freiburg, Germany, since 1990, studied harpsichord at the Amsterdam Sweelink Conservatory (Soloist Diploma, 1974) and musicology at Harvard University (PhD, 1987). He performs and records extensively on harpsichord and fortepiano, and his research specialties include the manuscript transmission of keyboard music and performance practices.

TON KOOPMAN is Director of the Amsterdam Baroque Orchestra and Choir, which is presently engaged in recording the complete cycle of sacred and secular cantatas of

J.S. Bach. Professor of Harpsichord at the Royal Conservatory in The Hague and Honorary Member of the Royal Academy of Music in London, Koopman is featured as a soloist and conductor on a large number of recording labels, including Erato, Teldec, Philips, and DGG.

DANIEL R. MELAMED is Professor and of Music at the Jacobs School of Music at Indiana University. He is author of *Hearing Bach's Passions* (Oxford University Press, 2005) and *J.S. Bach and the German Motet* (Cambridge University Press, 1995); editor of *Bach Studies 2* (Cambridge University Press, 1995); and co-author, with Michael Marisssen, of *An Introduction to Bach Studies* (Oxford University Press, 1998).

MICHAEL OCHS is former Richard F. French Librarian of the Music Library at Harvard and music editor at W.W. Norton. He is also a past president of the Music Library Association and editor of its journal, *NOTES*. He has served on the boards of the American Musicological Society and the Boston Camerata, and he is editor of *Music Librarianship in America* (Harvard University, 1990) and author of essays in *Mozart-Jahrbuch* and other publications.

MARK RISINGER has published articles on the vocal and chamber music of Handel, the *Lieder* of Schumann, and the late religious works of Schoenberg. He serves on the American Committee of the Handel House Trust and completed a dissertation on the classification of Handel's borrowing procedures at Harvard University in 1996. A New York–based bass, he has sung leading roles with opera companies and orchestras throughout North America and Europe.

WILLIAM H. SCHEIDE has written on the music of J.S. Bach for close to fifty years, including articles in *Bach-Jahrbuch*, *Musikforschung*, *Journal of the American Musicological Society*, and *Bach-Studien*. His groundbreaking studies of Bach's first annual Leipzig cantata cycle and Bach's use of works by Johann Ludwig Bach are well known. Philanthropist and collector of books and manuscripts, Mr. Scheide is the owner of the 1748 Haussmann portrait of Bach.

HANS-JOACHIM SCHULZE is former director of the Bach-Archiv in Leipzig and editor (with Christoph Wolff) of *Bach-Jahrbuch*. A frequent contributor to *Bach-Jahrbuch*, *Beiträge zur Bachforschung*, *Beiträge zur Musikwissenschaft*, *Bach-Studien*, and many other journals, he is author of *'Ey! Wie schmeckt der Coffee süße* and editor of *Bach-Dokumente* (with Werner Neumann) and *Johann Gottfried Walther: Briefe* (with I.K. Beckmann).

DOUGLASS SEATON is Warren D. Allen Professor of Music at Florida State University. His research focuses on the music of Felix Mendelssohn, Romanticism in the history of music, and interdisciplinary approaches to music and literature. He has published extensively in American and European journals, and he is author of *Ideas and Styles in the Western Musical Tradition* (McGraw-Hill, 2007) and editor of *The Mendelssohn Companion* (Greenwood Press, 2001).

GEORGE B. STAUFFER is Dean of the Mason Gross School of the Arts and Professor of Music at Rutgers University. He has published extensively on the history and culture of Baroque music, including, most recently, *The World of Baroque Music* (Indiana University Press, 2006) and *Bach: Mass in B Minor* (Yale University Press, 2003). He has held Guggenheim, ACLS, Fulbright, IREX, and Bogliasco fellowships and is a past president of the American Bach Society.

ANDREW TALLE studied cello performance and linguistics at Northwestern University before receiving the PhD in musicology from Harvard University, where he studied with Christoph Wolff. Since 2004, he has taught music history at Peabody Conservatory and Johns Hopkins University. Current projects include a book-length study of Bach's *Clavierübung* I and its audience during the composer's lifetime.

KATHRYN WELTER holds the PhD in musicology from Harvard University. She is Executive Director of both the Boston Camerata and the Composers Conference and Chamber Music Center at Wellesley College. She is also Music Director at Peace Lutheran Church in Wayland, Massachusetts, and Choir Director of St. Mark's Coptic Church in Natick, Massachusetts. Her research focuses on the works of Johann Pachelbel and seventeenth-century liturgical practices.

INDEX

(Page numbers in bold indicate the entry is the principal topic of discussion.)

Index

The University of Illinois Press
is a founding member of the
Association of American University Presses.

Composed in 10/14 Janson Text
by BookComp, Inc.
for the University of Illinois Press
Manufactured by Thomson-Shore, Inc.

University of Illinois Press
1325 South Oak Street
Champaign, IL 61820-6903
www.press.uillinois.edu